In the Nam

MW01113639

THE ISLAMIC NATION

STATUS & FUTURE OF MUSLIMS IN THE NEW WORLD ORDER

Ali Nawaz Memon

Writers' Inc. International
Beltsville, Maryland

The Islamic Nation
Status & Future of Muslims in the New World Order

Ali Nawaz Memon

Library of Congress Cataloging-in-Publication Data

Memon, Ali Nawaz, 1941-
    The Islamic nation : status & future of Muslims in the new world order / Ali Nawaz Memon.
    p.   cm.
    Includes bibliographical references (p.   ) and index.
    ISBN 0-9627854-7-4 (pbk.)
    1. Islam--20th century. 2. Islamic countries.   I. Title.
BP163.M45 1995
909'.0976710829--dc20   95-6017
                                                         CIP

Printed in the United States of America
by International Graphics
10710 Tucker Street, Beltsville, Maryland 20705-2223
Tel. (301) 595-5999 - Fax (301) 595-5888

DEDICATION

Dedicated to: my grandfathers, Haji Wali Mohamad and Maulvi Rahmatullah, who introduced me to Islam; my father, Abdul Fatah, who made me aware of the need for Muslim solidarity; my mother, Aisha, my wife, Razia, and my sister Najma who made me sensitive to the issues facing Muslim women; my uncle, Nizamuddin, who made me aware of obligations to fellow humans; and my children, Kamran, Sadia, Reshma, Amer, and Nauman, who will, *insha'Allah*, help in making this a better world.

Contents

Media Experience and Policy; Moral Fiber; Strong Community Feeling; Belief in One Muslim Nation; Principles of Good Governance; In Summary

TABLES AND FIGURES

The Islamic Nation
Status & Future of Muslims in the New World Order

Introduction

Every day, as one looks at newspaper headlines or listens to the world news, one is struck by the misery and suffering of Muslims:

a. massacre and rape of Muslims in Bosnia;
b. starvation of Muslims in Somalia due to civil war among Muslim war lords;
c. occupation of and systematic violation of human rights in Palestine for the last 27 years;
d. killing and rape of Muslims in Kashmir by the Indian army; and
e. savage violence in Chechnya.

These are just a few instances. Locally, Muslims do not appear able to do much; internationally, the Organization of Islamic Conference (OIC), with approximately 50-member countries, has failed to provide remedies. United Nations Security Council resolutions, used promptly and effectively against Muslims in Iraq, Iran, Libya, etc., are seemingly disregarded when it comes to defense of Muslims. Superpowers, who act as world police when their own vital interests are involved, give protection of Muslims little urgency. There is much debate, but there is little practical action.

Muslims tend to look at problems in Muslim countries as a collective stigma and a collective responsibility. This is because the Qur'an repeatedly declares that Muslims are brothers.

The believers are but a single Brotherhood: so make peace and reconciliation between your two (contending) brothers; and fear Allah, that you may receive Mercy *(Surah 49:10).*

There are internal problems also. There is discrimination against Muslims by Muslims. As a member of a middle class educated family from a town called Larkana, in the province of Sind, in Pakistan, the author has been reminded many a time that he is a second class citizen: (a) in Larkana, for not being from a landed, feudal, aristocratic family, or from a *syeid* (holy) family; (b) in Karachi (capital of the Sind province), dominated by an Urdu-speaking population for daring to speak the Sindhi language; and (c) in Islamabad, dominated by the powerful Punjab

Province for being only a Sindhi. Millions of people (less fortunate than the author) in Pakistan and other Muslim countries suffer daily in terms of social status, educational and employment opportunities, career advancements, and physical abuse for not belonging to the right group. While the discrimination at home can be dismissed as a common human failing, it is clearly against the teachings of Islam.

What are Muslims to do? To start with, as is commonly known, Muslims are not homogeneous. They are spread in over more than fifty countries. They have many identities based on their respective family, tribe, race, language, economic position, nationality, sect within the religion, etc. Which of the identities prevails at a particular time depends on the priority of the moment. Certainly, any identity which is threatened gets attention.

Obviously, today the Islamic Nation is a very weak brotherhood and nation. How can the Muslim nation develop so that it can (a) do justice at home, (b) defend itself against external threats, and (c) participate equally and effectively in the New World Order of the 1990's? This is a complex and perhaps impossible question. However, considering the magnitude of the problem and the collective heartache felt by Muslims everywhere, it is worthy of serious thought. Without a rational and peaceful solution, impetuous voices may prevail leading to drastic approaches harmful to them as well as Muslims in general.

The impressions given by the Western media are that Muslims: (a) are an irresponsible group; (b) have a limited positive role to play; and (c) are out to shatter the established world order by overthrowing their own legitimate governments and those of the West through arbitrary acts of violence and terrorism. Muslims know that these impressions are wrong. Most Muslims are taught to be God-fearing rather than terrorists. Muslims want to raise themselves up and help each other, including non-Muslims, rather than hurt anyone. They have genuine concerns about the New World Order, and seek an equitable role.

At the same time, there is fear within Christian groups that Muslims seek to spread Islam at any cost, and convert the entire human race. Muslims are obligated to demonstrate the goodness of their faith to all. However, the Qur'an teaches that there is no compulsion in Islam.

> Invite (all) to the way of thy Lord with wisdom and beautiful preaching; and argue with them in the ways that are best and most gracious; for thy Lord knoweth best, who have strayed from His path, and who received guidance (Surah 16:125).

Muslims clearly do not wish to spread their religion by force or dominate people of other religions.

On the other hand, Muslims are worried about the lifestyle of Western societies and the temptations it presents to their youth and future generations. They worry about Muslim youths walking away from Islam as Christian youths have largely walked away from their own religion.

The tension between Muslims and the West is noticed by all. It led the Prince of Wales to remark at the Oxford Centre for Islamic Studies, on October 27, 1993:

> **... I believe whole-heartedly that the links between these two worlds matter more today than ever before, because the degree of misunderstanding between the Islamic and the Western worlds remains dangerously high, and because the need for the two to live and work together in our increasingly interdependent world has never been greater . . .**

The objective of this book is to examine the problem from a perspective common to Muslims, without losing sight of the key interests and concerns of the West. The book barely scratches the surface. Nevertheless, the author prays that Muslims and their leaders can look at the *Ummah* (world Muslim community), examine their strengths and weaknesses, and make themselves stronger in the process. It is also hoped that:

a. the citizens and leaders of the West can understand Muslims in a better light as people who wish to improve their lot and make this world better for all;

b. major differences between Muslims and non-Muslim powers (broadly referred to as the "West" in this book) can be resolved peacefully, and coexistence will be possible;

c. Muslims and the West can live as equal partners on this small planet earth in peace; and

d. Muslim citizens of the West can have a chance to share political power with other religious groups.

The author may be condemned by both Muslims and non-Muslims for some thoughts presented in this book. Muslims may assume that the author has lived in the West too long, does not understand Islam, has already become "Westernized," and is too eager to compromise and coexist with the *kuffaar* (disbelievers). Non-Muslims may feel that the author has generalized too much, is too anti-Western, is a Muslim supremacist, and does not deserve to be heard in the West. In any case, the thoughts are on the table for discussion.

I believe that my proposals are entirely consistent with the teachings of Islam as I understand them, that they will serve the best interest of Muslims, and that they pose no threat to the West. I see a win-win situation. I only hope that the book will not be totally ignored and will lead to some good for all concerned.

Most informed observers feel that only a major miracle will change Muslims enough to make them equal partners in the New World Order; it is hopeless to dream of that happening in our life time. I know it is a tall order. However, I believe in God and that He will help in this worthy cause. I pray for a Divine intervention. I pray for angels to descend into the hearts of people of goodwill among Muslims and the West. I pray for angels in the form of humans who will be selfless, and work hard for the sole purpose of making this a better world. I hope that they start with helping all the needy ones with food, shelter, medicines, education, jobs, etc. and move on to be peacemakers for Muslims and the rest of the world. I invite all men and women to become those angels.

The Middle East peace movement could be the start of the miracle many have been waiting for. I am convinced that development of Muslims and their effective participation in the New World Order will make this a better world for all.

Thoughts contained in this work are not all original. The author has been thinking, reading, and writing about the subject for years. I have a copy of an article that I wrote when I was in the ninth grade. It was titled, "Independence," touched on similar issues, and was published in my school magazine in the Sindhi language in 1956. I have been influenced by many. My father's books (*Oil and Faith* and *Invitation to the New Society*) dealt with a similar subject matter and made me think about it. Years of travel, personal and in my job for the World Bank since 1967, and almost continuous monitoring of world events have influenced my thinking, too. I gratefully acknowledge all those whose thoughts and material are reflected in this work; may Allah bless and compensate all those who have contributed to it directly or indirectly. To the best of my knowledge, the book does not contain any confidential information from my employer. This is my personal statement of the agenda for reform of the Muslim *Ummah*.

1.

A. Definitions

1.   Allah is the name for the Supreme Being, or the Absolute. In Islam, it is the proper or true name of God through which humanity calls upon its Creator, the Essence of Reality. The name Allah is not confined to Islam, for Allah is the Name by which Christians of the Oriental churches call upon God.[1] Allah is the God of Abraham, Jacob, Jesus and all the prophets of Christianity and Judaism.

2.   A **Muslim**, literally, is a person "who has surrendered to God," from the Arabic word *aslama,* which means "to surrender, to seek peace." Also, from this Arabic root comes the name of the religion Islam. A Muslim, therefore, is one who follows the teachings and principles of Islam. The word "Moslem", less frequently used today, is the westernized form and it means the same as Muslim. This book will treat Muslims as one group of people. In part of the discussion, all Muslims, including those living in countries where Muslims are a minority, will be covered.

3.   **Muslim Countries** refer to nations with a majority Muslim population. Such a country is usually a member of the Organization of Islamic Conference (OIC). Currently about 50 countries are members. Muslim countries are also identified as belonging to Asia, the Middle East, and Africa. A few of them are rich, others belong to the middle income group, many are poor. Among Muslim countries there is great diversity, but also much in common, principally because common Islamic teachings and practice unify them.

4.   **Development** means balanced advancement in spiritual (including education and science), economic, military, and political (including legal) fields. Such development is meant to lead to increased prosperity, higher standards of living and improved quality of life. For Muslims, it also means eventually becoming a respected member of the community of world powers.

---

[1] Cyril Glassé, *The Concise Encyclopedia of Islam* (San Francisco: Harper & Row, 1989), p. 35.

5.   **New World Order.** The world had been dominated by two superpowers, i.e., the United States and the Soviet Union, from the post-World War II period beginning in the late 1940's up to the breakup of the Soviet Union in the early 1990's. Since then, only one superpower has been dominant. The United States, though in a uniquely powerful position, has exercised power in consultation with permanent members of the United Nations Security Council, in particular with its European allies.

Prompt decisions of the Security Council following the Iraqi attack on Kuwait, leading to military action in the Gulf War but lack of military action in Bosnia, are examples of the decision-making under the New World Order. In the first case, the United States persuaded the Security Council; in the second case, it did not.

It may be noted that Christianity is the religion of a vast majority of people living in the United States and Europe. However, in the U.S. and in European countries religion is explicitly separated from government. Religion may motivate the hearts of leaders of these countries, but their governments are predominantly secular. Often, church groups are alarmed at the lack of attention given to religion. The question then becomes whether the New World Order is to be based on a secular or spiritual foundation.

Islam does not have any special positive role or influence in the New World Order. Muslims seek such a positive role, and hope for an equitable world order.

6.   **The West.** The word "West" is used in this book to refer to the informal economic and political alliance led by the United States; it includes the European Union (EU), Japan, Canada and Australia. Indisputably, the United States is the most powerful nation militarily, but it also leads in economic and political areas.

7.   **Participation.** This concept means joining, enrolling, and sharing with others in specific activities of common concern. The level of participation of Muslims in the New World Order is low. Muslims appear to be observers and peripheral players. The fact that they are divided casts doubt on their ability to participate as a significant entity in the sphere of world events. In addition, Muslims often choose to ignore issues of apparent significance to the West, preferring to remain aloof.

8.   The **Islamic Nation,** *Ummah,* or the world Muslim community, signifies the universal Muslim brotherhood and unity of state. Though fragmented into nation states, the *Ummah* remains a viable conceptual

reality in the minds of Muslims. There is a resurgence of Islam almost everywhere. In some places, militancy is visible. A genuine renaissance is not widely visible yet.

B. Brief History

9.   From 570 AD to World War I. Prophet Muhammad (PBUH)[2] invited men and women to submit themselves to Allah, alone, in the early seventh century. The new religion of Islam spread in Arabia within a few short years. Soon thereafter, Islam spread from Central Asia to Spain. A majority of the population accepted Islam. Arabic became widely used. Muslim societies developed distinctive forms of government, codes of moral behavior, literature, architecture, the arts, the sciences, culture, and a way of life.

The Prophet (PBUH) and the four Caliphs (*al-Khulafa' ar-Rashidun*) who succeeded him were followed by Muslim kings. Government by consensus was replaced by autocracy and passive obedience. Nevertheless, the Islamic imprint continued on most of the known world for almost 12 centuries. Though provincial governors challenged their political unity on many occasions, in 1700, there were four major Muslim world powers, Mamluk Egypt, Ottoman Turkey, Safavid Persia, and Mogul India. The Moguls were defeated by Europeans around 1720, and the Mamluks around 1800. The Safavids disappeared in 1723. Only the Ottoman Empire continued as a world power up to modern times.

The Ottoman Empire (14th century-1923) was based in Turkey and was controlled by Turks. It ruled all Arabs in the Middle East and North Africa, as well as the Greeks, Yugoslavs, Albanians, Rumanians, and Bulgarians in the Balkans. Its forces advanced upon Vienna in 1683, but were unable to capture it. The subjects began to rebel because the government became (a) autocratic, with concentration of power in the hands of the Sultan; (b) corrupt, with a disproportionate flow of public money into private hands; (c) inefficient, with increasing disorder in many parts of the Empire; (d) discriminatory; and (e) cruel.

Greece was lost through a revolution by 1829. Cyprus, Serbia, Montenegro, and Rumania were lost at the Congress of Berlin (1878) following the Russo-Turkish War (1877-78). As a result of the Balkan Wars (1912-13), the Ottoman Empire lost all European territory, except for Constantinople and a small surrounding area. The remaining empire was

---

[2] Peace and blessings [from God] be upon him.

located in the Middle East and North Africa. It was almost entirely Muslim. It entered World War I on the side of Germany in 1914. The total breakup of the Empire and the centralized Muslim government *(Khilaafah* or Caliphate) occurred shortly after World War I.

Before the decline was complete, or as part of it, Turkey instituted numerous reforms called *tanzimat*, which were designed to "westernize" the country. This led to the stirring of Turkish nationalism which eventually led to the secularization of the nation and the loss of Muslim identity, under the rule of Mustafa Kemal Ataturk.[3]

10.   **Between World Wars I and II.** Having dreamed about conquering the Middle East for centuries, the Western powers succeeded after World War I. The remaining Ottoman Empire, which was the symbol of Muslim political and governmental unity, was divided in 1922. The Caliphate which was a symbol of Muslim religious unity was abolished. The accord of 1922 included the following:

    a. Russia's territorial claim over Muslim areas in Central Asia was recognized through the draft constitution of the USSR promulgated at the end of 1922;

    b. Creation of a Turkish national state confined to a part of the Turkish speaking portion of the dissolved empire;

    c. France's mandate from the League of Nations to rule Syria and Lebanon;

    d. Britain's mandate from the League of Nations to rule Palestine and Transjordan; and

    e. The Treaty of Iraq which effectively allowed British rule in that newly created country.

Colonial rule was expanded and strengthened in most Muslim countries between the two World Wars. Muslims became increasingly acquainted with the Western world and were introduced to the complexity of twentieth century civilization. Muslims started to learn the languages of their colonial masters, learning English, French, Dutch, and German. They travelled to Europe, saw the Western world for the first time, and were introduced to drink and dance but also to advanced science and technology.

Muslim were educated in medicine, engineering, politics, economics, and law. Railways, airplanes, and modern industry came to much of their

---

[3] *The Concise Encyclopedia of Islam*, p. 306.

world for the first time. They absorbed culture and values from their colonial rulers but also started to dream about independence. At times, these liberation movements were crushed ruthlessly; sometimes they were tolerated, and were even encouraged.

11. **World War II.** During World War II, Muslim countries were expected to support their respective colonial masters. In India, Hindus and Muslims joined the British army. They received military training in modern warfare, fought on behalf of Britain in distant lands and helped protect British rule at home. In return, self-rule and eventual independence was promised.

12. **Post World War II.** The colonial masters of Muslims (Britain, the Netherlands, Italy, Germany and France) were weakened by World War II. Simultaneously, the nationalistic independence movements grew stronger and more organized. The rift between the victorious allies and the subsequent Cold War contributed considerably to the demise of colonialism. Gradually, independence came to almost all colonialized Muslims. Indonesia became independent in 1945; Pakistan in 1947; Nigeria in 1960; Kuwait in 1961; Malaysia in 1963.

Independence was not without its cost for Muslims. The colonial powers would not leave a united Muslim nation as had existed, before World War I, in the Ottoman Empire. They followed a "divide and rule " policy, granting independence to fragmented nation states. Arbitrary straight line boundaries were drawn with utter disregard for rivers, mountains, and other forms of natural boundaries. New boundaries often cut through tribal and ethnic units, disrupted traditional access to water and grazing lands, and redistributed natural resources. Many boundaries remain disputed to this day and have been a cause of several wars. It is likely that they will continue to be disputed among the natives for years to come.

In 1948, a United Nations vote created Israel, a new Jewish state in the Middle East. This has been the single most significant event of the post World War II era. It has led to several wars and many battles between Arabs and Israelis and has kept the region and much of the Muslim world in turmoil. Israel and Palestine represent one of the most critical international issues for Muslims in the New World Order.

Since regaining independence, several Muslim states have remained busy defending their new national states and their arbitrarily-drawn borders. Muslim countries have often needed, requested, and received military equipment and training from former colonial masters. Frequently, the ex-rulers supported two warring parties, then played the role of arbitrator.

Muslim republics, under Soviet control since the end of World War I, became independent only recently. Their impact on Muslim development and on the New World Order cannot yet be accurately evaluated.

C. Objectives

13.   **Integrated Development**. Development of Muslims requires four components: spiritual development; economic development; political development; and military development. Basic objectives in each of the four areas need to be established.

14.   **Spiritual Development.** Spiritually, Muslims believe in the one God, Allah, and His messenger Muhammad (PBUH); the Qur'an as the authentic source of all knowledge; the temporary nature of life in this world; and the Day of Judgment. All Muslim sects appear to believe in these basic points. However, different interpretations arise as one gets into greater details. Muslims would benefit from greater tolerance, allowing diversity of opinions as long as the basic beliefs are affirmed. Declaring each other a disbeliever, *kaafir,* is unproductive. It would also be advantageous for Muslims to consider each other a part of the same nation; develop greater economic ties; settle disputes among each other peacefully; and defend each other against non-Muslims.

15.   **Economic Development.** The basic needs of all Muslims, food, shelter, education, and health care should be met. This can best be achieved through adequate employment opportunities at reasonable wages in the private and public sectors. Muslim countries as a group are currently at the lower/middle income level. Through better distribution of resources, a greater portion of basic human needs can be provided. Several Muslim countries have not achieved a reasonable level of development or equitable economic distribution, in spite of numerous recent efforts. It is unrealistic to expect to improve in this area without meaningful development in other areas.

Muslim countries need to advance economically, both individually and collectively, in order to achieve their desired economic objectives. This implies that Muslim countries, as a group, should be able to take care of each others' unexpected but essential expenses. Economic interdependence and trade among all nations of the world are essential and unavoidable. Dependence on non-Muslim nations, however, for economic survival is inappropriate from economic, political, and spiritual perspectives. For example, to most Muslims, reliance by Somalia, Sudan, or Bosnia on non-Muslims, even for minimum food supplies, would represent neglect and disregard of fundamental Islamic beliefs.

16. **Political Development.** Islam neither requires nor prohibits government based on "one man one vote." However, Islam requires consultation, mutual consent, freedom of speech, justice, and support for good and avoidance of evil. Muslim countries as a group would benefit from a form of government based on these fundamental principles. Periodic opportunities to express their opinion about their rulers appear to be desired by Muslim people. Islam endorses stable government and urges citizens to follow their rulers, as long as they do not stray from the right path.

> **Oh ye who believe! Obey Allah, and obey the Messenger, and those charged with authority among you. If ye differ in anything among yourselves, refer it to Allah and His Messenger . . .** *(Surah 4:59).*

It should be noted that Islam expects governments to be run in a righteous manner, and requires that Allah and His teachings be used as the source of arbitration. Islamically, the rule of those who do not have the welfare of Muslim citizens and the pleasure of Allah as their prime objectives is illicit. Establishment of representative government is the key political objective.

17. **Military Development.** Militarily, it is in the best interest of Muslim countries to be strong enough to defend their own borders and to render help to other Muslims in defense of their vital interests. Several Muslim countries have for years been dedicating noticeably large budgets to their military establishment.

There are about one billion Muslims in the world, but most have received no military training. Muslims have about 4.5 million persons under arms. Most Muslim countries have adequate conventional equipment and the capacity to produce more or acquire more. However, Muslims are decades behind in the capability to produce modern military weapons. The West has been increasingly reluctant to help Muslims acquire or develop high technology. In the final analysis, Muslims are far from being able to defend their own borders and render help to other Muslims.

If Muslims were to become more unified and pool their resources, they would represent a significantly greater force than they currently do. Adversaries, real or imagined, are determined to prevent such unity. Ultimately, the success of any military effort depends on:

a. a just and moral cause;
b. wisdom, bravery, and sincerity of the leadership;
c. sense of the proper timing of action, suitable for the political conditions and physical circumstances;
d. the required number, organization, discipline of the troops; and
e. superior equipment.

Assuming a just and moral cause, Muslim countries, as a group, appear to possess the number of troops for defense in major confrontations, but are lacking in all other areas at the moment. Some individual Muslim countries do have some elements of each of the other requisites.

18.   **Participation in the New World Order**. Ironically, a unified Muslim alliance would likely play an important role in the international arena. If Muslims were stronger or at least more united, they would seek increasing levels of participation in the New World Order contributing significantly to the preservation of world peace, particularly among Muslim nations. However, the fear engendered in non-Muslims by a united "Islamic Nation" is so great that opposition to such a development is likely to continue and probably increase.

There are shared fundamental values and morals among the monotheistic religions of the world, including Judaism, Christianity, and Islam. There is every reason for followers of these religions to live in peace, participating as equals in development and progress of this world.

D. Qur'anic Guidance

For Muslims, the Qur'an is the source of guidance. The Qur'an describes worship of Allah as the primary purpose of human existence; Islam translates worship to be a complete way of life with emphasis on life in this world and in the hereafter. Muslims seek to excel in both worlds. Accordingly, in Islam, the development of Muslims is an act of worship and a very desirable goal.

To remain consistent in their affirmations, Muslims must seek solutions to all issues in their religion, specifically in the Qur'an. Verified and agreed-upon prophetic traditions (*ahadith)* can be used if clear answers cannot be found in The Qur'an.

The purpose of this chapter is to understand the existing spiritual, economic, political, and military conditions of Muslim countries. The statistical tables deal with 50 Muslim countries most of which are members of OIC. Some of them, like Nigeria and Lebanon, have large non-Muslim minority populations. Other countries, like China and India, have large Muslim minority populations but are not covered in these tables (India alone has more than 120 million Muslims). Data for Bosnia was not available, therefore, it has not been included.

Of the 50 countries listed below, 24 are located in the northern and central parts of Africa; the rest are located in the southern, central and eastern parts of Asia and the Middle East.

A. Existing Economic Conditions.

19.   **Population**. The population of 50 countries with Muslim majorities, for which data was available, was estimated at 988 million in 1992, out of a total world population of 5,438 million, or about 18 percent of the total world population. Reliable data for some countries (Lebanon, Iraq, Sudan and Afghanistan) are not available and therefore not included; if the populations of these countries were included, the total would be over one billion.[4] Some Muslim countries have rather small populations. Eleven countries have populations of less than two million. (The membership of Organization of Islamic Conference has increased recently.)

The following Table 1. presents statistical data on fifty countries with majority Muslim populations.[5]

---

[4] Based on earlier estimates, the population of Lebanon is 2.8 million, Iraq 18.8 million, Sudan 30 million, Afghanistan 18.1 million.

[5] The economic data presented here have been primarily extracted from the World Bank's *World Development Report of 1994*. The data itself is mostly for years 1990 through 1992.

Statistical Data

	COUNTRY	AREA '000 SQ. KM	POPULATION MILLION 1992	PER CAPITA GNP US $ 1992	TOTAL GNP US $ MILLION	ANNUAL % GROWTH 1980-92	% ANNUAL INFLATION 1980-92
1	Afghanistan	652	NA	NA	NA	NA	NA
2	Algeria	2,382	26.3	1,840	48,392	-1	11
3	Azerbaijan	87	7.4	740	5,476	NA	NA
4	Bahrain	1	0.5	7,130	3,565	NA	NA
5	Bangladesh	144	114.4	220	25,168	2	9
6	Benin	113	5.0	410	2,050	-1	2
7	Brunei	6	0.2	HI			
8	Burkina Faso	274	9.5	300	2,850	1	4
9	Cameroon	475	12.2	820	10,004	-2	4
10	Chad	1,284	6.0	220	1,320	3	1
11	Comoros	2	0.5	510	255	-1	6
12	Djibouti	23	0.5	NA	NA	NA	NA
13	Egypt	1,001	54.7	640	35,008	2	13
14	Gabon	268	1.2	4,450	5,340	-4	2
15	Gambia	11	1.0	370	370	NA	18
16	Guinea Bissau	36	1.0	220	220	2	59
17	Guinea	246	6.1	510	3,111	NA	NA
18	Indonesia	1,905	184.3	670	123,481	4	8
19	Iran	1,648	59.6	2,200	131,120	-1	16

	COUNTRY	AREA '000 SQ. KM	POPULATION MILLION 1992	PER CAPITA GNP US $ 1992	TOTAL GNP US $ MILLION	ANNUAL % GROWTH 1980-92	% ANNUAL INFLATION 1980-92
20	Iraq	438	NA	NA	NA	NA	NA
21	Jordan	89	3.9	1,120	4,368	-5	5
22	Kazakhstan	2,717	17.0	1,680	28,560	NA	NA
23	Kuwait	18	1.5	16,150	24,225	NA	NA
24	Kyrgyzstan	199	4.5	820	3,690	NA	NA
25	Lebanon	10	NA	NA	NA	NA	NA
26	Libya	1,760	4.7	5,310	24,957	NA	NA
27	Malaysia	330	18.6	2,790	51,894	3	2
28	Maldives	.03	0.2	500	100	7	NA
29	Mali	1,240	9.0	310	2,790	-3	4
30	Mauritania	1,026	2.1	530	1,113	-1	8
31	Morocco	447	26.2	1,030	26,986	1	7
32	Niger	1,267	8.2	280	2,296	-4	2
33	Nigeria	924	101.9	320	32,608	0	19
34	Oman	212	1.6	6,480	10,368	4	-3
35	Pakistan	796	119.3	420	50,106	3	7
36	Qatar	11	0.5	16,750	8,375	-11	NA
37	Saudi Arabia	2,150	16.8	7,510	126,168	-3	-2
38	Senegal	197	7.8	780	6,084	0	5
39	Sierra Leone	72	4.4	160	704	-1	61

15

	COUNTRY	AREA '000 SQ. KM	POPULATION MILLION 1992	PER CAPITA GNP US $ 1992	TOTAL GNP US $ MILLION	ANNUAL % GROWTH 1980-92	% ANNUAL INFLATION 1980-92
40	Somalia	638	8.1	170	1,377	NA	NA
41	Sudan	2,506	NA	NA	NA	NA	43
42	Syria	185	12.5	1,160	14,500	-1	14
43	Tajikistan	143	5.6	490	2,744	NA	NA
44	Tunisia	164	8.4	1,720	14,448	1	7
45	Turkey	779	58.5	1,980	115,830	3	46
46	Turkmenistan	448	3.9	1,230	4,797	NA	NA
47	Uganda	236	17.5	170	2,975	NA	NA
48	United Arab Emirates	84	1.7	22,020	37,434	-4	1
49	Uzbekistan	447	21.5	850	18,275	NA	NA
50	Yemen	472.1	12.5	520	6,500	NA	NA
	TOTAL	30,563	988.0		1,015,502		
	PER CAPITA INCOME			1,034			
	LOW-INCOME COUNTRIES	38,229	3191.3	390	1,244,607	4	12
	LOW/MID-INCOME	40,903	941	1,590	1,496,190	NA	41
	HIGH-INCOME	31,709	828.1	22,160	18,350,696	2	4
	WORLD	133,378	5438.2	4,280	23,275,496	1	17
	MUSLIM WORLD %	23	18.2	24	4		

NA = Data Not Available   HI = Estimated As High Income, $8,356 or more
Source: The World Bank, *World Development Report, 1994*, Table I, Basic Indicators.

16

20. **Per Capita Income**. The following general observations may be made about the income levels of Muslim countries:

    a. Twenty-seven countries belong to the low-income group with 1992 GNP per capita income of $670 or less. The poorest Muslim countries are located in sub-Sahara Africa and South Asia.

    b. Fourteen countries belong to the lower middle-income group of countries with per capita between $670 and $2,730.

    c. Five countries (Malaysia, Bahrain, Gabon, Oman, and Saudi Arabia) belong to upper-middle income group of countries with income between $2,730 and $7,510.

    d. Three countries (UAE, Kuwait and Qatar) were in the high income group of countries; data for another country belonging to this group (Brunei) is not available.

    e. Six Central Asian republics are going through a major transition. Estimates of their income levels were revised downwards during 1993-94.

Based on the same data, these additional comments may be made:

    a. Per capita GNP of Muslim countries ranged between $160 per year for Somalia and Uganda to $22,020 for UAE.

    b. Out of 50 countries with Muslim majorities for which some data were available, only eight belonged to upper middle income or high-income categories.

    c. Weighted average per capita GNP for all of the low-income countries in the world amounted to $390; middle-income countries $2,490; and high-income countries $22,160. Per capita GNP for the world as a whole amounted to $4,280.

    d. Muslims as a group had per capita GNP of about $1,034, placing average Muslim citizens of the world in the lower middle-income category.[6]

21. **Purchasing Power**. Purchasing power of the per capita income mentioned above, in relation to those of the high income countries (in US $) may be much higher than that suggested by the figures. In case of Pakistan, the 1992 per capita income is $420. However, based on the purchasing power, World Bank calculations indicate an income of $2,130

---

[6] Reliable data for Sudan, Lebanon, Iraq, Afghanistan and Brunei are not available and hence not included.

or 5.1 times larger. Similarly, purchasing power is estimated at $1,230 for Bangladesh (i.e., 5.6 times); $1,440 for Nigeria (4.5 times); $2,970 for Indonesia (4.4 times); $3,670 for Egypt (5.7 times); $5,170 for Turkey (2.6 times); $5,280 for Iran (2.4 times); and $8,050 for Malaysia (2.9 times). The purchasing power of Muslims, as a group, is probably at least three times the amount suggested by the per capita figures.[7]

22.   **Gross National Product.** During 1992, the world had a total GNP of $23,275 billion. Muslim countries, for which data are available and listed above, had a total GNP of $1,022 billion or about 4.4. Given the disparity between the dollar figures and purchasing power, as shown above, Muslims probably had about 10 percent to 15 percent of the world's purchasing power. The four Muslim countries with the largest economies were: Iran $131 billion; Saudi Arabia $126 billion; Indonesia $123 billion; and Turkey $115 billion.

23.   **Underdevelopment.** Several Muslim countries are under-developed in important ways. They can be characterized by:

    a. poverty conditions for a large percentage of the population;
    b. poor distribution of already low income;
    c. large portion of manpower illiterate and poorly trained;
    d. sizable unemployment and under employment;
    e. inadequate infrastructure;
    f. low expenditure on the health, education, and welfare of the people;
    g. heavy dependence on foreign aid; and
    h. low savings and investment rate.

Some of these points are discussed in detail later. Inadequate response to these issues is likely to result in continued underdevelopment.

    The following Table 2. presents economic data on fifty countries with majority Muslim populations.

---

[7] The World Bank, *World Development Report, 1994*, Table 30, p. 220.

Economic Data

	COUNTRY	LIFE EXPECTANCY YEARS (1992)	ADULT ILLITERACY DATA (1990)	AGRICULTURE % GDP (1991)	INDUSTRY % GDP (1991)	EXTERNAL DEBT% GNP (1991)	DEBT * SERVICE % EXPORT GS
1	Afghanistan	43	71	NA	NA	NA	NA
2	Algeria	67	43	14	50	70	74
3	Azerbaijan	71	NA	NA	NA	NA	NA
4	Bahrain	69	23	NA	NA	NA	NA
5	Bangladesh	55	65	36	16	56	20
6	Benin	51	77	37	14	70	6
7	Brunei	74	NA	NA	NA	NA	NA
8	Burkina Faso	48	82	44	20	35	9
9	Cameroon	56	46	27	22	58	19
10	Chad	47	70	43	18	47	5
11	Comoros	56	NA	NA	NA	NA	NA
12	Djibouti	49	NA	NA	NA	NA	NA
13	Egypt	62	52	18	30	133	17
14	Gabon	54	39	9	45	88	7
15	Gambia	45	73	NA	NA	NA	NA
16	Guinea Bissau	39	64	46	12	NA	NA
17	Guinea	44	76	29	35	95	18
18	Indonesia	60	23	19	41	66	33

	COUNTRY	LIFE EXPECTANCY YEARS (1992)	ADULT ILLITERACY DATA (1990)	AGRICULTURE % GDP (1991)	INDUSTRY % GDP (1991)	EXTERNAL DEBT% GNP (1991)	DEBT * SERVICE % EXPORT GS
19	Iran	65	46	21	21	12	4
20	Iraq	65	40	NA	NA	NA	NA
21	Jordan	70	20	7	26	227	21
22	Kazakhstan	68	NA	NA	NA	NA	NA
23	Kuwait	75	27	NA	NA	NA	NA
24	Kyrgyzstan	66	NA	NA	NA	NA	NA
25	Lebanon	66	20	NA	NA	NA	NA
26	Libya	63	36	NA	NA	NA	NA
27	Malaysia	71	22	NA	NA	48	8
28	Maldives	62	NA	NA	NA	NA	NA
29	Mali	48	68	44	12	105	5
30	Mauritania	48	66	22	31	215	17
31	Morocco	63	51	19	31	80	28
32	Niger	46	72	38	19	73	50
33	Nigeria	52	49	37	38	109	25
34	Oman	70	NA	4	52	29	NA
35	Pakistan	59	65	26	26	50	21
36	Qatar	71	NA	NA	NA	NA	NA
37	Saudi Arabia	69	38	7	52	NA	NA

	COUNTRY	LIFE EXPECTANCY YEARS (1992)	ADULT ILLITERACY DATA (1990)	AGRICULTURE % GDP (1991)	INDUSTRY % GDP (1991)	EXTERNAL DEBT% GNP (1991)	DEBT * SERVICE % EXPORT GS
38	Senegal	49	62	20	19	63	20
39	Sierra Leone	43	79	43	14	168	NA
40	Somalia	49	76	NA	NA	NA	NA
41	Sudan	52	73	NA	NA	NA	NA
42	Syria	67	36	30	23	104	NA
43	Tajikistan	69	NA	NA	NA	NA	NA
44	Tunisia	68	35	18	32	66	23
45	Turkey	67	19	18	34	48	31
46	Turkmenistan	66	NA	NA	NA	NA	NA
47	Uganda	43	52	51	12	109	70
48	United Arab Emirates	72	NA	NA	NA	NA	NA
49	Uzbekistan	69	NA	NA	NA	NA	NA
50	Yemen	53	62	22	26	88	7
	Weighted Averages						
	Low-income	62	40	NA	NA	NA	NA
	Low/middle Inc Count	67	35	NA	NA	42	21
	High Income Countr's	77	4	NA	NA	NA	NA
	World	66	35	NA	NA	NA	NA

* GS = Goods and services; data is for 1991

Source: The World Bank, *World Development Report, 1993 and 1994.*

24.   **Infant Mortality.** In spite of considerable progress in child survival and development, five million children under the age of five die in OIC countries every year due to lack of clean water, poor sanitation, malnutrition, and common diseases, including diarrhea and measles. Millions more are seriously disabled by diseases preventable at low cost. According to a recent report, 76 countries have a high mortality rate for children under five year of age; 25 of these countries are members of OIC.

25.   **Growth Rate.** During the 13-year period ending in 1992, while the world as a whole had a positive growth rate, at least 18 Muslim countries had a negative growth rate. Most others had a very low rate of growth. Indonesia, Oman and the Maldives enjoyed the highest growth at 4.0 percent, 4.1 percent, and 6.8 percent respectively; all others had lower rates. Most oil exporting Muslim countries had negative growth. This has meant continued poverty for many Muslims around the world. In contrast, some non-Muslim developing countries have experienced large growth rates, including Korea at 8.5 percent, Thailand at 6 percent, and China at 7.6 percent.

26.   **Inflation.** During the same 1980-92 period, high-income countries were generally able to control their inflation. However, many low-income and middle-income countries suffered from very high inflation rates. Muslim countries followed the same pattern. Some poor African countries and Turkey were particularly hard hit and experienced inflation of over 40 percent per year. On the other hand, some Muslim oil exporters actually experienced negative inflation rates.

27.   **Agricultural Production.** During 1991, agriculture accounted for 29 percent of gross domestic product (GDP) in low-income economies of the world. For low- and middle-income countries combined, agriculture accounted for 31 percent in sub-Sahara Africa; 19 percent in East Asia; 31 percent in South Asia; and 14 percent in the Middle East and North Africa. For fuel exporters as a group, agriculture accounted for 12 percent of GDP. Among the high income countries of the West, agriculture accounts for 3 percent to 6 percent of GDP. Muslim economies are located in Africa, Asia, and the Middle East, and tend to follow the regional pattern. In several low-income Muslim countries, agriculture accounts for more than 40 percent of GDP, which indicates relatively low levels of industrialization and development of the economy.

28.   **Industrial Production.** During 1991, industry accounted for 34 percent of GDP in low-income economies. For all low- and middle-income economies, industry accounted for 29 percent in sub-Sahara Africa; 41 percent in East Asia and the Pacific Rim countries; and 26 percent in South Asia. Most Muslim countries in sub-Sahara Africa registered industrial production of less than 20 percent. Others appear to follow the pattern. For Muslim countries for which data is available, industry accounts for more than 30 percent in only 12 countries. In only five, Indonesia, Algeria, Gabon, Oman, and Saudi Arabia, did it account for more than 40 percent. It is fair to say that as a group, Muslim countries are far behind in industrial development.

29.   **External Debt and Debt Service.** Total external debt as a percentage of gross national product (GNP) amounted to 45 percent for low-income economies in 1991; 53 percent for lower middle-income; 33 percent for upper middle-income. For severely indebted countries as a group, external debt amounted to 46 percent of GNP. With exception of a few, all Muslim countries (for which data is available) are severely indebted. For at least eight Muslim countries, external debt is over 100 percent of GNP. This suggests high levels of external debt by Muslim countries.

Recently, Saudi Arabia and Kuwait have borrowed heavily while Indonesia, Pakistan and others have increased reliance on commercial borrowing (as compared to softer borrowing from international agencies). This suggests that the external debt and debt service problems of Muslim countries have become worse than indicated.

B. Existing Political Conditions.

30.   **Types of Governments.** Governments in most Muslim countries fall into the following categories:

  a. one party rule headed by former military rulers;
  b. military rule;
  c. kings;
  d. democracy; and
  e. guided democracy.

Military rulers in several Muslim countries have tried to legitimatize their rule through new constitutions and hurried elections since the fall of the Soviet Union and the concomitant increased power of the democratic West. Invariably, one party (headed by the national ruler) is used and justified for reasons of accelerating national development and maintaining national unity. At least six countries are still ruled directly by the military. Nearly all others are managed under the eyes of powerful military leaders. Nine countries are ruled by kings.

Few Muslim countries, (e.g., Malaysia) have democratically elected governments. Several have some form of "guided" elected government (e.g., candidates for high office are screened); for example, in Turkey and Pakistan, candidates require the military's "approval" while in Iran, they require the clergy's "approval." Some observers assert that approval or an indication of "no-objection" is required from Washington for holders of top offices in at least some Muslim countries, in particular, those economically and militarily dependent or seeking assistance. Good relations with foreign powers frequently translate into political, economic, and even military success at home.

31.   **Limited Democracy**. In most developing countries, including Muslim countries, democracy is not government of common people, for common people, nor by common people. In many of these countries:

a. the constitutions do not reflect the prevalent thinking of the nation as represented by the parliament and as interpreted by the judiciary; and constitutional rule does not preclude arbitrary rule;
b. the legitimate role of opposition parties is denied by resorting to their oppression;
c. the absence of a viable opposition means unlimited powers in the hands of government officials and their illicit enrichment, persistent violation of human rights, and denial of civil liberties;
d. law and law enforcement agencies are used as instruments of state tyranny; and
e. the military is the most important power broker if not the actual holder of power; instead of dealing with each other for resolution of political issues, politicians deal directly with the military and further weaken the democratic political process.

Several Muslim countries are implementing democracy. Some military-led governments have introduced new and more democratic constitutions during the last five years. The list includes Bangladesh, Azerbaijan, Benin, Gabon, and Guinea. Many have elected new presidents.

32. **Islamic Democracy**. Although Islam requires leadership based on consultations, it does not explicitly mandate a particular form of government for its followers. Instead it exhorts leaders to rule with the fear of God in their hearts, honorably and with justice. In practical terms, Islam recognizes that the form of government matters little if the hearts of the rulers do not reflect the spirit of Islam. The form of government, be it monarchy, republic, theocracy, or empire, is called into question, Islamically, when it fails to uphold the *shari'ah* or Islamic law and abandons sacred traditions. For this reason, Muslim governments rarely categorize themselves according to traditionally Western ideas of government.[8]

Few modern Muslim countries offer much choice of leadership to their populace. Even the provincial and local government leaders are generally appointed on the basis of loyalty to the national leadership. Most leaders gain and retain power on the basis of "might." In political affairs, Muslims have relatively little experience with elective forms of government; their traditions and cultures do not recognize such politics as particularly beneficial or necessary. To some orthodox Muslims, elected government represents a foreign concept at odds with their culture, imposed or advocated by the former colonial masters or their trained puppets.

In contrast, most Western governments wielding significant power are headed by elected officials. They have come into power on the basis of support for their ideas from the general public. They remain in power at the pleasure of their respective citizenry. Western leaders see themselves representing a sacred heritage, established by honored statesmen and philosophers and implemented by glorious revolutions against oppressive authorities. It is not surprising, therefore, that Muslim and Western heads of governments do not share common objective on politics. Behind diplomatic courtesies, many Muslim leaders are commonly held in contempt and ridiculed by Western politicians, the media, and intellectuals.

The following Table 3. presents political and military data on fifty countries with majority Muslim populations.

---

[8] Some scholars, including Dr. Imad A. Ahmad, point out that Islam is a "nomocracy" or a government ruled by law.

Table 3. Political and Military Data

	COUNTRY	YEAR OF INDEPENDENCE	GOVERNMENT	MILITARY '000 PERSONS				RATING
				ARMY	NAVY	AIR	TOTAL	
1	Afghanistan	(d)	Civil War	NA	NA	NA	NA	Medium
2	Algeria	1962	Military	120,000	7,000	12,000	139,000	Modern
3	Azerbaijan	1991	Elected President	30,000	NA	NA	30,000	Modern
4	Bahrain	1971	King	5,000	500	650	6,150	Modern
5	Bangladesh	1971	Prime Min./ Parliament	93,000	7,500	6,000	106,500	Modern
6	Benin	1960	Elected President	12,000	0	0	12,000	Basic
7	Brunei	1984	King	3,600	550	300	4,450	Modern
8	Burkina Faso	1960	Elected President	7,000	0	200	7,200	Basic
9	Cameroon	1960	Elected President	6,600	0	0	6,600	Basic
10	Chad	1960	Prime Minister	25,000	0	0	25,000	Basic
11	Comoros	1975	Pres./ Military Influence	700	0	0	700	Basic
12	Djibouti	1977	Pres./ Military Influence	3,680	100	100	3,880	Basic
13	Egypt	1922	Elected President	290,000	20,000	100,000	410,000	Modern
14	Gabon	1960	Elected President	3,250	500	1,000	4,750	Basic
15	Gambia	1965	Elected President	800	0	0	800	Basic
16	Guinea Bissau	1974	Elected President	6,800	300	100	7,200	Basic
17	Guinea	1958	President	8,500	400	800	9,700	Basic
18	Indonesia	1945(f)	Pres. Elect By Assembly	215,000	44,000	24,000	283,000	Modern
19	Iran	(d)	Elected President	475,000	18,000	35,000	528,000	Modern

	COUNTRY	Year of Independence	GOVERNMENT	MILITARY '000 PERSONS					RATING
				ARMY	NAVY	AIR	TOTAL		
20	Iraq	1932	1-party Rule, Life President	350,000	1,000	30,000	381,000		Modern
21	Jordan	1946	King	8,500	400	14,000	22,900		Modern
22	Kazakhstan	1991	Democracy/Military	NA	NA	NA	NA		Modern
23	Kuwait	(a)	King	7,000	1,000	200	8,200		Modern
24	Kyrgyzstan	1991	Democracy/Military Veto	NA	NA	NA	NA		Modern
25	Lebanon	1945	President by Natl Assembly	17,500	500	800	18,800		Modern
26	Libya	1951	Leader per Assembly	55,000	8,000	22,000	85,000		Modern
27	Malaysia	1948	Prime Minister	105,000	10,500	12,400	127,900		Modern
28	Maldives	1953(b)	Elected President	NA	NA	NA	NA		Basic
29	Mali	1960	Elected President	6,900	50	400	7,350		Basic
30	Mauritania	1960	Elected President	10,500	450	150	11,100		Basic
31	Morocco	1956	King	175,000	7,000	13,500	195,500		Modern
32	Niger	1960	Military Rule	3,200	0	100	3,300		Basic
33	Nigeria	1960	Military Rule.	80,000	5,000	9,500	94,500		Modern
34	Oman	1951	King	20,000	3,400	3,000	26,400		Modern
35	Pakistan	1947	Prime Min./ Parliament	500,000	20,000	45,000	565,000		Modern
36	Qatar	1971(c)	King	6,000	700	800	7,500		Modern
37	Saudi Arabia	(d)	King	45,000	9,500	18,000	72,500		Modern
38	Senegal	1960	Elected President	8,500	700	500	9,700		Basic
39	Sierra Leone	1961	Military Rule	3,000	150	0	3,150		Basic

27

	COUNTRY	Year of Independence	GOVERNMENT	MILITARY '000 PERSONS				RATING
				ARMY	NAVY	AIR	TOTAL	
40	Somalia	1960	Civil War in Progress	NA	NA	NA	NA	Basic
41	Sudan	1955	Military Rule	NA	500	6,000	71,500	Medium
42	Syria	1941	Elected President	300,000	4,000	100,000	404,000	Modern
43	Tajikistan	1991	Democracy/Military Veto	NA	NA	NA	NA	Modern
44	Tunisia	1956	Elected President	27,000	4,500	3,500	35,000	Modern
45	Turkey	(d)	Democracy/Military Veto	470,000	52,000	57,200	579,200	Modern
46	Turkmenistan	1991	Democracy/Military Veto	NA	NA	NA	NA	Modern
47	Uganda	1962	Military	70,000	NA	NA	70,000	Basic
48	Un. Arab Emirates	1971	King	40,000	1,500	2,500	44,000	Modern
49	Uzbekistan	1991	Democracy/Military Veto	NA	NA	NA	NA	Modern
50	Yemen	1953(e)	Elected President	60,000	3,000	2,000	65,000	Medium
	Total Muslims			3,739,03	232,700	521,700	4,493,43	

(a) The new constitution of Kuwait was prepared in 1962.

(b) The Maldives became a republic in 1953.

(c) Qatar joined the UN as a member in 1971.

(d) Afghanistan, Iran, Turkey, and Saudi Arabia have maintained independence in different forms for a long time.

(e) Freedom fighters claimed independence in Yemen in 1953.

(f) The Netherlands ceded sovereignty on December 27, 1947.

Sources: Year of independence: *Encyclopedia Britannica* and *The World Almanac 1995*; Profiles of Islamic countries: *Islamic Propagation Organization, Tehran 1989*; Military data: *The Europa World Year Book, 1992*; Military rating by author.

C. Existing Spiritual Conditions.

33. Religious Differences.

As for those who divide their religion and break up into sects, thou hast no part in them in the least: Their affair is with Allah: He will in the end tell them the truth of all that they did *(Surah 6:159)*.

As in Christianity, Islam encompasses several denominations. While there are two main Muslim divisions, *Sunni* and *Shi'ah*, there are many subdivisions, with varying degrees of differences. The majority of Muslims identify themselves as *Sunni*. Only a few countries have sizeable *Shi'ah* populations. *Shi'ites* comprise a majority in Iran, Iraq, Azerbaijan and Bahrain. About 30 percent of the population in Kuwait and Lebanon is *Shi'ah*. The *Sunni* majority is, itself, divided into four main schools of thought: *Hanafi; Maliki; Shafi'i;* and *Hanbali.* The differences between these are not considered major.

There is much disagreement among Muslims regarding important issues such as *Hadith*, Islamic jurisprudence (*Fiqh*), and succession to the Prophet. *Sunnis* believe that the order of succession was correct. *Shi'ites* believe that Ali ibn Abi Talib (RA[9]) should have succeeded the prophet, and that the *Khilaafah* (Caliphate) should have remained within the prophet's family. There is violence between *Shi'ites* and *Sunnis* every year, particularly during the month of *Muharram*, over succession issues.

Among the other relatively small sects, Ismailis believe in the Aga Khan as their spiritual leader; in the U.S., Elijah Muhammad established The Nation of Islam which produced boxing champion Muhammad Ali and Malcolm X. Despite major differences in dogma, Elijah Muhammad's "Black Muslims" made the Pilgrimage to Mecca as Muslims.

The Ahmadiyya sect, while themselves professing to be Muslims and observing the prescribed rituals, are generally not permitted to perform the Pilgrimage and are widely considered to be outside the pale of Islam. They were expelled primarily because they believe that Ghulam Ahmad, their movement's founder, was himself a prophet. Other groups with direct or indirect origins in Islam include the Bahá'í and the Sikhs, neither of which is part of the Muslim *Ummah*, nor do they consider themselves Muslims.

---

[9] May Allah be pleased with him.

34.   **Belief Versus Practice.** Spiritually, Muslims are strong yet vulnerable. Their belief in Allah, Muhammad as Allah's prophet, the authenticity of the Qur'an as the final revelation, and the Day of Judgment, continues to be proclaimed unhesitantly. Often however, belief is not reflected in day-to-day practices. Increasingly, this laxity in religious practices is causing serious friction in the Muslim social order. Many urban Muslims, particularly those with higher education, acquire Western views as part of their interaction with non-Muslims. Further, the influence of the Western media cannot be underestimated.

Ironically, the United States, frequently accused of pandering irreligious values to Muslim countries, recently experienced the electorate's outcry for moral values. This seems to echo the Islamists' call for a return to basic religious affirmations. Throughout the Islamic world, there is a spiritual renaissance which seems most fervent among young Muslims.

Muslims all believe in Prophet Muhammad (PBUH) as the model for human behavior. His life, day-to-day conduct, and sayings are documented in great detail. Many Muslims place great emphasis on following his traditions *(Sunnah)* in physical terms: correct beard; dress; and etiquette. Innovations are considered detrimental if not ruinous to the religion. Others argue that following his spiritual example, faith in Allah, humility, tolerance and generosity, is more important, particularly in modern times.

35.   **The Qur'an.** Muslims profess deep respect for the Qur'an. It is kept in a high, clean place, never allowed to touch the ground, often kissed. Most solemn gatherings start with a recitation from the Qur'an, which is heard in solemn reverence. In Qur'anic recitation competitions, prizes are given to the best reciters. However, relatively few outside the Arabic-speaking world can read it correctly. Fewer understand it. Most read translations and explanations in other languages but are reminded by scholars of the multi-faceted meaning and rich nuances of the Qur'anic language which are being missed. Even fewer truly practice its teachings.

36.   **Day of Judgment.** Muslims believe in the eventual occurrence of the Day of Judgment. Death is seen occurring among elders, contemporaries and even the young ones. Yet, few actions in the life of most Muslims are truly guided by the certainty of death, the Day of Judgment, and the final settlement with Allah.

D. Existing Military Situation

37.   **Military Manpower.** Based on the data from *The Europa World Year Book, 1992,* military manpower data for Muslim countries are

summarized in the table above. The data for army, navy, and air force are as of June 1992 in some cases, and June 1991 for others. Data for several countries known to have large armed forces are not available, including five of the Central Asian republics and Afghanistan. Information on the recent increase in the strength of Saudi Arabia and Kuwait is also not available. Nevertheless, based on the data available, the total strength of all Muslim armed forces amounted to about 4,493,000; of which armies had 3,739,000; navies had 232,000; and air forces had 521,700. By all measures, Muslim countries have very large armed forces.

The following table summarizes the comparative strengths of military manpower in the U.S.A., India, the U.K., Japan, Israel, China and includes the number of total Muslim forces:

COUNTRY	ARMY	NAVY	AIR FORCE	TOTAL
USA	731,700	779,500	517,400	2,028,600
India	1,100,000	55,000	110,000	1,265,000
UK	149,600	61,800	88,700	300,100
Japan	156,000	44,000	46,000	246,000
Israel	134,000	10,000	32,000	176,000
China	2,300,000	260,000	470,000	3,030,000
All Muslims	3,739,030	232,700	521,700	4,493,930

Figure 1: Military Strength.

Numerically, the total Muslim forces are large enough to command considerable respect. They can match any other power on earth. While years of distorted spending have deprived Muslim economies of much needed economic development, they have developed large and reasonably-equipped forces for defense purposes. Also, each country has paramilitary and police forces which are generally used for domestic law and order. (Members of on-going resistance movements, some of whom may be very well trained, are not here included.) Except for major civil wars (e.g., Somalia), forces have been sufficient to maintain order at home.

38. Military Equipment. Many Muslim countries have relatively modern military establishments. Turkey, Pakistan, Indonesia, Egypt, Syria, Iran, and Saudi Arabia are relatively advanced. Other countries such as Bangladesh, Nigeria, Morocco, Tunisia, Jordan, Malaysia, Algeria, and Kuwait are reasonably equipped. These groups, working together, can satisfy each others' total need for manpower and conventional equipment.

Combined, their forces are capable of defending Muslim countries against most enemies. Individually, the forces of most Muslim countries are small, weak, and dependent on foreign troops for support.

39.   Morale. Since the military attacks on Iran and Kuwait by Iraq, and on Libya and Iraq by the United States, the morale of individual countries has been low. Many are anxious to improve bilateral ties with the West, particularly the United States. By contrast, Muslim countries appear reluctant to support each other militarily, or even financially. Accordingly, there exists a common feeling of vulnerability and isolation. To some extent, this appears to change as Islamic political affirmation increases.

40.   Dependence on External Technology. All Muslim countries are, to some degree, dependent on the West, Russia, or China for state-of-the-art military equipment and technology. With advanced military-industrial establishments, Western nations face little threat from Muslims in technological areas. However, manufacturing capacity for conventional equipment exists in several Muslim countries. While most military procurements are currently made abroad, military budgets of Muslim countries for conventional equipment can be diverted to purchase from other Muslim countries or for domestic production of weapons. Trained scientists are available to satisfy requirements for such production.

41.   Military Objectives. The objective of Muslims should be to live as peaceful, but equal, partners under the New World Order, as justified by their demographic, political, economic, and military positions. Most agree that to think beyond peaceful coexistence in the world would be folly for Muslims. Nevertheless, Muslims must continue to improve the quality of their military capability and promote self-sufficiency in military equipment and technology primarily for individual and collective self-defense. Given the number of military conflicts which affect Muslims, it should be possible to assure those who may be concerned that the intentions are genuinely defensive and not offensive.

There does not appear to be a unifying military objective which Muslim nations share. Their divergent religious, economic, social and political views preclude any significant solidarity. Among those Muslim nations with modern military capabilities, political and economic cooperation is rare. The obvious example is the continuing conflict between Iran and Saudi Arabia. It is unlikely that any one Muslim country will emerge as the leader of all Muslims. It is more likely that Muslim countries will consider an economic union such as the European Union (EU) a military alliance such as NATO.

Muslims have many strengths. Most are listed in this chapter. Muslims themselves need to identify, acknowledge and assess their strengths and weaknesses. This is necessary in order to (a) understand existing problems, (b) enhance self-confidence, (c) reinforce strengths, and (d) remedy weaknesses. The world media often point to sleeping giants, China and India in particular; sometimes they include Muslims. Muslims can be considered a major world power once they recognize their own strengths.

> **. . .And hold fast, all together, by the Rope which Allah (stretches out for you), and be not divided among yourselves; and remember with gratitude Allah's favor on you; for you were enemies and He joined your hearts in love, so that by His Grace, you became brethren . . .** *(Surah 3:102-103).*

42.   **The Qur'an.** As noted above, Muslims share a common religious bond based on the revelation from Allah to Prophet Muhammad (PBUH), the Qur'an. All Muslims agree on the purity of the Qur'an's Arabic text; it has not changed from the original transmission to the Prophet through the angel Gabriel. While translations differ in minor ways, as do commentary and interpretation, all Muslim read the same Arabic text.

43.   **Brotherhood.** Regardless of sectarian, cultural, and ethnic divisions, Muslims affirm a strong brotherhood based on the Qur'anic injunction that they should hold steadfast to their religious bond. This is regularly invoked during the five daily prayers.

44.   **Ritual Language.** Though the vast majority of Muslims are not Arabs and do not speak Arabic, all Muslims, to some extent, study and learn Arabic. This is essential in order to read the Qur'an and to perform the five daily prayers. Muslims are comfortable within a mosque in any country of the world, ignoring political boundaries during their worship services.

45.   **Pilgrimage.** Unlike Christianity, Muslims, regardless of denomination, annually observe a common and unifying ritual, the Pilgrimage to

Mecca, Saudi Arabia. More than any other ceremony, the *Hajj* serves to identify Muslims as a unified body, an *Ummah*. From the death of Prophet Muhammad (PBUH) to the present, differences between Muslims have only increased. Yet, the Pilgrimage to Mecca, along with the Qur'an, remains intact, unifying Muslims throughout the world.

46.   Belief in the Day of Judgment. All Muslims acknowledge the temporary nature of life in this world. They share a common conscience, often weak but persistent, which recognizes the need to do good and avoid evil.

47.   Benefits of Prayer and Fasting. Prayers five times a day (before sunrise, around noon, late afternoon, at sunset, and before going to bed) have many benefits, in addition to spiritual rewards:

a. Ablution (cleaning of hands, mouth, nostrils, face, arms, head, neck, and feet) ensures a clean body at the five prayer times. In practice it encourages Muslims to remain clean throughout the day. Such an emphasis on cleanliness encourages the believers to avoid all kinds of mischief throughout the day.

b. The prayer requires clothing that is clean and protective of the modesty of both males and females. It encourages all to wear clean clothes and to avoid any form of nudity.

c. The prayer involves physical movements (standing straight, bending, prostrating, and sitting) several times in each prayer. It provides aerobic exercise for several minutes each time, five times a day.

d. The prayer involves direct communication with God and is at least a form of meditation. The meditation part is highly recommended by the medical profession.

Even Pope John Paul II is much impressed by the Muslim prayer. In *Crossing the Threshold of Hope,* the Pope writes:

In the Declaration *Nostra Aetate* we read: "The Church also has a high regard for the Muslims, who worship one God, living and subsistent, merciful and omnipotent, the Creator

of heaven and earth (*Nostra Aetate 3*)." As a result of their monotheism, believers in Allah are particularly close to us.[10]
[T]he religiosity of Muslims deserves respect. It is impossible not to admire, for example, their *fidelity to prayer*. The image of believers in Allah who, without caring about time and place, fall to their knees and immerse themselves in prayer remains a model for *all those who invoke* the true God, in particular for those Christians who, having deserted their magnificent cathedrals, pray only a little or not at all.[11]

The month of *Ramadhan* requires fasting from sun rise to sunset each day. Besides the spiritual cleansing, it provides a wonderful opportunity to diet and achieve desirable body weight. Being hungry and thirsty all day makes you recognize the plight of the poor who are forced to remain hungry. It inspires you to contribute generously to those in need. Muslims believe that Allah bestows special rewards for charity and other good deeds performed during the month of fasting.

48.   **Large Population.** Muslims comprise a majority of the population in about 50 out of about 170 independent countries of the world. They represent one of the largest blocks of nations in the United Nations. Muslim observers assert that were Muslims to cooperate sufficiently, they could, as a block, justifiably demand and get a permanent seat and veto power at the Security Council under the New World Order.

Out of about five billion people, about one billion in the world are Muslims. In addition to Muslim majority countries, practically all other nations of the world have conspicuous Muslim populations. India alone has about 150 million Muslims. The United States, Russia, China, Europe, and Israel all have significant numbers of Muslims. The literacy rate for the group is low. Nevertheless, a large well-trained pool of manpower exists. Unemployment among the educated classes is high.

49.   **Diversity.** Muslims belong to all races, cultures, and ethnic groups. Muslims come in black, white, brown, and yellow, and many combinations. Muslims officially claim to be free from racism since the Qur'an and

---

[10] Pope John Paul II, *Crossing the Threshold of Hope* (New York: Alfred A. Knopf, Inc., 1994), p. 91.

[11] *Ibid.* p. 93.

the traditions of the Prophet specifically reject it. However, cultural, nationalistic and ethnic differences always remained; these were strategically heightened by colonialism.

Muslims can find themselves at home in all continents, most countries and cultures. They speak many languages, live in deserts, plains, mountains, and on seashores. They are at home just about anywhere in the world. Their diversity is often exploited and turned into weakness. In an ever shrinking world, it is a major asset from political, economic and military points of view; this diversity can be a force for good in the world.

50.   **Vast Land and Natural Resources.** Muslims occupy about 30 million square kilometers or more than one fifth (23 percent) of the world land area. Parts of it are barren, and inhospitable but include all types of terrain and known natural resources.

Muslim countries are particularly rich in oil and gas resources; this has induced the West to take measures to control those areas. In spite of Muslim dominance of the Organization of Petroleum Exporting Countries (OPEC), the oil-rich kingdoms appear to have assured the West in recent years that they have no intention of withholding these resources. The Gulf War was an obvious illustration of the importance of Muslim lands to the West.

Much of the current political and military pressures asserted against Muslims is based on the need to ensure that Muslim leadership remains hospitable to the energy interests of the West. Any group whose politics oppose Western domination of, or significant influence over, Muslim resources is bound to be depicted as an enemy of peace, democracy, human rights, and even civilization.

51.   **Large Financial Resources.** Muslims possess large financial resources in the form of (a) official reserves amounting to several billion dollars, (b) private holdings in the form of cash and commercial property, and (c) gold which is the most common form of financial reserve held by even the poorest of Muslim families. Gold holding is conservatively estimated at 0.5 ounces per family of six persons, which would amount to about 83 million ounces. At the rate of $350 per ounce, this would be valued at $29 billion.

Muslims do not lack financial expertise. In fact, they own and manage hundreds of financial institutions in the world.

It may be noted that much Muslim wealth is invested in the West. In the cases of Iran and Iraq, assets were frozen when their political stance changed. Others, including Saudi Arabia and Kuwait, have lost tens of billions of dollars in expenses incurred during the Gulf War, and continue to incur expenses for troops stationed on their soils. Ironically, this forced cooperation among Muslim countries and the West resulted in strange alliances in the Gulf War, with Saudi Arabia, alongside the United States and Israel, fighting against Muslims in Iraq, with Iran standing by neutral.

The wealth in natural resources found in Muslim lands can be a source of great strength; it also represents a divisive factor. Such is the financial stake in the region that the Islamic bond has often been weakened considerably, if not severed completely, when these huge financial resources have been threatened.

52.   Sizeable Industrial Base. Several Muslim countries have firm industrial bases, at least for consumer and medium level technology. Several Muslim countries are largely self-sufficient in consumer goods such as textiles, and shoes, processed agricultural products, and basic electronics such as radios and televisions. Muslims produce most other items under licenses from foreign manufacturers. Some Muslim countries can manufacture capital assets and machinery to produce other goods. Some are using nuclear technology for peaceful purposes. One is reportedly able to produce nuclear weapons. Industrial raw materials exist in abundance.

53.   Trained Manpower. Although the literacy rate is very low, many well-educated Muslims are available inside and outside Muslim countries. Doctors, engineers, scientists, and other professionals are currently employed in all aspects of economic development. Many more are under training at home and abroad.

The current problem is not shortage, but excess supply of professionals. Economic growth is not large enough to absorb many who are unemployed or underemployed. Difficulty in finding suitable jobs is discouraging many from devoting their full energy to education. As far as trained manpower is concerned, Muslims are capable of undertaking a much larger level of economic activity.

54.   Media Experience and Policy. Muslims in more than 50 countries provide their own print, audio, and visual media. They (a) own and operate television and radio stations, (b) publish daily newspapers and monthly journals in almost all the languages of the world, (c) have thousands of journalists in all fields of specialization, and (d) have contacts and working relations the with media all over the world. Media coverage (particularly

TV) in less-developed areas of Muslim countries is poor but can easily be improved; all they need is finance.

The world is facing an explosion of Western television broadcasts beamed by satellites across national borders. CNN, Star TV, and Australian TV are examples. Anyone with a large antenna can receive the signals. Broadcasters depend on revenue from advertisement rather than user fees in many cases. Some countries are happy to allow access to their citizens. Others like Malaysia are concerned that the news, views, and culture of the sending nations are being propagated.

Muslims are beginning to consider the implications of their media policy. To become an important and reputable media alternative at the global level, there are technical and financial considerations. The new broadcasting technology has to be mastered, or purchased. However, there is also a need for being thorough in information or data collection, analytical in data sorting, and comprehensive and fair in presentation.

55.   **Moral Fiber.** The Islamic message throughout the Qur'an and *Hadith* encourages Muslims to be good and clean people, to take a long-term view beyond life in this world, and to cooperate with each other. Accordingly, a vast majority of Muslims have never touched alcohol or used illegal drugs. Most have a great deal of patience and are willing to sacrifice for the life hereafter. Given the moral decay all over the world, these are valuable messages in today's world and a valuable strength that should be reinforced.

56.   **Strong Community Feeling.** There is a strong "community feeling" among all Muslims, a continuing sense of a brotherhood that transcends political boundaries. They share the pain when they hear of conflicts among Muslims or injustices at the hands of non-Muslims. An outcry was heard when Muslim fought Muslim in the Gulf War and when Serbs slaughtered Muslims in Bosnia. Though the feeling is largely passive because of inability to actively respond, Muslims regularly offer prayers for their fellow Muslims experiencing hardships in foreign lands. At the Friday prayers, the rhetorical call is regularly made for strong and sincere leadership who will lead them in defense of fellow Muslims.

57.   **Belief in One Muslim Nation.** Muslims have been declared to be one "Ummah or nation" in the Qur'an. Implications of this can be enormously beneficial to Muslims if put into practice. This implies open

borders, the free flow of manpower, capital, and goods and services among more than 50 countries.

The EU and other common markets would be small in comparison to such an Islamic union. How to put this "declaration" in practice is one of the biggest challenges to Muslim leadership, particularly to OIC. Poorer countries with surplus labor are in favor or it; richer ones are not too keen. They need to remember the teachings of the Qur'an:

Never did we send a warner to a population, but the wealthy ones among them said: "We believe not in the (message) with which you have been sent." They said: "We have more in wealth and in sons [than the faithful]. And we cannot be punished." Say: "Verily my Lord enlarges and restricts the provision to whom He pleases, but most men understand not *(Surah 34:34-36).* **"**

Whether or not the rich follow religious teachings in this regard, Muslims need to demonstrate that the idea of "one Muslim nation" is attractive for rich as well as poor Muslim nations. They should analyze the reasons richer EU nations cited for joining the poorer ones, and why the United States and Canada joined much poorer Mexico in the North American Free Trade Agreement (NAFTA). The EU has been economically helpful to all member countries. Belief in and implementation of one Muslim nation is likely to improve the conditions of all Muslims, both rich and poor.

58.   **Principles of Good Governance.** Islam and good governance have much in common. The Qur'an and the Prophet's traditions offer numerous examples of mutual consultation, public service, protection of the weak and poor, equality of all under God, charity, learning (education and human resource development), human rights, spending for public welfare, and simple taxation based on the value of assets. These are just a few. The governance in Muslim countries in practice, however, leaves much to be desired and is discussed below.

59.   **In Summary.** Muslims have many geopolitical strengths which are envied by others. Some are listed below:

    a. ownership of oil and gas resources;
    b. large armed forces;

  c. ownership of strategic areas; and
  d. political power of more than 50 countries.

Muslims have many strengths. However, much of their strength is focused on keeping regimes in power in individual Muslim countries. No price, including use of corrupt practices and repression, is considered too high for perpetuation of power. Muslims have been unable to use their strengths collectively for the common good of the *Ummah*. They have been unable to put their powerful message, strong community feeling, belief in one Muslim nation, principles of good governance, and geopolitical strengths to common use. Their other strengths (e.g., media experience, financial resources, industrial bases) can be of greater value if united. However, in relation to non-Muslims, Islamic countries remain far more divided than their beliefs profess.

Muslims are hampered by many weaknesses. As a people, they are divided, often manipulated, and compromise their values for financial gain. Spiritually, they conflict in interpreting Islamic teachings, lack religious leadership, do not understand Arabic, arbitrarily restrict the role of women, neglect their beliefs, and are beguiled by Western customs. Some make Islam more difficult to practice than it is. All agree that reform is needed, individually and collectively. This chapter briefly analyzes the spiritual issues and suggest some ideas for corrective action.

> **As for those who divide their religion and breakup into sects, you have no part in them in the least: Their affair is with Allah: He will in the end tell them the truth of all that they did** *(Surah 6:159).*

Muslims are divided people in terms of nationality, ethnicity, religious denomination, language, race, and economic position. Muslims have no hesitation in fighting each other, or questioning each others' "true faith" based on any of these factors.

Somalia is a recent example. Civil war there among various tribal warlords resulted in mass killings, starvation, and the breakdown of law and order. Pakistani Muslims were among the United Nations military peace keepers in Somalia in early 1993. It is unclear how, but Pakistanis and Somalis came to shoot each other; one result was that United States marines invaded Mogadishu. It appears that Muslims often contribute to the destruction of each other.

Afghanistan is another tragic example of civil war among Muslims. The current instability started in the 1970's after President Daud tried to improve relations with Muslim neighbors in Pakistan and Iran while reducing reliance on the Soviet Union. A few coups by Soviet puppets later, the Soviet military arrived in force to support their local communist partners. The West and most Muslims in Afghanistan and abroad united, and struggled for years to defeat the communists. After thousands of casualties on both sides, and destruction of much of the country, the Soviet forces withdrew. Left on their own, the Afghan freedom fighters are now fighting among themselves, using heavy weapons to destroy cities, productive infrastructure, and life, in a way unparalleled in the country's violent history. Unlike Somalia, the main groups are all led by well known religious leaders each of whom claims Allah to be on his side.

Muslim unity occurred in Afghanistan because the Western countries supported it to counter the Soviet Union, financed it, and persuaded diverse groups to join the effort. Now that the Soviets are no longer a threat, the West sees a new threat, Muslim unity and a possible fundamentalist government in Afghanistan. The West was content with the earlier king, and would prefer to bring him back. As in the Iran-Iraq War, Western leaders have no interest in stopping bloodshed among Muslims. Their past policy for dealing with Muslims has been to promote disunity among them and allow them to fight each other. Some argue that by providing arms to their favorite groups, Pakistan, Saudi Arabia, and Iran are indirectly helping Western strategy and are contributing to the continued bloodshed.

Another example is Bangladesh. A civil war in Pakistan resulted in brutal action by the Pakistani army in East Pakistan. India intervened, capturing more than 90,000 Pakistani soldiers. This eventually led to the breakup of the Islamic Republic of Pakistan and the establishing of a new Muslim nation. The leadership in Bangladesh has publicly accused Muslim brethren of the Pakistani armed forces of having committed more than a million rapes. Ethnic strife continues in the remaining Pakistan, inflamed by differences in language, culture, and education.

In the Gulf War, Muslims joined with non-Muslims to fight Muslims. The Iran-Iraq War pitted *Sunni* Muslims against *Shi'ah* Muslims and Arab Muslims against non-Arabs Muslims. Even in the United States, followers of W. D. Muhammad bitterly oppose the followers of Louis Farrakhan, while both groups, predominantly African-American, find little in common with immigrant Muslims, predominantly from the Middle East and Asia.

Several Muslim countries have domestic discontent. Sind province in Pakistan is an example. Sind was the first province to accept Islam in the subcontinent, and is known as a gateway of Islam. Sindhis are devoted Muslims and very proud of their role in the creation of Pakistan. However, Sindhis have been treated as second class citizens in Pakistan ever since independence in 1947. Sindhis feel that they have not received an equitable share of economic development in terms of physical infrastructure, human resource development, commerce and industry, and above all, civilian and military jobs. Small towns and villages in Sind lack electricity, water, health facilities, schools, and minimal housing. Instead of getting facilities and support for the development of their language and culture (like Urdu, Punjabi, and Pushtu-speaking people have received), people taking interest in the Sindhi language and culture are harassed and suspected of anti-

Pakistan activities. At the same time, Urdu-speaking citizens are struggling to restore law and order in Karachi and to secure their economic rights. Past governments in Pakistan have been accused of creating and fanning communal strife. This genuine discontent in Pakistan, and similar domestic discontent in other Muslim countries, obviously needs to be addressed.

> **If two parties among the believers fall into a fight, make ye peace between them: but if one of them transgresses beyond bounds against the other, then fight ye (all) against the one that transgresses until it complies with the command of Allah; but if it complies, then make peace between them with justice, and be fair; for Allah loves those who are fair (and just). The believers are but a single brotherhood so make peace and reconciliation between your two (contending) brothers; and fear Allah, that ye may receive Mercy** *(Surah 49:9-10)*.

Muslims must try to reduce the divisions among themselves as commanded by Allah.

60.   **Cultural Differences.** Observers assert that cultural differences between Muslims are quite significant and cannot be overcome to achieve common spiritual or secular goals. Arab Muslims, South Asian Muslims, Black African Muslims, and European Muslims are all very different, culturally, from each other. The point was made rather strongly by some press reports that Bosnian Muslims brought to Pakistan for refuge would rather go back to their killing fields than stay in Pakistan. Reportedly, they have made clear that they are Europeans and unable to cope with the South Asians' living conditions and their brand of Islam.

To refute such reports or deny that differences exist is folly. The differences need to be recognized. Standards of living, tolerance in spiritual practice, political freedoms, and even hygienic conditions are factors which make for a cultural composite. Muslim leaders must struggle to minimize differences.

61.   **Different Interpretations of Islamic Teachings.** The Qur'an is available to all Muslims in Arabic. It has been translated into the vast majority of native languages spoken by Muslims and is studied by them from childhood. Although there is full agreement among the scholars as to its authentic content and principles, complete unity of opinion does not exist regarding some practices.

Religious leaders and denominations vie with each other in interpreting the application of Qur'an, *Hadith* and *shari'ah,* willing to go to extremes to assert their own view while condemning that of others. Some conflicts among Muslims are centuries old; civilian strife in modern Muslim countries often reflects historic prejudices and controversies. Each group considers all others to be misguided, not hesitating even to declare war against them. Military action in Bangladesh, current massacres in Afghanistan, annual riots on the Muharram in several Muslim countries have been justified on this basis. The fundamental teaching of the Qur'an on Muslim unity is routinely ignored.

162.   Lack of Religious Leadership. Islam teaches that every individual is responsible to Allah for actions in this world. Allah's direct word is available to each Muslim and non-Muslim alike through the Qur'an; hence, there is no need for a middle man. Accordingly, Muslims (particularly the *Sunni* majority) do not have established religious leadership.

Nevertheless, after the death of the Prophet, the *Khalifah* (Caliph or successor to the Prophet PBUH) acted as the religious leader as well as head of state. Some form of succession continued until early in the twentieth century. Since the loss of even the nominal *Khalifah* (Caliph) based in Turkey after the end of World War I, there has been no central Islamic authority. Local *imams, muftis,* and even internationally known scholars have not been able to fill the vacuum.

An acknowledged leader supported by a suitable organizational structure and human and financial resources could deal with the pressing issues of the community; likewise, it could deal with world powers regarding religious, moral and financial issues just as the Pope does for Catholics. If the person was respected and accepted by them, many conflicts among Muslims could be prevented, and disputed interpretations of the religious teachings could be clarified. Such a leadership is urgently needed. Attempts by religious scholars, political leaders of individual countries, and the OIC have done little to prevent conflicts in Pakistan, Afghanistan, and Somalia.

It may be noted that some minority sects who have established leadership have succeeded in achieving greater unity and a higher level of progress for their followers. The Aga Khan has that role for Ismailis, the *Khalifah* for the Ahmadis, and the Grand Ayatollah for *Shi'ites.*

In the 1920's, when the office of *Khalifah* (Caliph) was abolished, there was much protest among Muslims. For example, Muslims of the Indian subcontinent launched a movement for restoration of the *Khalifah.*

In recent years, there has been renewed discussion of the *Khilaafah* (Caliphate) concept.

The King of Saudi Arabia enjoys considerable respect as guardian of the holy places in Mecca and Madinah. In addition, as sponsor of OIC and many Islamic and charitable programs, he is the focal point of many Muslim activities. However, the role of *Khalifah* has not been assigned to anyone yet. The International Muslim *Khilaafah* Conference, held in London in August 1994 focused on this subject. Questions about how, when, where, and who were controversial then and remain so today. While the need is acknowledged by most Muslims, implementation in the near-term is improbable.

63. Low Education Level of Religious Leaders.

Religious leadership in Islam is largely left to people having little education, secular or religious. Religious leaders, particularly in rural areas where a majority of Muslims reside, may not be even high school graduates. Apprenticeship with the existing *imam* (leader) and memorization of some verses from the Qur'an, often without even understanding the meaning, can be sufficient qualification for becoming the *imam* of a mosque. The Friday sermons, which are the dominant means of religious communications, are often repetitive focusing on rituals, irrelevant issues of dogma or fine points of Islamic jurisprudence. Communication between the common Muslim and his *imam* is a one way lecture on basic rules. Opportunities for weekly gatherings in millions of mosques around the world are vastly under-utilized. The tradition of Muslims in the mosques inquiring of the Prophet (PBUH) and his rightly guided successors on spiritual, political, economic, and political issues are hardly in practice today. Such a practice would result in better guidance for the community and improved communications among Muslims.

Lack of wise and dynamic leadership is one of the main reasons why educated Muslims have abandoned full observance of Islam. Their inability to translate traditional Islam into modern practice creates what they consider a conflict between religion and everyday existence. Without spiritual leadership to address the modern needs of Muslims, many succumb to worldly distractions exhibiting apathetic Islamic practice at best, adopting Western secularism at worst. An urgent need is present for upgrading the training and broadening the education of *imams*.

64. Deficient Observance of Islam.

While lack of spiritual leadership may be identified as a reason for apathetic observance of Islam by many Muslims, in Islam, each individual is responsible for his action and must affirm his beliefs on that basis. As in the case of all religions, many who are born and raised under Islam take for granted much of what the religion teaches. The practice of Islam as a complete way of life is rare. A vast majority of professed Muslims ignore it; "traditionalists" have largely restricted it to rituals of prayers, fasting, and Hajj; "modern Muslims" wish to forget about the "rituals" and focus on "good humanitarian" conduct in day to day life only. The traditionalists and the modern Muslims look at each other with some contempt, each feeling a sense of superiority over the other. There is a need to advocate a balanced approach to performing the duties owed to Allah and the duties owed to mankind.

65.   Difficulty of Understanding Arabic.

Had We sent this as a Qur'an (in a language) other than Arabic, they would have said: "Why are not its verses explained in detail? What! a foreign (tongue) and (a Messenger) an Arab?" Say: "It is a guide and a healing to those who believe; and for those who believe not, there is a deafness in their ears . . . (Surah 41:44)."

The Qur'an was revealed in Arabic partly because the Prophet (PBUH) was an Arab, and was initially dealing with Arab people. Today, the majority of Muslims are non-Arabs (about 80 percent) who do not speak Arabic. Some non-Arab Muslims have learned Arabic, but most have not. For them, the Qur'an is a holy book, to be touched and kissed reverently, recited beautifully, and respectfully listened to only in a state of cleanliness. Understanding and subsequently acting on most of the instructions contained in the Qur'an, beyond commonly known duties, has been decidedly neglected. Mosques are often full of worshipers who do not understand what has been said in the prayer.

Muslims believe that Arabic is a very rich language with multiple meanings. Accordingly, the Qur'an cannot be fully translated. It has to be read in Arabic in order to understand fully the essence of each verse. Not knowing Arabic leaves most non-Arab Muslims with a sense of inadequacy. It provides an excuse for not understanding even the basic agreed translation. Turkey's attempt to hold prayers in their own language has not been well received by other Muslims. In any case, there is a need for making Islamic knowledge more accessible to common Muslims. There is an urgent need to deal with the language issue in order to ensure wider understanding of the Qur'an.

A possible remedy may be available in *ijma* (consensus) and *ijtihad* (individual endeavor or adaption). These would allow Muslims to consider several options including compulsory study of Arabic in all Muslim countries, and greater use of their local languages in religious matters. Of course, leaders participating in *ijma* and *ijtihad* must understand the Qur'an and the *Sunnah* fully, either on their own account or with the help of Arabic language experts who are readily available in almost every country. It would be a mistake to restrict participation only to religious scholars or those who have direct command of Arabic. All practicing Muslims must have a voice (either directly or through their chosen representatives) in resolving outstanding issues.

66. Easy to Manipulate. Western media have played a malevolent role in accentuating Muslim differences. They are eager to point out the "aspirations" of Berbers in Algeria, Kurds in Turkey, Iran, and Iraq, Sindhis in Pakistan, etc. They appear to sympathize with the oppressed minorities, who may indeed have genuine complaints, yet the Western media's politically-based agenda often seeks to divide Muslims rather than help the minorities. Muslim national governments make themselves vulnerable to such criticism when they ignore the genuine interests of their subjects. Ironically, fickle Muslim officials often are more distressed by the Western media's criticism of their conduct than by the protests of their citizens or the warnings in their own Scripture.

67. Easy to Corrupt. For reasons of greed or disbelief, Muslim officials are easy to corrupt. It is sardonically asserted that Muslim government officials can be compromised by a smile from a Western dignitary, an invitation to a cocktail party, companionship of a pretty woman, a visa, etc. If nothing else works, a well-placed threat soon leads to compliance, obedience and even treachery. National interests are often relegated to secondary position in relation to personal interests. Books written by former Western officials have sighted many such instances of Muslims' debasement.

68. Poor Treatment of Guest Workers. Muslims in poor countries are grateful for job opportunities in oil-rich Arab countries. There is a large demand for every available job. Such competition and excess supply of labor has given rise to a number of abuses: confinement of workers; payment of less than contracted wages; delayed payment of wages; sexual abuse of female workers; use of small children as camel jockeys in races; etc. These are just a few types of the reported abuses. Private employers as well as the host governments have the obligation to stop un-Islamic practices. It may be noted that:

    a. without respect for contractual rights, Muslims are undermining their own Islamic beliefs and Qur'anic affirmations;

    b. Muslims cannot pressure non-Muslim governments to end mistreatment of Muslims (e.g., Germany's mistreatment of its guest workers from Turkey), if Muslim Arabs cannot treat foreign Muslims well;

    c. if the idea of a unified Islamic Nation is ever implemented, labor would freely flow across national boundaries, at least in the initial phases.

69.   **Restricted Role of Women.**

The believers, men and women, are protectors, one of another: they enjoin what is just, and forbid what is evil... *(Surah 9:71).*

In spite of its relatively benevolent treatment of women 1,400 years ago, "Islamic society" today finds women frequently mistreated, abused, and even deprived of some basic Islamic rights. Many Muslim women openly complain of the way Islamic scholars interpret certain doctrines, including: teachings relating to men simultaneously having up to four wives; extra covering to be worn; half the value given to their testimony in some courts of law; exclusion of women from mosques, even for Friday prayers; general discrimination against women in daily life; etc. These concerns exist and are frequently underscored by critical Western media.

In many Muslim countries, discrimination against girls and women is visible, particularly in low-income and rural families. Education beyond religious teachings is given low priority. Girls are removed from schools at a much earlier age than boys and are kept under a strict eye at home. Employment outside the home is frowned upon. In the work place, female workers are paid less than men for the same work. Political participation by women is discouraged and rare. Economically, they are expected to remain dependent on their fathers, brothers, and husbands.

The Struggle of Muslim Women, by Dr. Kaukab Siddique, deserves special attention. Documented from the Qur'an and *Hadith*, it puts Islamic teachings relating to women in proper historical context, demonstrating the equality that men and women share under Islam. Among other things, the book indicates that:

a. Permission for more than one marriage is reluctantly granted under specific and difficult conditions.
b. The Qur'an has expressly prohibited harsh treatment of women.
c. Islamic dress and modesty are ordained for both men and women. The extra head covering for women was meant to "dignify women and to stop men from approaching them as sex objects."
d. The punishments for adultery and fornication are identical for both men and women.

The theory that women cannot lead is not correct. From the Qur'an, Dr. Siddique cites examples of a female ruler named Bilquis (known to Christians as the Queen of Sheba) who continued to rule by process of consensus even after she became a Muslim. He has also mentioned the example of Ayesha Siddiqa, the wife of the Prophet (PBUH) who led the army from Mecca to Basra.

Theologically, Christianity and Judaism accord lower status to women in comparison to that of men. As the Prince of Wales remarked at the Oxford Center for Islamic Studies on October 27, 1993:

> . . .Remember if you will, that Islamic countries like Turkey, Egypt, and Syria gave women the vote as early as Europe did its women -- and much earlier than in Switzerland! In those countries the women have long enjoyed equal pay and the opportunity to play a full working role in their societies. The rights of Muslim women to property and inheritance, to some protection if divorced, and to conducting of business were rights prescribed by Qur'an 1400 years ago, even if they were not everywhere translated into practice. In Britain at least, some of these rights were novel even to my grandmother's generation!

At the time of this writing in 1995, there are women heading government in three Muslim countries, Turkey, Bangladesh, and Pakistan. These leaders, in turn, have appointed many more women to high positions in their respective countries. Nevertheless, much more visible and widespread change has occurred for women in Western society during the last 50 to 100 years. Accordingly, many Muslim women look at Western women with envy, not fully understanding the differences between appearance and substance, and often ignoring the destructive impact such changes are having on family life and society in general.

Throughout Muslim countries, an urgent need exists for greater empowerment of women. For any change to occur, however, it must be based on a definitive interpretation of what the Qur'an and *Hadith* command regarding women. Islamic scholars need to discuss the issue with all interested parties (historians, sociologist, representatives of women, etc.); they must reach a consensus and adopt it.

70.   Need for Self-Reform.

Do you enjoin right conduct on the people, and forget (to practice it) yourselves and yet you study the Scriptures? Will you not understand? *(Surah 2:44).*

There is an urgent need for Muslims to look inside themselves to verify that they are on the right path. The answers are clear; the corrective steps are very difficult. Nevertheless, it is almost impossible to reform others when one is so clearly unable to reform himself. Many problems facing Muslims would be solved if they listened to their conscience.

71.   **Attraction to Western Lifestyle.** Many Muslims, particularly educated ones, have a strong affection for the Western way of life. They desire a Western education, job, income, home, and conveniences, if not for themselves, at least, for their children. A majority of Muslims who come to visit or study wish to remain in the West, particularly in the United States. This may be due to (a) poor economic conditions or a lack of political freedom back home; (b) better economic opportunities or greater political freedom in the West; (c) for women, freedom from in-laws and opportunities to run a separate household; or (d) hope for a better future for children.

Whatever the reason, most Muslims prefer to stay in the West and they make exceptional efforts to do so. It may be argued that this is not "un-Islamic." The desire to travel, explore the world, and live a comfortable life is perfectly Islamic, as long as it is earned through honest means. However, an obvious danger exists that the lure of the West may not stop there but continue until Islam is fully compromised. Some Muslim scholars argue that Muslims have no business in the West other than to propagate Islam. To them, any desire to leave a Muslim country for material reasons is unacceptable Islamic behavior.

In a spiritual sense, Muslims exposed to the modern world often compare Islam to Western philosophies and test its teachings against the norms of today, which happen to be the norms of the West. In doing so, they negate the essential attribute of revelation, substituting human concepts and ideas for Divine commands.

By contrast, Muhammad Asad noted in his book, *Islam at the Crossroads,* that:

> **The outcome of such an endeavor might be emergence of a new *Fiqh* [jurisprudence] exactly conforming to the two sources of Islam -- the Qur'an and the life example of the Prophet -- and, at the same time, answering to the exigencies of present life: just as the older forms of *Fiqh* answered to the exigencies of a period dominated by Aristotelian and Neoplatonic philosophy and to the conditions of life prevailing in those earlier ages.**[12]

Such a systematic assessment of Islamic doctrines against conditions of the twentieth and the twenty-first century requires a large effort, involving much thought and research. However, it would help regain the lost self-confidence of many Muslims; such an undertaking would ultimately benefit Muslims.

72.   Making Religion More Difficult Than It Is.

O ye who believe! Make not unlawful the good things which Allah hath made lawful for you, but commit no excesses. . . *(Surah 5:87).*

Increasingly large number of Muslims are being attracted to modern comforts and freedoms. Even in the smallest towns around the world one can see the relaxed Western life on TV. The desire to have a similar life is powerful if not overpowering. Is it all against Islam?

Islam has a code of conduct with prohibitions. However, some clarifications are needed to determine what is allowed and what is not. To be on the safe side, some Muslims deny themselves (and others) almost all pleasures and comforts. Some refuse even to take cough syrup because it has alcohol in it. Others feel that an occasional drink is allowed as long as one does not get drunk. Muslims of financial means in the Middle East are able to keep four wives and frequently change them without "violating the religious law."

---

[12] Muhammad Asad, *Islam at the Crossroads* (Islamabad: Da'wah Academy, 1990), p. 82.

Islam does not deny pleasure. It claims to be the most natural religion for mankind. Accordingly, there is need for sincere scholarly research to determine what "pleasures" are allowed by Islam. Such a determination would help keep those Muslims who may otherwise give in and walk away from Islam. Some orthodox Muslims may argue that such "weaklings" are not needed in Islam, that Muslims need not apologize for what Allah has commanded. Others may ask who gives anyone the right to make Islam any more difficult than it is meant to be by Allah?

73.   **Non-Muslim Minorities.** Historic evidence shows that Muslims have generally been tolerant of non-Muslim minorities within their boundaries. Jews, after being expelled from Spain, lived under Muslim protection for years. Nevertheless, in recent times, non-Muslims in Islamic lands have complained of feeling like second class citizens. Accordingly, they are the most vocal proponents of secular governments in Muslim majority countries. In Lebanon, for example, the non-Muslims have assured their identity and power by constitutionally dividing Muslims into two groups (*Sunni* and *Shi'ah*) with the help of the French colonial masters. Subsequently, they used military power and even an alliance with Israel to avoid Muslim rule.

Whatever can be done to build confidence and protect the interests of minorities within Muslim countries deserves further study. As usual, the answer should be found in the practices of the Prophet regarding the various classes of non-Muslims existing under the Islamic state.

74.   **Muslim Marriage Arrangement.** In the early days of Islam, Muslims married at a very young age -- typically as soon after reaching puberty as possible, around the age of 14. Marriages were frequently among closely allied families, children of well-known friends and distant relatives. Accordingly, in spite of the required separation of sexes starting from the age of puberty, the bride and the groom were well acquainted from childhood, had shown some romantic interest, and willingly gave the required consent for the marriage.

In addition, marriage to four wives at a time was allowed and practiced by men. Divorce and remarriage was easy for each partner. Some *Shi'ites* allow temporary (*mut'ah*) marriages during travel. These arrangements made it easy to confine sex to married life, from puberty until death. This is one reason why Islam claims to be a most natural religion.

Behavior has changed significantly since then. Marriages are now commonly delayed until the groom has secured a reasonable job -- the late-twenties or even thirties. In many cases, there has not been any social contact -- the two have simply seen each other's face once or twice before marriage. Increasingly, marriages are taking place outside the auspices of the family. Even though physical contact between the bride and the groom prior to the marriage is still avoided, traditional Islamic patterns, which had facilitated the acquaintance of each, are being abandoned.

Many Muslim countries prohibit polygamy. Divorces and re-marriages have become very difficult. Muslims have taken a very natural religion and gradually made it very hard for themselves. The changed sexual behavior has meant introduction of sexual abuse including frequent masturbation, homosexuality, and unhappy marriages. There is a need to review Muslim marital behavior to make it as natural as intended and practiced earlier.

75.   **Muslim Appearance.** Muslim dress codes have been under attack for some time. To some, it is synonymous with Arab garb; it has always looked strange to the Western eye. Some Muslims are themselves disowning it, while others continue to stress the need to maintain an Islamic appearance.

In the 1920's, Turkey banned the "Islamic dress" for reasons of anti-Arab feeling. It was viewed as "inefficient in the work place," and "to look Western" became the style. During the Gulf War, American and European Muslims were afraid to be seen in Arab clothing for fear of being labelled Iraqis. In 1993, Arab Algeria, involved in a mortal struggle with so-called Islamic fundamentalists banned state employees from wearing it.

Should Muslims be concerned about this? To be forced to do anything is repugnant to many. It is interesting to note that the appearance of orthodox Jews (e.g., long beards; head wear) has become accepted and even respected as symbolic of Jewish power and pride. Muslim dress is not synonymous with Arab or Pakistani or Malaysian dress, but there are prescribed rules. The right to wear Islamically prescribed clothing cannot be denied or abridged without Muslims compromising their beliefs; legal recourse to safeguarding such rights is essential for the long-term survival of Muslims in Islamic countries and in the West.

It may be noted though that Islam does not require a veil over the face of believing woman and yet some religious leaders in some countries, particularly in India and Pakistan, require it.

And say to the believing women that they should lower their gaze and guard their modesty; that they should not display their beauty and ornaments except what (must ordinarily) appear thereof; that they should draw veils over their bosoms

**and not display their beauty except to their husbands, their
fathers . . .** *(Surah 24:31).*

Islam gives permission to both men and women to go out of the house,
with some restrictions, and yet some Muslims confine their women to their
homes. These Muslims ought to reconsider this practice.

76.   **Food and Drink.**

**They ask [you] concerning wine and gambling. Say: "In them
is great sin, and some profit for men: but the sin is greater
than the profit."** *(Surah 2:219).*

**O ye who believe! Intoxicants and gambling, sacrificing to
stones, and (divination by) arrows, are an abomination. . .**
(Surah 5:90).

The vast majority of Muslims around the world avoid alcoholic drinks.
Most of the nearly one billion Muslims have never touched an alcoholic
drink in their entire lives. Some dedicated ones will even refuse cough
syrup in sickness because it contains alcohol. However, some ignore the
implied injunction against any kind of intoxication. Large numbers of
Muslims have become addicted to heroin and other modern drugs in recent
years. The addiction has reached alarming proportions in Pakistan and
Afghanistan. For a long time, many Muslims have used drugs and plants
such as opium, charus and bhang to induce various levels of euphoria.

   Khat, a bitter tasting and mildly narcotic plant, is chewed by
millions in Somalia, Djibouti, Yemen, Kenya, and Ethiopia. According to
the World Health Organization, *khat* triggers a rush of adrenalin that raises
body temperature, blood pressure, and emotions. Users experience a lifting
of spirits and enhanced erotic activity. A few hours later, the user sinks
into lethargy. Many who can least afford it spend a large amount of money
on sustaining this addiction. Trade in *khat* has reportedly reached a
hundred million dollars a year or more. Local Islamic scholars have ruled
that while the Qur'an is not specific about *khat,* it is clearly a gray area,
and that Muslims should stay clear of it. Millions have not paid much
attention.

   While a majority of Muslims follow Islamic teachings and avoid eating
pork and drinking alcohol, other substances, such as those mentioned
above, which have similar or even worse effects are gaining popularity in
Muslim countries. These substances are expensive and destructive to their
users. Countless families have been destroyed in Pakistan, Afghanistan, and

Somalia because of their use. Careful study and more effective regulation by governmental authorities in conjunction with religious leaders would be of great benefit to these societies.

77.   **Violence Against Each Other.** Muslims are willingly using violence against each other at the personal, national and international level to assert their own point of view. In recent times, Muslims have killed and injured millions of fellow Muslims in (a) the civil war in East Pakistan; (b) the Iran-Iraq war; (c) the Iraqi civil war against Kurds and *Shi'ites*; (d) the Jordanian military action against Palestinians; (e) Syrian action against internal opposition; and (f) the Somali civil war and subsequent famine. Such violence is extending at an alarming rate into Algeria, Egypt, Pakistan, Somalia, Kuwait, and elsewhere. Some sadly point out that the number of Muslims killed by other Muslims far exceed the number killed by non-Muslims. Violence of brother against brother is most destructive physically and spiritually.

Laws against violence to others exist in every Muslim society, whether they are based on civil and criminal jurisprudence inherited from colonial masters or based on *hudud,* the restraint or limit laws of Islam.

The recompense for an injury is an injury equal thereto (in degree): but if a person forgives and makes reconciliation, his reward is due from Allah; for (Allah) loveth not those who do wrong *(Surah 42:40).*

The judiciary in many Muslim countries is accused of corruption and lack of independence. The judiciary of such countries must be streamlined, reformed and strengthened to provide prompt justice at home. They must not forget that for those who transgress, **"defying right and justice: for those there will be a penalty grievous"** *(Surah 42:40).*

At the international level, conflict resolution mechanisms offer some hope (e.g., OIC), but the ultimate solution can only be found in those Islamic values of unity and brotherhood which are so basic to the religion.

78.   **Historic Misunderstandings Among Muslims.** There are historic "misunderstandings" among Muslims. For example, some Turks have not forgotten the Arab collaboration with Britain in the Ottoman Empire's breakup. Since then, Turks have been luke warm in their support of Arab causes. Similarly, Arabs and Iranians often find each other at opposite ends of "Muslim opinion." Historically, some Iranians look at Arabs as uncivilized. Arabs and Iranians (Persians) have been competitors for some

time; the Iraq-Iran War is just one of the recent examples. The Prophet (PBUH) had a high opinion of both. Based on *Hadith* (Tirmidhi):

> **Abu Hurairah reported that the Apostle of Allah recited this verse: "If you turn back, He will replace a people other than you and then they will not be like you." They said: "O Apostle of Allah! Who are those about whom Allah said that if we turn back, He will replace them in our place and then they will not be like us? He struck the thigh of Salman, the Persian, and then said: He and his people. Had there been religion near Pleiades, some of the Persians would have certainly secured it."**

In the West, Germany has reconciled with its enemies of World Wars I and II. Japan is an ally of the United States though the latter dropped atomic bombs on Japanese citizens. Muslims, too, would find great benefit in reconciling their past disputes.

> **But indeed if any show patience and forgive, that would truly be an affair of great resolution** *(Surah 42:43).*

79.   **Self-Interest of Regimes in Power.**

> **. . .Obey Allah and obey the Messenger, and those charged with authority among you . . .** *(Surah 4:59).*

In most Muslim countries, the narrow interests of the regime in power are paramount. Each ruling group is much more interested in its own power, prestige, and short-term objectives. This is particularly true for dictatorships and monarchies. Their supporters have often used the above verse to justify continued support of the people. They often forget the following instruction about not following the unworthy ones:

> **But fear Allah and obey Me; and follow not the bidding of those who are extravagant -- who make mischief in the land and mend not (their ways)** *(Surah 26:150-152).*

In short, Islam supports the stability provided by the righteous ruler, but also expects the government to be run in a righteous manner. Islam encourages disobedience to and even overthrow of the corrupt ruler.

For Iran (which has held frequent elections), increasing its own national influence, spreading *Shi'ah* theology, and teaching a lesson to the

West at times appears to be of higher value than Islamic solidarity. Muslim governments benefit when they realize that individually they have little power in the world and can be manipulated easily. As the EU is demonstrating in Europe, Muslims, together in a block, are capable of extraordinary accomplishments.

It may be noted that kings and strong rulers are not prohibited by the Qur'an. The Jewish Prophets who were also kings include Saul, David, and Solomon; also, Joseph was employed by the King of Egypt. The Qur'an refers to these kings without condemnation of their title or their authority. However, there are many heads of Muslim governments whose primary objective is to remain in power. They may be kings wishing to perpetuate their dynasties or dictators wishing to stay in power for life. They do not hesitate to crush their own Muslim populace or invite non-Muslim foreign powers to protect their rule.

Today, Muslim rulers often look to the West, particularly the United States, for protection, persuaded by its power and record of coming to the aid of "current" friends. However, the United States' record of dumping old friends (Pakistan, Iran or Iraq) and of freezing assets (Iran, Iraq, etc.) is often forgotten. Ignoring their shared beliefs, Muslim leaders apparently cannot find anywhere else to go for help except the West. Even though, Iran has lost considerable wealth as a result of the asset freeze, and Arab kings had to "contribute" huge sums to pay for United Nations military action in the Gulf War, the idea of Muslims relying on Muslims appears to be too far fetched to be taken seriously.

80. Principles of Conflict Management.

The Believers are but a single Brotherhood: so make peace and reconciliation between your two (contending) brothers; and fear Allah, that you may receive Mercy *(Surah 49:10).*

Many issues among Muslims involve the need for conflict resolution. Susan L. Carpenter, and W. J. D. Kennedy in their book, *Managing Public Disputes* discuss means for conflict resolution and present a valuable analysis.[13] They note that if a dispute is left unresolved for a long period of time, conflict emerges, sides form, positions harden, communications

---

[13] Susan L. Carpenter, and W. J. D. Kennedy, *Managing Public Disputes* (Jossey-Bass, San Francisco, 1988).

stop, resources are committed by each side, conflict goes outside the community, perceptions become distorted, and a sense of crisis emerges.

Conflicts have several psychological effects on the parties: increased anxiety; intensification of feelings; hardening of positions; inability to perceive neutrals; militant hostility; sense of urgency; momentum of conflict beyond individual's control; and motivation based on revenge. Accordingly, conflicts deserve attention and resolution as soon as possible.

Based on the judicial reforms mentioned above, each country can use its own court system to settle issues within its jurisdiction. However, with regard to international issues among Muslims, a system of conflict management based on mediation is not well developed. Delegations sent to OIC to resolve the Iran-Iraqi and Kuwait-Iraq Wars and other conflicts have been ineffectual, partly because they lacked a well-defined approach. The problem is further complicated by the fact that Muslim governments are able to cite passages from the Qur'an and *Hadith* to support their respective points of view. Therefore, there is a need for a conflict management mechanism. It can be used to get to the core of the problem.

81.   **Conclusion.** Islamic history has been full of religious teachers, legists, and traditionalists such as Imams Abu Hanifah, Malik ibn Anas, ash-Shafi'i, Ibn Hanbal, al-Bukhari, Muslim, al-Ghazali, Ibn Taymiyah, and others. There have been reformers such as Jamal ad-Din al-Afghani, Shaikh 'Abd al-Wahhab, Shah Wali Allah, and others. They have tried to clarify issues which needed clarification during their times. At this juncture, there are many outstanding spiritual issues, some of which have been pointed out above, which need resolution. Muslims must use the Qur'an, *Sunnah*, knowledge of the available scholars, collective thinking of practicing Muslims, and individual reasoning and effort to resolve the issues. Muslims must get on with resolving the differences of opinion and conflicts, and implement the resolutions as soon as possible.

Muslims face many economic issues; in general, they are economically weak. They are faced with low per capita income, widespread poverty, poor distribution of resources, considerable illiteracy, poorly-trained manpower, extensive unemployment, corruption, misuse of resources, and excessive dependence on foreign aid. As noted above, Muslims make up about one fifth (18 percent) of the world population. However, the GNP of Muslim-majority countries represents less than one twentieth (4.4 percent) of it. The relatively small size of their economies is one of the reasons Muslims lack influence in a predominantly materialistic New World Order. Many of the economic issues facing Muslims are discussed below. However, it is important to understand how basic Islamic economics differs from other economic systems.

A. Comparative Economic Systems.

78. **Capitalism.** A capitalist is a possessor of wealth who invests it in commercial ventures with the objective of making a profit. He also bears the risk of possible loss. Capitalism includes several basic principles:

a. private ownership of the means of production, with market competition, i.e., freedom to compete with other producers and suppliers of goods and services resulting in improved quality and cheaper prices.
b. free enterprise, i.e., freedom to conduct business without government restrictions;
c. profit motive, i.e., freedom to conduct business in such a way as to maximize profit and to avoid a loss;

Pure capitalism leaves individuals unrestricted for purposes of maximizing efficiency and profit. It has little concern for those who cannot operate efficiently.

79. **Communism.** Karl Marx, founder of communism or "scientific socialism," viewed history as a struggle between the capitalists (bourgeoisie) and the workers (proletariat). He felt that under the capitalist system, workers were paid little more than subsistence wages, while the owners

retained all surplus as profit. He believed that workers could get justice through a revolution against the bourgeoisie. In the *Manifesto of the Communist Party*, he envisaged achievement of the following:[14]

    a. Abolition of private ownership of land and application of rents of land to public purposes.

    b. A heavy progressive income tax.

    c. Abolition of all rights of inheritance.

    d. Confiscation of the property of all emigrants and rebels.

    e. Centralization of credit in the hands of the state, by means of a national bank with state capital and an exclusive monopoly.

    f. Centralization of the means of communication and transport in the hands of the state.

    g. Extension of factories and instruments of production owned by the state; the bringing into cultivation of waste lands and the improvement of soil.

    h. Equal exposure of all to labor. Establishment of industrial armies, specially for agriculture.

    i. Combination of agriculture with manufacturing industries; gradual abolition of distinction between town and country by a more equitable distribution of the population over the country.

    j. Free education of all children in public schools. Abolition of children's factory labor. Combination of education with industrial production, etc.

80.   **Communism vs. Socialism.** Though both communists and socialists are inspired by Marx, in practice they differ, *inter alia,* on the following:

    a. Communism can be achieved only through revolution; socialism can be achieved through a peaceful transfer of power through elections.

    b. To protect the revolution, a communist government must be a dictatorship of the proletariat; a socialist government must be a democracy based on political liberty and economic justice.

---

[14] Karl Marx and Friedrich Engels, *Manifesto of the Communist Party, 1848*, as summarized in W. Sahakian and M. Sahakian, *Ideas of the Great Philosophers* (New York: Barnes & Noble, Inc., 1966), pp. 80-81.

c. Communism requires governmental ownership and operation of all means of production and distribution; socialism requires nationalization of only the major industries.[15]

81.   **Christian Economic Approach.** Even though most of the capitalist world is Christian, they all do not necessarily follow the economic teachings of Christianity. The Bible discourages accumulation of material possessions, and suggests difficulties for the wealthy on the Day of Judgment. In addition, interest income was forbidden for centuries until the Protestant Reformation made concessions for its use.

82.   **Muslim Economic Approach.** Islam has laid much emphasis on economic issues. Allah has fixed night for rest and day for work.

...But Allah doth appoint night and day in due measure... *(Surah 73:20).*

And when the prayer is finished, then may ye disperse through the land, and seek of the bounty of Allah: and celebrate the praises of Allah often (and without stint): that ye may prosper *(Surah 62:10).*

As explained by Dr. Imad A. Ahmad in his paper "An Islamic Perspective on the Wealth of Nations":

The Qur'an deals with a number of specific economic issues. Private property is protected *(Surah 2:188).* **The fulfillment of obligations is commanded** *(Surah 2:177* **and** *Surah 5:1),* **and is accompanied by details of contract law** *(Surah 2:82-283).* **There is prohibition of fraud** *(Surah 26:181)* **and a call for establishing clear standards of weights and measures** *(Surah 55:9).*[16]

---

[15] Summarized from Irving L. Gordon, *Reviewing World History* (Amsco School Publication, 1964), p. 294.

[16] Imad A. Ahmad, "An Islamic Perspective on the Wealth of Nations" presented at the International Conference on Comprehensive Development of Muslim Countries from an Islamic Perspective (Subang Jaza, Malaysia, August 1994), in press.

Islam believes in private property, free trade, free market, minimal governmental intervention, and reward for personal effort. However, Islam aims at human welfare in this world and in the hereafter. Material gain is important but not the final objective. Islam encourages individuals to maximize efficiency and profit, as does capitalism, but Islam also encourages individuals to help and protect the weak.

Dr. M. Umar Chapra has summarized an Islamic economic strategy well in *Islam and the Economic Challenge*. It consists of reorganizing the entire economic system with a set of four indispensable and mutually-reinforcing elements:

  a. a socially agreed filter mechanism;
  b. a strong motivating system to induce the individual to render his best in his own interest as well as in the interest of society;
  c. restructuring of the whole economy, with the goal of realizing the key *maqasid* (objectives) in spite of scarce resources; and
  d. a strong and positive goal-oriented role for the government.

The issue of resource allocation is particularly tricky. The Islamic approach emphasizes: (a) universal brotherhood of Muslims; (b) human freedom; (c) treatment of resources as a trust; (d) fulfillment of basic needs for all; (e) humble life-style; (f) equitable distribution of income and wealth; (g) respectable source of earning for all; (h) growth; and (i) stability.

Poverty, poor distribution of resources among countries and within countries, unemployment and underemployment, exclusion of manpower (women) from the economy, large dependence on foreign aid, inability to collect *zakat*, lack of loan capital without interest, illiterate and untrained manpower, and scarcity of water -- these are a few of the immediate problems facing Muslim countries. The four elements noted above, if applied sincerely, address these economic issues. In modern times, Muslims have yet to demonstrate Islamically-based approaches to their problems.

B. Poverty

83.   **Low Per Capita Income.** As mentioned above, most Muslim countries had negative or small growth rates in per capita GNP during the 1980-92 period. All low-income countries, excluding China and India, grew at an average rate of 1.2 percent per year. At zero growth rate, per

capita remains constant for ever; at 1 percent it doubles in about 70 years. At 2 percent it doubles in 35 years; at 3 percent it doubles in 24 years; at 4 percent it doubles in 18 years. Per capita income of selected Muslim and non-Muslim countries at varying growth rates will be expected to double in the indicated year:

Country	Per Capita 1992 ($)	1% Growth YR. 2062	2%Growth YR. 2027	3%Growth YR.2016	4%Growth YR.2010
Uganda	170	340	340	340	340
Pakistan	420	840	840	840	840
Egypt	640	1,280	1,280	1,280	1,280
Muslims Average	1,034	2,068	2,068	2,068	2,068
USA	23,240	46,480	46,480	46,480	46,480
Switzerland	36,080	72,160	72,160	72,160	72,160

Figure 2   Growth of Per Capita Income

Obviously, if the current patterns of economic development continues, the gap between the rich countries and the poor countries will increase. For example, the average growth rate for Muslims as a group for the 1960-1992 period was 1 percent. At this rate, while Uganda's per capita income increases by $170 in the next seventy years, Switzerland's per capita income would have increased by $36,080. At higher growth rates, it will take less time. However, Muslims must grow at a much higher rate than the West or else they will never be able to catch up.

Unless drastic improvements occur in development policies of Muslim countries, there is no reason to expect any higher growth rates. All major factors affecting economic development, including revenue mobilization, expenditures, borrowing, human resource development and defense, must be reconsidered to improve the outlook. Economic growth at rates of 2 percent or 3 percent looms ominously for most Muslim countries. They must achieve much higher rates of return (as in China and Korea) in order to narrow the gap. Muslim leaders must agree to implement ambitious five, ten, twenty, and fifty year plans of development.

The former caretaker Prime Minister of Pakistan, Moeen Qureshi, identified the following causes for the poor economic performance of his country in a speech in December 1990:

    a. inadequate economic management and policy without a clear long-term course;

    b. low social investment resulting in inadequate development of human resources;

    c. low investment in physical capital which is partly a result of a declining investment rate as a percentage of gross domestic product;

    d. weak competition and incentive system;

    e. complex and anomalous tax system which discourages exports; and

    f. absence of political and social institutions capable of mobilizing the nation for development.

As an example of long-term policies for economic development, Mr. Qureshi recommended the following goals and corrective actions for his own country:

    a. double the size of the economy in ten years which translates into 7 percent annual growth for the economy or about 4 percent growth in per capita income after allowing for the population growth;

    b. sharply increase the investment rate through reform of the tax system and administration;

    c. obtain a national consensus on the level and sources of resource mobilization and priorities of expenditure in terms of sectors of economy (e.g., defense) and regional spending;

    d. create an open economy with the government assuming the role of regulator rather than manager; promotion of the private sector; and liberalization of the trade and exchange system;

    e. establish a program of social development with emphasis on basic health coverage and education for all; and

    f. give greater freedom to financial institutions in the conduct of their affairs.

During the 1980-91 period, Thailand achieved 5.9 percent annual growth, China 7.8 percent, and the Republic of Korea 8.7 percent. At 8 percent rate, per capita will double each nine years. At that rate, Pakistan, for example, could have per capita income of $840 by year 2001, and $1680 by year 2010. Such would be a minimal target. Even then, the per capita income will be a fraction of that in the U.S. or in other developed countries.

Each Muslim country has an existing endowment of labor, land, capital, and the people (entrepreneurs) who can put it all together to increase the GNP. In simple language, the goal is to produce much more output per unit of input. Others have done so through techniques such as mass production, economies of scale, product specialization, improved technology and increased efficiency. This requires correct work ethics and environment. Emphasis has to be put on human resource development, provision of incentives to entrepreneurs, and change in legal frame work to make it all possible. There are models which can be adapted to satisfy fundamental Islamic requirements. However, Muslim countries experiencing political and economic instability will find it difficult to achieve such high rates of growth.

84.   Reduction of Poverty.

Satan threatens you with poverty and bids you to conduct unseemly. Allah promises you His forgiveness and bounties. And Allah careth for all and He knoweth all things *(Surah 2:268).*

Poverty is from evil *(shaytan)*. Muslims must resist and fight poverty and seek the bounties of Allah. Reducing poverty is a long and complex matter. Singapore, Malaysia, Hong Kong, Korea, and Indonesia have made good progress in the last few years. Muslim governments must analyze their economic policy, public expenditures and national institutions with the objective of poverty reduction. The focus must be on: incentive policies for everyone to produce more; wage and employment policies which will make effective use of millions of unemployed and underemployed workers; cost effectiveness of public expenditures, in particular for developing human resources; and cost effectiveness of the safety net for the poor. Governments and the private sector must increase allocations for financing programs and projects that support and enhance poverty reduction.

Policy for each sector (agriculture, rural and urban infrastructure, health, education, etc.) must focus on poverty reduction. Design and implementation of each project must involve the poor directly. Targets must be clearly set. Country performance must be monitored at the highest levels of the government to ensure achievement of targeted improvement in social and economic indicators.

Each government must coordinate its efforts with other OIC members, donors supporting poverty reduction, and other interested groups at home and abroad to maximize learning based on experience and assistance. Lessons must be learned from relatively successful efforts of Muslims in Malaysia and Indonesia. Only with well-directed and sincere efforts, can Muslim governments expect to reduce poverty.

85.   **Removal of Hunger.** Allah has required all Muslims to help the needy ones. Nevertheless, many people in Muslim countries continue to go hungry. Well publicized, widespread starvation in parts of Somalia and Sudan, and large number of beggars on the streets of most Muslim countries in Asia and Africa illustrate the problem of hunger. In addition, the look on the faces of people in many countries indicates undernutrition.

In addition to the usual hunger associated with poverty, a classified U.S. intelligence report has depicted sub-Sahara Africa as "the most strife-torn region in the world, with around 30 million people there at the risk of malnutrition or death without emergency aid. Those at varying degrees of risk include some people of the Muslim majority countries of Sudan, Somalia, Sierra Leone, Chad, Mali, and even Nigeria. Muslims in Bosnia, Afghanistan, Azerbaijan, and Tajikistan are expected to continue to need some assistance, too.[17] Corrective action is available and has been successfully taken by the World Bank and other international agencies in several countries of East Asia and elsewhere. Action is required at the international, national, and household level. Muslims, as a group and in cooperation with others, need to:

a. increase supply of food through more research, extension work, and conservation of natural resources;
b. stabilize supply through maintaining sufficient stocks, paying attention to early warning signals, and doing more research in relevant areas; and
c. accelerate shared growth in Muslim economies which empower all to get the needed quantity of food.

Individual Muslims can help through acts of charity and provision of economic opportunities for the needy. Allah says in the Qur'an:

> **So woe to the worshipers who are neglectful of their prayers, those who (want but) to be seen (of men), but refuse (to supply even) neighborly needs** *(Surah 107:4-7).*

---

[17] *Washington Post,* December 17, 1994, page A22.

By no means shall ye attain righteousness unless ye give (freely) of that which ye love; and whatever ye give, of truth Allah knoweth it well *(Surah 3:92).*

The Prophet (PBUH) said that charity will be a shade for believers on the Day of Judgment where there will be no shade; and that charity appeases the wrath of Allah and removes the pangs of death.

At the national level Muslims need to (a) increase level of income through GNP growth or timely mobilization of aid in money or kind; (b) increase supply through increasing production of food, importing needed quantities in a timely manner, maintaining adequate stocks, and eliminating post harvest losses; (c) stabilize supply through maintaining adequate stocks, facilitating trade, and putting in place/monitoring early warning signals of coming shortfalls; (d) improving distribution; and (e) taking steps to increase consumption as needed.

At the household level, there is a need for: (a) increased production; (b) better income distribution through social security, unemployment insurance, and food subsidies or vouchers; (c) increased consumption through emergency and drought relief, feeding and nutrition programs, and subsidized food rations; and (d) improved nutrition and health through education and information, better water supply and sanitation; etc.

86.   The Conference on "Overcoming Global Hunger." This conference, held in Washington in late 1993, emphasized the following points which are applicable to Muslims too:

a. Each country and its people are ultimately responsible for over-coming hunger. International agencies can only help.
b. Too many international agencies are involved in hunger issues. Each has own prescription. They must increase coordination among themselves, and be prepared to change policies as needed to meet the requirements of the poor in each specific country.
c. Many poor countries particularly in sub-Sahara Africa have weak governments. International agencies wishing to help must assess and understand the capacity of the country involved and its leadership, and provide practical advice. Programs must be specific to each country and the situation. There must be hands-on support ensuring that capacity is built within the country. Special attention should be given to ensuring involvement of women.

d. International agencies must ensure that none of their actions harms the poor. In the past, some structural adjustment schemes may have harmed the poor. They should listen to the poor and their representatives, and provide incentives to their staff for helping the poor through their operations.

87.   **Poor Distribution of Resources.** Economic resources are unevenly distributed in practically all parts of the world. The top 10 percent of the population often owns 50 percent or more of the resources while the lowest 20 percent or more survives below the poverty line. The poor distribution is particularly painful in Muslim countries of South Asia and Africa. This is partly demonstrated by the uneven per capita income in Muslim countries, as discussed above. Islam recognizes the right of people to have their basic portion (*nisaab*) provided and encourages the establishing of mechanisms to address these needs.

C. Economic Management.

88.   **Need for Decentralization.** The limited resources available to Muslim countries are generally controlled by the central governments. Given widespread non-representative forms of government, the national resources often become concentrated in the hands of a few people, resulting in the poor distribution as discussed above. One way to deal with this problem is establishing democratic institutions. Another is decentralization, having authority and responsibility exercised at the lowest level of government possible. The Prophet (PBUH) and the rightly-guided *Khulafa'* (Caliphs) delegated much authority and responsibility to the local communities and their leaders.

Citizens at the village, municipal, and provincial levels feel that they best understand their local problems. If allowed to do so by the centralized governments, they frequently find the solutions. Under such an arrangement, provision of local services such as water supply, sanitation, local transport, area development, etc. would be in local government hands. Some political parties which favor greater decentralization have gone as far as limiting the central government powers to defense, foreign affairs, and currency.

People living in poor areas feel that they are being excluded from opportunities at the national level. They wish to introduce affirmative action for the weak by reserving for themselves, at the least, economic opportunities in their own areas. They wish to:

a. expel all non-local people; reserve employment opportunities for local citizens; and introduce a system of work permits for the exceptional cases of non-local workers;

b. give high priority to provision of basic nutrition, clothing, medical care, shelter, and justice to the locals at as low a cost as possible;

c. actively promote local language and culture;

d. curb special privileges obtained by local feudal lords for services rendered to former colonial masters or local dictators;

e. provide technical assistance and credits to locals in order to enable them to become entrepreneurs;

f. reform the educational system, curricula, and targets with the aim of reaching full literacy and employment;

g. collect and keep all taxes locally, and pay only the required amounts for agreed functions to the central government; and

h. control local law and order with the assistance of local police or militia.

Many Muslims object to such affirmative action. Under the concept of one Muslim *Ummah*, doors to opportunities have to be open to all Muslims. This argument sounds very convincing at first glance. However, this argument has been used by people of power, money, and comparative advantage at the national level to enrich themselves. In turn, the weaker, poorer, and relatively disadvantaged Muslims have been left farther behind. Free competition among equals is healthy and produces good results. However, free license to the strong ones to exploit the weaker ones in the name of competition cannot be Islamic.

Some regulation is essential. When people are allowed to develop and prosper in their own area, chances for exploitation are reduced. After minimal development is achieved with local effort, and financial and technical assistance from non-locals, then greater national and international competition from all Muslims can be achieved.

Each government must determine the optimal degree of decentralization that is desirable, or the best division of powers among central, provincial, and local governments. There is merit in increased decentralization and it should be considered by all Muslim leaders.

89. Large Illiterate and Poorly Trained Manpower. Based on 1991 data, the adult illiteracy rate was 4 percent for high income countries; 35 percent for the world as a whole; and 40 percent for low-income countries. At least 17 Muslim majority countries had adult illiteracy rates of 50 percent to 82 percent. In many countries of Muslim Africa, more than 70 percent were illiterate. In Pakistan and Bangladesh 65 percent were illiterate; 52 percent in Egypt; 46 percent in Iran; and 43 percent in Algeria. It reflects the sizable loss of human resources among Muslims, both in relative and absolute terms.

Some Muslim countries are making efforts to improve their situation by spending a reasonable part of their central government's budget on education. Others are not. Overall data are not available for all countries, and some such as the United States, fund education through property taxes collected and spent by local governments. However, some comparative data is illustrative. Singapore spent 19.9 percent of the central government's expenditures on education, in spite of insignificant illiteracy in 1991. Israel spent 10 percent. Many African countries and Bangladesh spent about 10 percent too. The Pakistan central government spent only 1.6 percent. It is possible that provincial governments of Pakistan provided a part of the remaining needed amount.

As is typical of developing countries, Muslim countries are far behind in science and technology. Tariq Husain (in a yet to be published paper) has pointed to interesting numbers: Japan has 3,500 scientists and engineers per million of population; the United States has 2,700; Europe has 1,600; Asia (minus Japan) has 100; and Africa has 50. While the data for Muslims as a group are not available, the number of scientists and engineers is probably somewhere between 50 and 100 per million. This, in part, explains the advancement of the West and the obvious backwardness of Muslims. The same report suggests that 90 percent of world research potential is concentrated in about 35 countries with 25 percent of the world's population.

The importance of education and learning is emphasized in several places in the Qur'an and *Hadith:*

O my Lord! Advance me in knowledge *(Surah 20:114).*

But teach (the Message): For teaching benefits the believers *(Surah 51:55).*

Nevertheless, large numbers of Muslims remains illiterate and poorly trained. In the areas of science and research, Muslims are even farther behind. The result is that Muslims are almost totally dependent on Western countries. During the years of the Cold War, scientists and researchers from many Muslim countries had access to advanced research in the West. Such access is decreasing.

Muslims can expect to continue lagging in basic knowledge, scientific research and advanced technology unless shifts in education policy, accompanied by major increases in expenditure for education, are made. Long-term commitments to technology and science are essential; in addition, transfers of technology and cooperation with the West in scientific endeavors would be beneficial. Muslim religious scholars often point out the detrimental impact some modern technology has had on Western society, and on the family unit in particular. Ecological disasters, newly developed illegal drugs, the immoral entertainment industry, and pollution are cited. Muslims are required, of course, to support good and reject evil.

90. **Large Unemployment.** Allah expects Muslims to work. The Prophet (PBUH) was employed. Allah encourages Muslims to "seek His bounty" through work. Yet, with the exception of a few oil-rich exporting countries, all Muslim countries face serious unemployment. Lack of employment opportunities is the single most important economic issue in countries such as Bangladesh, Pakistan, Egypt, and most of the Muslim countries in Africa. Considering the fact that in Muslim countries women are not frequently employed outside their homes, and elderly parents and needy relatives are a part of the extended family, each job provides sustenance for at least one family. Despite having a family support system, without that job, it is difficult for that family to survive. Related problems of underemployment, low wages, lack of job security, etc., are also critical, but the first need is to have a job as a source of income.

Muslim governments have been trying to increase employment opportunities in both rural and urban areas. The United Nations, the World Bank, and the International Monetary Fund have prepared comprehensive economic reports for each country. Each report generally addresses the problems of labor and unemployment. Much advice and many large investments later, Muslim countries have not been able to keep pace with the demand for employment. There are a variety of reasons:

a. inadequate employment generating capacity due to low rate of overall economic growth;
b. fast increase in labor force due to high birth rates;
c. movement of labor from areas of high unemployment within the country; and/or
d. immigration of job seekers from neighboring countries.

Many skilled and unskilled workers have been seeking and getting jobs abroad, largely in the oil-rich kingdoms. The unemployment problem continues. Current economic wisdom emphasizes the need for:

a. high economic growth policies;
b. low population growth;
c. accelerating rural development in order to discourage large scale movement of labor to already congested urban areas;
d. well-designed and directed public works projects;
e. support for schemes which maximize labor utilization;
f. discouragement of high minimum wages;
g. incentives for self-employment;
h. incentives for employment generation in the private sector;
i. effective educational policy, matching skills with job opportunities; and
j. removal of discrimination against ethnic, racial, tribal, and gender groups.

All Muslim governments need to accord high priority to reduction of unemployment; close cooperation with the private sector is needed. As a group, Muslims can plan and implement a well-coordinated and effective action program.

95.   Corruption.

And do not eat up your property among yourselves for vanities, nor use it as bait for the judges, with intent that ye may eat up wrongfully and knowingly a little of (other) people's property *(Surah 2:188).*

Obtaining money illegally is the most common form of corruption. It happens in the form of cash bribery in exchange for favors; loans from government banks without intention of repayment; real estate transactions perceived to be legal yet are immoral, etc. It can be found in all parts of the world.

In developed countries, the common man does not need to pay extra money for getting routine chores done; the rich and powerful may, if they desire, pay extra to obtain special favors in manners that are unique. In many Muslim countries, common people pay for even the simplest and most routine work. There are extra payments: to police in connection with investigations; to judges for favorable consideration; to government engineers for approving private construction jobs; to bankers for approving loans; to custom officials for allowing imports to enter the country; to income tax officials for assessing lower taxes, etc. Most of these payments are concealed and are difficult to calculate.

It is also believed that 10 percent to 30 percent of government expenditures are syphoned off in payoffs to government officials. Using gross national product (GNP) data, a rough estimate of the payoffs on central government expenditures can be made in millions of U.S. dollars.

				(In Million US $)	
Country	GNP (1992)	Central Govt. Exp. % GNP	Govt. Exp.	[Estimated Payoffs] 10% Govt. Exp.	30% Govt. Exp.
Bangladesh	25,168	15.0	3,775	377	1,131
Pakistan	50,106	21.7	10,873	1,087	3,261
Indonesia	12,348	19.2	23,708	2,370	7,110
Tunisia	14,448	32.8	4,737	473	1,419
Egypt	35,008	39.6	13,863	13,861	4,158

Figure 3 Estimated Government Payoffs

Assuming that (a) average central government expenditure for Muslim governments amounts to 20 percent of GNP, and (b) that the payoff equals 20 percent of the expenditure, the total pay-off would amount to more than $40 billion per year. The above figures do not include expenditures by provincial and local governments, nor do they include many other types of payoffs referred to above. The total economic leakage would easily exceed the total foreign aid received by Muslim countries.

In Pakistan, the constitution provides the president, prime minister, federal ministers, provincial governors, chief ministers, and ministers with blanket amnesty for all acts performed during their tenure of office. These officials often use their powers, particularly the discretionary ones, to benefit themselves without any fear of prosecution.

There is a general notion that corruption is everywhere and nothing can be done to stop it. Every government has an anti-corruption department. Many lower level officials are caught. The cases against the high level officials never seem to result in convictions and they always seem to get away. Once in a while there are major purges of senior officials, however the corruption tends to grow. The 1993 interim government in Pakistan took some steps to force high officials to repay loans. There are so many legal loopholes and "political considerations" that the big robbers of the *Ummah* often go free.

South Korea's first civilian president in 32 years, Kim Young Sam, has made a dent by simply demanding that all bank accounts bear the names of their true owners. The Iranian Revolution reportedly stopped corruption for many years. Corruption is a large and unnecessary burden on people. The Muslim *Ummah* and governments should not tolerate it.

96.   Exclusion of Women from Market Economy. Muslims forget the importance that the Prophet gave to women in the economic area. He worked for Khadijah (RA) who was a prosperous business woman of his time. After their marriage, she continued working as a successful business woman. It was she in whom the Prophet (PBUH) confided when he received the Divine Revelation. Islam was the first religion which granted the right of inheritance to women, more than fourteen hundred years ago.

Women in Pakistan, An Economic and Social Strategy (The World Bank 1990) describes a common situation which may be even worse in other Muslim countries. It suggests that a major obstacle to the country's transformation into a dynamic middle-income country is under-investment in people, particularly women. Women, who make up half of the population, cannot participate effectively either as contributors or as beneficiaries.

In many social contexts, women are accorded esteem and importance; but on certain counts, the status of Pakistani women is among the lowest in the world. Within the family, women are responsible for training children, and are preferred service providers for three quarters of the population, i.e., women and children. However, they perform well below their potential.

Women's education is essential to improve the health and education of the entire family; to allow family size to remain at the size desired by the family itself; and to increase economic productivity. Women's income is very important for the survival of poor families. Without education, women can only play the traditional role of home caretaker. Outside the home, they remain ignorant and dependent. They produce more children than desired by the family, lose more of them than necessary, and remain poor.

There is a need to remove overt legal and regulatory discrimination against women. Political leadership, Islamic scholars, and the media can play a vital role. Increasing opportunities for women will be essential to improve economic performance and promote equity. Improvements in their access to employment, credit, new technology, commercial activities and markets may allow women to raise their productivity, and hence contribute to family welfare and overall economic development. Current efforts in these areas (e.g., credit schemes for women in Bangladesh) have to be increased to have a visible impact.

97.   **Family Economic Uncertainty.** Many Muslim heads of households feel that there is no need to think of the economic future for themselves or their families. In case of death of the head of household who is often the only bread winner in a vast number of Muslim families around the world, all has been left to Allah.

> **Let those (disposing of an estate) have the same fear in their mind as they would have for their own if they had left a helpless family behind: let them fear Allah and speak words of appropriate (comfort)** *(Surah 4:9).*

In the above verse, attention is drawn to the plight of helpless families left behind. Muslims should engage in economic planning for their loved ones.

98.   **Need for Improved Health Services.** Health standards are generally low in most Muslim countries; this is reflected in low average life expectancy and high infant mortality. All families are ultimately responsible for their own health. However, their ability to make correct decisions are a function of their education, particularly health education, and financial position, i.e., ability to pay for required health services. The poor are generally lacking in both areas. Governments can help by:

a. carrying out economic development policies to benefit the poor;
b. increasing cost effectiveness of health expenditure programs;
c. expanding investment in schooling and health education, particularly for girls;
d. financing and ensuring delivery of basic clinical services including immunization against all childhood diseases;
e. minimizing external threats to public health through controls over infectious diseases, including the spread of AIDS, environmental pollution, and the availability of illegal drugs and addiction ;
f. raising educational and professional standards of medical personnel;
g. removing theft and corruption in publicly owned medical facilities;
h. improving management of government medical facilities through decentralization to the extent possible;

    i. encouraging public and private suppliers to compete in terms of provision of drugs and clinical services;

    j. ensuring provision of basic services to all citizens;

    k. encouraging social or private insurance for clinical services outside the essential services; and

    l. facilitating continual increase in scientific knowledge in preventive, diagnostic, and curative areas.

99.   **Misuse of Own Resources.** National revenue of most developing countries including a majority of Muslim countries is not sufficient to meet even debt service payments, the cost of military, and the cost of government employees. Development expenditure is almost entirely met from foreign borrowing and aid. The national budget of Pakistan for the year 1993/94 shows revenue of $7.227 billion; debt service payments of 4.96 billion (69 percent of revenue); and defense 3.3 billion (46 percent of revenue). Much of the costs of establishment (employees) and practically all of the development budget have to be borrowed at home or abroad. How this stage of national bankruptcy and total dependence on others has been reached is a tale of great sadness. Whether several Muslim countries can continue to survive as viable entities is highly questionable.

100.   **Dependence on Foreign Aid.** While there is much talk of self-reliance, Muslims have not worked out alternate arrangements to replace tied foreign aid from non-Muslims. Muslims are afraid that regardless of their own self-interest, if they take any step which is perceived to be against the interest of the West, they will be punished economically or even militarily at a later date by the powerful and well-organized West. Dependence on foreign aid from non-Muslims must be reduced. This does not imply closing the doors to mutually beneficial cooperation with international agencies or to assistance without undue strings. Lessons in self-reliance may be learned from experiences of (a) China from 1940's through 1970's; (b) Iraq since the end of the Gulf War; and (c)Iran since the Revolution. It will mean hardship and lowering of an already low living standard. However, eventually Muslims will emerge as stronger, and will be able to deal with the rest of the world on equal terms.

101.   **Payment of *Zakat*.**

> **And be steadfast in prayers and give *zakat*. And whatever good ye send forth for your own souls before you, ye shall find it with Allah; for Allah sees well all that ye do *(Surah 2:110).***

Payment of *zakat* (alms tax) is one of the most fundamental rules of Islam. It is estimated to be about 2.5 percent of the value of one's assets. It is to be paid annually. Some important exemptions are allowed. Priorities for the payment in terms of recipients are also indicated, with first preference being given to needy relatives.

They ask thee what they should spend (in charity). Say: Whatever wealth ye spend that is good, is for parents and kindred and orphans and those in want and for wayfarers and whatever ye do that is good, -- Allah knoweth it well *(Surah 2:215).*

Data are not available about either the total value of Muslim assets on which *zakat* could be levied; or how much the *zakat* will amount to, if all Muslims paid their due share. However, as shown above, the gross national product (GNP) of Muslim countries for year 1992 amounted to the equivalent of $1,022 billion; 2.5 percent (the standard *zakat* rate) of GNP would alone amount to about $25 billion. Normally, total value of accumulated assets on which *zakat* will be levied will be several folds larger than the GNP of one year alone. It can be safely assumed that the *zakat* will amount to over $25 billion. For comparison purposes, it may be noted that the total amount lent by the World Bank annually to all countries of the world (Muslims and non-Muslims combined) is less than $25 billion. The amount will be certainly sufficient to provide a safety net for all needy Muslims and may exceed total foreign aid received by all Muslim countries from all sources, bilateral and multilateral.

However, there are other unresolved issues. Under the Islamic rule during the days of the Prophet (PBUH), *zakat* was a tax on the Muslims' income and assets.[18] Today, Muslim governments already levy several taxes on their Muslim citizens, income tax, property tax, sales tax, customs duty, etc. Are Muslim governments supposed to abolish all other taxes, and simply collect *zakat*? Muslims should study taxation options including *zakat*, and improve arrangements for collection of agreed taxes. An improved taxation system, and its efficient collection could greatly reduce fiscal deficits, and the need for foreign aid from non-Muslims.

---

[18] Of the other taxes, *jizyah* was levied on non-Muslims in lieu of *zakat* and military service; *sadaqah* was voluntary; *khums* related to spoils of war; and *kharaj* related to land.

It may be noted that payments for community development played a very important part in strengthening Islam in early days. The Jewish community and also some Muslim sects, e.g., Ismailis, have improved their lot greatly through mandated payments as well as through the generosity of individuals.

102.   Resource Mobilization Without Payment of Interest.

The Muslim economic system encourages private enterprise and free trade as personally conducted by the Prophet (PBUH). It is not much different from the capitalistic system with an understanding that "moral filter" has to be applied to each transaction. However, there is a clear ban on usury. Many Muslims feel that interest is prohibited in any form.

The word used in the Qur'an is *riba'* which means excess or an addition. While a majority of scholars have held that *riba'* and interest are synonymous, others, including the present *mufti* of Egypt, have argued that it refers to excessively high interest rates.[19]

> **Oh ye who believe! Devour not usury, double and multiplied; but fear Allah. . .** *(Surah 3:130).*

Normal interest rates do not result in the quick doubling of money; accordingly banning interest under all circumstance is not intended. A ban on charging interest can be justified when someone helps an individual who is suffering a financial crisis. However, in the case of borrowing money for business investment, the lender deprives himself of use of his savings; his money may then be losing value due to inflation or other economic factors.

Dr. Imad A. Ahmad has argued in his paper, "Riba' and Interest: Definitions and Implications," that such a loss of value to the lender, "whom the Qur'an has guaranteed shall suffer no such loss," is unjust[20].

> **. . .But if ye turn back (from usury) ye shall have your capital sums; deal not unjustly, and ye shall not be dealt with unjustly** *(Surah 2:279).*

---

[19] *The Economist*, "Survey of Islam - The Cash-flow of God," August 6, 1994.

[20] Dr. Imad A. Ahmad, "Riba' and Interest: Definitions and Implications," a paper delivered at the 22nd meeting of the American Muslims Social Scientists, October 15-17, 1993, Herndon Virginia; in press.

Dr. Ahmad also mentions the example of the financial needs of an inventor to whom no one is ready to provide capital for his radically innovative idea even if a high level of profit sharing is promised. He has argued that the restrictive interpretation of *riba'* has led to the lack of availability of venture capital in Muslim countries resulting in the decline of inventions and technical innovations in the Muslim world.

In contrast, availability of such capital at a reasonable rate of interest has provided a definite boost to inventions and to the technical advantage to the West. Muslim students of economics belonging to this school of thought feel that *riba'* does not refer to all interest, but rather the overcharging of it.

Muslims need to agree on the definition of *riba'*. If the flexibility mentioned above is not accepted, then a way to mobilize the capital of those who do not wish to share in profit and loss should studied. This is a big obstacle in mobilization of savings for much needed investments.

103. **Scarcity of Water and Water Resources Management.** The lives of over a billion people around the world are at risk drinking unsafe water. More than 130 million Africans are dying of starvation due to drought. The Senegal River in West Africa which irrigates much of Senegal, Mauritania, and Mali is drying up. There is a water shortage in the Nile River basin, which supports up to 250 million people in Egypt, Sudan, etc. These are just a few relevant news headlines. What is not openly mentioned is that a very large number of people affected are Muslims. Issues of water quantity and quality are involved. A look at the world map shows that most of the Middle East, North Africa, and the Sahel are deserts. Most of the OIC member countries are located in these regions.

Even Bangladesh which is crossed by about 250 rivers, and is faced with excess water most of the year, faces severe shortages due to the unilateral withdrawal of Ganges River water by India through the Farakha barrage located in the upper stream. Some 40 million people living in the Ganges-Padma basin are facing drought. Years of bilateral talks between the two countries have not solved the problem for Bangladesh which is now seeking help from the United Nations.

Much technical data and studies exist on the water issues. Many countries have already performed assessments of water resources, considered policy options, and chosen the suitable ones. Similarly, many have developed master plans and identified investment projects to meet their requirements. Numerous projects are being implemented in many countries with the help of international organizations. However, with large population growth in Muslim countries, the investments are barely sufficient to maintain current levels of supply for agriculture, industry, and human consumption. Muslims, as a group, should examine the issues relating to scarcity of water. In most cases, appropriate action for sustained long-term management of water resources focuses on:

   a. collecting or catching the maximum quantity of water;
   b. improving delivery of water to the poor;
   c. consolidating fragmented responsibilities within the public sector;
   d. measures to reduce pollution and improve quality of water;
   e. realistic pricing which ensures availability of the minimum needed quantity to all, discourages waste and encourages conservation;
   f. ensuring user participation in demand and supply management;
   g. increasing private sector participation in public sector investment and management;
   h. increasing the reliability of supply;
   i. timely planning;
   j. timely investments; and
   k. research.

Some studies suggest a need for up to $600 billion in investments over a ten-year period for water resources in all developing countries. About 40 percent of these countries have majority Muslim populations. Accordingly, Muslim countries as a group will need roughly 40 percent of the investment or approximately $240 billion. In comparison to the resources available within Muslim countries or the donors as a whole, the amount is extremely large and not likely to be available to Muslims for many years.

104.   **In Summary.** Muslims face many economic challenges. Individually, each Muslim country is trying to solve its economic problems. All are receiving monetary and technical assistance from donors. Progress is slow. A fresh approach has been presented above for consideration.

> **O ye who believe! If ye will aid (the cause) of Allah, He will aid you, and plant your feet firmly** *(Surah 47:7).*

Fight in the cause of Allah those who fight you, but do not transgress limits; for Allah loveth not transgressors *(Surah 2:190)*.

A. Military Concerns of Muslims

105. A Just and Moral Cause. The desires to defend one's own borders, to render help to an aggrieved Muslim ally, and to protect vital interests constitute just and noble causes. All can agree on this and no one would seriously object to military development for such reasons. This is distinct from military adventure to conquer lands of others or to dominate them.

What creates doubts and fears are the political manifestations of spiritual affirmations, in the words of the West, "Holy War." The secular countries of the West not long ago were spiritually inspired to affirm such concepts as "manifest destiny" and "the White-man's burden." History is replete with the accomplishments of spiritually motivated movements. It is the fear of Islam as a political philosophy leading to a military power that is threatening to some non-Muslims, in the East and in the West. It is the perception that Islam is becoming the new Cold War threat seeking to bury Western civilization that generates the hostile reaction.

106. Military Superiority of Non-Muslim Nations. The contemporary military situation finds non-Muslims having a clear edge over Muslims in military and economic power, as well as in science and technology. In addition, non-Muslim nations enjoy greater unity, objectives and strategies, and a well-defined mechanism for cooperation among each other (e.g., EU, NATO, UN). Muslims have yet to strengthen themselves in these areas.

107. Muslims' Potential Perceived As a Threat. Muslims represent a potentially powerful group if seen as a united front transcending national boundaries. Those leaders and peoples who consider Muslims their adversaries, whether in the West or in the East, whether Russian or Jewish, American or Arab, feel threatened by such Islamic unity and are working to prevent it. The first challenge for Muslims is to effectively assure their assumed adversaries that they are developing themselves for the welfare of their people and to achieve positive goals, in the path of right. It is the perceived intentions of a few militant Muslims that creates the hostile environment. Muslims as a group are not militant and they should make that clear at every opportunity.

108.   **Wisdom, Bravery, and Sincerity of the Leadership.** During any war, a reckless general is easily killed. If he is afraid of dying, he is easily captured. If quick-tempered, he is easily provoked. If too sensitive about his honor, he is easily insulted. If overly concerned about his men, he is easily harassed. In recent wars, opponents have questioned the wisdom, bravery, and sincerity of Muslim leadership. It is alleged that Muslim leaders, including generals, have become too fat, too rich, too greedy, and too concerned about personal welfare to effectively defend the cause of Islam, or even their respective national causes.

Intelligence officers of adversary nations need only to offer a dinner invitation, a visa for a family member, or a scholarship for a child to win undying personal gratitude and friendship. Their own eventual defeat at the hands of adversaries is presumed by cynical Muslim leaders. Their primary concern is to arrange for personal safety and security at home, or preferably in the comforts of the West.

In contrast, untrained Muslim civilians are fighting sophisticated military machines, at times with nothing more than stones. They have shown the willingness to self-destruct for their Islamic cause. It is this dedication that wins wars; it also engenders fear, suspicion, and eventually repression. If misused it can kill prospects for peace and start wars.

109.   **Proper Timing.** Right timing in terms of suitability of the political conditions and physical circumstances (climate, terrain, adequate logistical support, etc.) is very important. Many of the conflicts erupting in Eastern Europe are the direct result of deteriorating political conditions in various republics of the former Soviet Union and increased Islamic awareness, particularly since to the Iranian Revolution.

Wars are destructive in terms of lives and material. Islam means peace through submission to God's will; the acknowledged purpose of Muslims is to worship their Creator. Despite these affirmations, the perception that Muslims are militant terrorist has been exploited by opponents of Islamic movements to combat the appeal of Islam and obstruct whatever sympathy may be engendered by Muslim causes.

Muslims, as has every world leader seeking peace with honor and coexistence, have generally avoided war through strategy, including formation of alliances, seizing opportunities for peace as they arise.

Conflict has been the last resort in most cases since usually there has been little advantage to be gained and only slight assurance of victory.

110.   Size, Organization, and Discipline of the Troops. The strength of Western powers in conventional war has been well demonstrated in their conflict with Iraq. Nuclear, biological, chemical, and other weapons of mass destruction are known to be available and in reserve. The provocation of war with the West under such circumstances is quite futile. The more likely scenario and the one most often mentioned is guerilla warfare, including terrorist acts of sabotage. It is this picture that is most often painted in the media, with sufficient conjectural evidence to elicit fear and mobilize enmity toward Muslims.

As in the case of the Palestinians in the Holy Land, Muslims pose little military threat. They represent a serious threat to any leadership when they are willing to sacrifice their own lives in face of great oppression.

111.   Performance of Muslim Armies in Recent Times. The military in Muslim countries is often criticized. Their relatively poor performance against external enemies, such as Israel in the case of Arabs and India in the case of Pakistanis, is one reason. Muslim armies have rarely been victorious on the battlefield in the last fifty odd years. In some instances, they have stood firm (e.g., the Pakistan-India War of 1965; and Arab-Israeli War of 1973); in others, their performance has been lamentable.

By contrast, Muslim armies have been able to destroy each other with relative ease and success (e.g., Iran-Iraq war, Iraq-Kuwait war, and numerous civil wars in East Pakistan, Afghanistan, Somalia, etc.). In addition, internal repression by the military has been reported in several Muslim countries. Many believe that the primary purpose of the military is to protect the ruling classes from their disgruntled masses.

112.   High Cost. Standing armies in Muslim countries, as in the West, consume the lion's portion of the national budget. Muslims continue to spend a large part of their national budgets on military equipment and personnel. This results in a significant reduction in urgently needed expenditures for health, education, and welfare. Political leaders are often obligated by the overwhelming influence of the military to increase military budgets year after year.

Soldiers retire young. Accordingly, military pensions represent one of the largest expense items in many national budgets. In addition, tradition has been established in some countries to award valuable land, licenses, and assets to retired military personnel. Additional benefits and privileges are made available through foundations and trusts for the welfare of "soldiers."

Few dare to question the volume of resources allocated to the military. Such criticism would be labelled unpatriotic or as coming from enemies of the nation and from foreign agents. As in the West, the costs and benefits of military expenditures are not always evaluated objectively in Muslim countries. Often military objectives are vague and expenditures are made for public display, for nationalistic pride or even to satisfy political obligations.

At times it appears that the people hired to defend the country have forcibly taken control of the national wealth, while most of the rest of the nationals are living hand to mouth. Given the performance of the Muslim military on the battlefield, it is only a matter of time before public sentiment reacts in one way or another against such conditions.

Reduction of military expenditures without sacrificing national defense is a common problem for Muslims, as it is for Western nations. This is not surprising considering that most of the Muslim military have been trained by Cold War veterans who viewed the arms race as the solution to their military responsibilities. Muslims buy their arms with the same gusto that characterized the Kremlin and the Pentagon. As in the Gulf War, weapons in the hands of a friend today may be in the hands of an enemy tomorrow.

Observers have made recommendations for solving the problem. They propose substantial reduction in permanent standing armies as an economic remedy. Also, universal military training for all citizens with increasing reliance on a national draft or conscription would reduce military costs. The development of armament industry would reduce dependence on foreign sources but would require massive capital investments resulting in the classical exchange of weapons for butter. Finally, acquisition of advanced conventional equipment from abroad is an expensive and uncertain method.

Muslim countries may consider any or all of these options, but without first establishing definite short and long-term objectives based on affirmed beliefs, there is little likelihood that they will be implemented in a meaningful way. As with any strategic plan, complete commitment to clearly defined goals and objectives must be accepted by the implementing leadership.

113.   **Professionalism.** The military in Muslim countries is frequently criticized for lacking high professional standards. This is partly the result

of the control of leadership positions by royal families or ethnic groups, and the total or partial exclusion of large segments of the population. In addition, attempted or actual take-overs of many Muslim governments by military leaders have eroded morale at the lower ranks.

In the few Muslim countries which have some form of democratic government, the military frequently has the role of king-makers, through interference in politics . Several Muslim countries use military personnel for police duties in maintaining domestic law and order. Others impose martial law over a disgruntled citizenry. Likewise, judicial and administrative powers in the hands of military personnel often bring the temptations of appropriating personal benefits.

Few Muslim countries exercise civilian control by elected officials over management of military affairs. Civilian defense ministers often are rubber-stamps for decisions of the military itself.

114. Nuclear Weapons and Technology. It is quite apparent that non-Muslims have total control over nuclear technology and weapons. The United States, France, the U.K., China, and four republics of the old Soviet Union (Russia, Ukraine, Kazakhstan, and Georgia) have publicly acknowledged possession of nuclear weapons. Israel and India are reported to possess weapons and the technology. South Africa also was known to possess both, but may have dismantled them before transfer of power to the new "majority" Black government.

Most industrialized nations in Europe, particularly Germany, and Japan and Canada, are likely to be able to acquire or develop the technology quickly, if needed. Several developing countries including Pakistan, South Korea, North Korea, Argentina, and Brazil are also presumed to have nuclear capability, even though the quantity and quality of their weapons and the delivery system are inferior.

India possesses nuclear technology and has successfully tested atomic devices. In Muslim Pakistan, former Presidents Bhutto and even Zia might have lost their lives in trying to acquire nuclear technology. Former President Ghulam Ishaque of Pakistan has confirmed that he received many threats while in office for advocating a nuclear program. In addition, Pakistan has been denied hundreds of millions of dollars a year in aid from the United States and remains a candidate for declaration as a terrorist state mainly for the same reason. Iraq continues to pay heavily for aspiring to have a nuclear program. Similarly, Iran faces considerable opposition for developing nuclear technology.

Nuclear non-proliferation is the cornerstone of the foreign policy of Western governments seeking to continue military dominance. Only "responsible" new members are acceptable into the nuclear club. While Muslim Kazakhstan has acknowledged nuclear capability, other Muslim countries can expect to have their ambition for nuclear programs firmly opposed. Furthermore, alliances between Muslim countries to advance such programs are certain to be monitored and obstructed.

115.   **Pakistan's Dilemma.** Muslim commentators, particularly Pakistanis, have argued that if Pakistan does have the capability, then like India, it should publicly test a small nuclear device. It is asserted that such a move will deter aggression. Pakistan, if capable, should even announce possession of a small number of weapons. Such an action would earn the wrath of the West and could result in loss of even the remaining economic assistance from donors such as Japan. Some argue that eventually Pakistan would earn respect of all concerned. All agree that Pakistan must offer credible assurances of responsible behavior to India and to other interested parties on a reciprocal basis.

Based on the nuclear issue, pursuant to the Pressler Amendment, the United States stopped direct economic and military assistance to Pakistan around 1990. Pakistan has not suffered significant damage because the United States has maintained relatively cordial relations and has not fully implemented its declared policy. What is important is not just the direct military or economic aid from the United States, but the total financial resources, trade, and military power which it affects, including:

a. loans and assistance from international financial institutions such as the World Bank, the International Monetary Fund (IMF), the Asian Development Bank (ADB), and other UN agencies.
b. bilateral aid from several European countries and Japan;
c. bilateral aid from pro-American Arab countries;
d. international private investment;
e. investment by Pakistanis living at home and abroad who may be otherwise deterred by United States hostility to Pakistan;
f. U.S. signals to India, Israel, and others to go ahead with strategic de-stabilization of Pakistan; and
g. supply of military spare parts from its own stocks, or those of other friendly powers.

Based on disclosures of high level officials, few doubt Pakistan's de facto membership in the nuclear club. The argument continues whether Pakistan benefits more by the "perception" of having a nuclear bomb, or by actually tests. It is assumed that Pakistan has an adequate delivery system against its traditional enemy India; this is repeatedly validated by Indian and United States accusations of technical assistance and hardware support coming from China and North Korea to Pakistan.

In summary, the potential costs of the "nuclear proof" include: (a) the wrath of the United States resulting in condemnation and sanctions mentioned above; (b) reduction of economic assistance by Japan (the largest bilateral donor) and European countries; and (c) further hostile action in the economic, political, or even military fields by India.

The potential benefits include: (a) improved relationship with the West within a "relatively short" period, including resumption of aid, based on reassessed Western interests; (b) increased "respect," including financial assistance from rich Arab and other Muslim countries; (c) establishment of an effective determent to the Indian government (which may already exist), and Indian citizens (which may not exist now); (d) greater respect by non-Muslim Indians toward Muslim Indians, resulting in less communal violence, and better treatment of Kashmiri Muslims; and (e) increased self-confidence of Muslims.

116.   Buying and Selling Weapons. The non-Muslim nations have almost total control over production and marketing of conventional weapons. A report from the Stockholm International Peace Research Institute suggested that, in 1992, the United States maintained its position as the world's leading exporter of conventional weapons, accounting for 46 percent of the market, against 51 percent in 1991. Members of the European community boosted their share of sales in 1992 to 26 percent, up from 20 percent a year earlier. Exports from the former Soviet Union amounted to 11 percent in 1992, against 18 percent in 1991, and 34 percent in 1990. China accounted for 8 percent in 1992. European countries were the leading buyers in 1992, responsible for 36 percent of all purchases, followed by Asia at 30 percent and the Middle East at 22 percent.

Time Magazine (December 12, 1994, pages 47-48) reported that while the total size of the arms market was shrinking, the U.S. share was increasing. Since the collapse of the Berlin Wall in late 1989, U.S. overseas weapons sales have totalled $82.4 billion, far ahead of the $66.8 billion in sales reported by the rest of the world's nations combined. U.S.

arms-transfer agreements in 1993 totalled $22.3 billion, eclipsing second-place Russia's $2.8 billion and Britain's $2.3 billion third-place finish.

The Gulf War showed the critical importance of high technology. Even though Iraq was known to have much military hardware, and trained, motivated manpower as a result of the long war with Iran, it did not have the state-of-the-art technology brandished by the West. Advanced as it was, Iraq's weapons were no match for the more advanced Western alliance.

It is generally acknowledged that Muslim nations have purchased their military capabilities primarily from the West and the former Soviet Union. Whether as a deterrent or for protection against attacks, they have sought to have the best available weapons. However, it is not likely that Muslim governments will be militarily or technological competitive with the West in the future. Recognizing the current military superiority of non-Muslims, Muslim leaders, for the most part, have wisely avoided direct conflicts with the West.

B. Some Lessons

117.   Lessons of Past Wars. John G. Stoessinger has analyzed causes of major conflicts in the twentieth century in *Why Nations Go to War*. He has concluded that:

a. no nation that began major war in this century emerged a winner;
b. war between nuclear powers is suicidal;
c. wars between small countries with big friends are likely to be inconclusive and interminable;
d. small, friendless states can still settle scores against each other;
e. major powers win easily against friendless small states;
f. unless the defeated side is completely destroyed, the victor's peace is seldom lasting;
g. peace settlements negotiated on the basis of equality are much more permanent and durable;
h. personalities of leaders play a very important part in the outbreak of wars; volatile, irrational leaders start most wars;
i. misperception of a leader's image of himself and his adversary's character, intentions, or capabilities and power, is the single most important cause of wars;

j. wars usually end when the fighting nations perceive each other's strength more realistically[21].

118. Lessons for Muslims. It would be futile and self-defeating for the *Ummah* to start any war, either against each other or the West. As discussed above, the United States, Britain, France, Israel, and India are known to have nuclear weapons with long-range delivery capability. Among Muslims, Pakistan's limited nuclear capability may be enough to offset a threat from India. Pakistan's delivery capacity is known to be limited to nearby areas of India. Accordingly, a war by any Muslim country, singly or jointly, against any of the world powers is futile and suicidal. There is no merit in contemplating it.

War initiatives by any Muslim country, with covert or overt help from a major power, is likewise futile. Any adversary of a Muslim country, be it Muslim or non-Muslim, would be supported by one or several of the world powers. Such a war would be inconclusive at best, and would certainly be destructive to the Muslim country initiating hostilities. In cases of grievances against other countries, Muslim leaders are best advised to seek peaceful resolution. War should be, of course, only the last resort.

Muslims need to judge their leaders according to the highest standards provided in the Qur'an, opposing oppressive and irrational leaders, supporting dedicated and sincere reformers. Miscalculation of their own powers or the powers of potential enemies can lead to much destruction. Leaders should be prevented from embroiling their countries in whimsical conflicts which expose their people to suffering. They should be supported in their efforts to rid their nations of exploitation, corruption and degradation.

Gamal Abdul Nasser of Egypt, Ayub Khan, Yahya Khan, and Zulfiqar Bhutto of Pakistan, Colonel Qadhafi of Libya, and Saddam Hussain of Iraq are but a few of the controversial Muslim leaders who have engaged in conflicts. Only Allah can judge their actions, but their history remains quite vivid for other Muslim leaders to study.

119. Need for the Treaty of Hudaybiyah. Some Muslims have suggested that this is a time for a treaty comparable to the one concluded by the Prophet (PBUH) at Hudaybiyah, south of Mecca, six years after his migration to Madinah. Muslims were on their way to perform their

---

[21] John G. Stoessinger, *Why Nations Go to War* (New York: St. Martin's Press, 1992), pp. 205-212.

religious pilgrimage, but the leaders of Mecca would not allow it. At that time, both sides were ready for war. Muslims made a covenant of al-Ridwan to fight to the last man. But, the Prophet (PBUH) felt that peace was more important than war. In order to convince the Meccans that he was there to perform a holy pilgrimage rather than to fight, he set an example of patience and moderation:

a. he held respectful talks with several different delegations sent by the people of Mecca;
b. he prominently displaced the seventy sacrificial camels to demonstrate the intention of pilgrimage;
c. he forgave and returned unharmed the forty to fifty persons who had stoned the tents of Muslims and tried to provoke them into a fight; and
d. he sent his own delegations to Mecca including his dear friend and son-in-law Usman ibn Affan, at great risk to their safety.

The final treaty required Muslims to stay away from Mecca that year, and return for the pilgrimage the next year; and to return anyone from the Quraysh who wanted to join the Muslims, while anyone wishing to leave the Muslims would not be returned. The treaty was considered to be a great humiliation, and resented by Muslims. Many, including 'Umar ibn al-Khattab, were initially impatient. Yet, eventually, it turned out to be very useful for Muslims and proved the profound political wisdom and farsightedness of the Prophet (PBUH).

Once again, Muslims need peace. They need to make a covenant with themselves similar to the one made at al-Ridwan. They must sacrifice for the welfare of the *Ummah*, give assurances to the West through demonstrable actions about their peaceful intentions, ensure peace, and devote themselves to the welfare of each other.

Muslims clearly face many political problems. These include, but are not limited to, widespread mistrust of their own governments, military conflicts around the world, division among Arabs, limited freedom of the press, disagreement on the definition of Islamic government, human rights violations on a massive scale, Western fear of Islamic states, and the poor image of Muslims around the world. This chapter attempts to look at the political issues and makes some recommendations for the consideration of *Ummah* and its leaders.

A. Mistrust of Governments.

120. Lack of Sound Leadership. While Muslims do not have religious leadership to help resolve day to day spiritual issues, they also lack political leadership. Even more uncommon is the religious leader who has spiritual qualities and can also lead politically.

Successful leaders usually have many common attributes. Very few leaders of Muslim governments possess the requisite qualities. Seldom do they possess honesty and integrity or fulfill promised actions. Rarely are they competent and possess the required skills. Rarely are they forward-looking, visualizing future events and making them happen; providing inspiration for the people; mobilizing them for hard work and sacrifice for desired goals; enjoining the good and forbidding the evil; and recognizing that they do not have all the answers and therefore require mutual consultation. On rare occasions when their leaders have displayed one or more of the above qualities, people have responded and followed enthusiastically.

Over the centuries, Muslims have been ruled by *Khulafa'* (Caliphs), kings and monarchs, a few rightly-guided, many tyrannical. Little precedent exists for rule by the common people themselves. The rulers were frequently interested in protection of their own dynasties. At first, a traditional system of tribal representation and protection existed so that even a common person could question the actions of the *Khalifah* (Caliph). Eventually, unrepresentative governments developed in which no one was able to challenge the despot.

Muslims in general do not have trust in their governments. There are many reasons for it:

a. Many leaders are perceived by their citizens to lack honesty; competence; vision for the future; ability to inspire people; and genuine commitment to the welfare of citizens.

b. They lack of a voice in government; many governments are non-democratic (i.e., the people have no say in who holds power). In so-called elected governments, citizens openly question the results of elections or feel that priorities of elected leaders change when in power, becoming dedicated solely to continuing in power.

c. Protection and immunity are provided to the rulers under the law; hence, there is no accountability for election promises. Occasionally, a coup d'etat results in exemplary punishment for the deposed official, but in most cases, the rulers remain unpunished.

d. The democratic process is frequently interrupted by coups d'etat and often there is little choice among the candidates.

e. The national media are controlled and the local media are in a relatively less developed stages.

f. Through international TV and other media, citizens can compare economic progress in other countries, some previously poorer than their own; they also see a dramatic change in the economic condition of their leaders while seeing little change in the general populace.

121. **King Can Do No Wrong.** The concept of "the King can do no wrong" has been elaborated by Abdul Fatah Memon in *Protection of High Executives in Pakistan.*[22] Under British colonial rule, Section 306 of the Government of India Act of 1935 stated:

(1) No proceedings whatsoever shall lie in, and no process what soever shall issue from any court in India against the Governor General, against the Governor of a province, or against the Secretary of State, whether in a personal capacity or otherwise and, except with the sanction of His Majesty in Council, no proceedings whatsoever shall lie in any court in India against any person who has been the Governor General, the Governor of any province, or the Secretary of State in respect of anything done or committed to be done by any of

---

[22] Abdul Fatah Memon, *Protection of High Executives in Pakistan* (unpublished).

them during his term in office in performance or purported performance of the duties...

Elected officials do not wish to be left behind. Article 248 of the Constitution of the Islamic Republic of Pakistan, 1973, has even extended the protection to a larger number of persons. It states:

(1) The President, a Governor, the Prime Minister, a Federal Minister, a Minister of State, the Chief Minister and a Provincial Minister shall not be answerable to any court for the exercise of powers and performance of functions of their respective offices or for any other act done or purported to be done in the exercise of these powers and performance of these functions...

During the period of subsequent military rule, similar blanket amnesty was granted to a large number of military personnel. This puts the rulers above law. No wonder that elected officials (and military officials during the martial law) become so corrupt. Once they are in office, they are above the law. They use their powers to the full extent for personal benefit, fully realizing that they cannot be legally touched. Even the opposition party keeps quiet. They recognize that they will be able to use the same laws for their own benefit when their turn comes.

An Islamic government, of course, does not allow for such provisions. In part, it is the fear of such reform that motivates some Muslim governments to oppose religious reformers. In any event, whether secular or religious, a government must remain accountable.

The political situation of Muslims in Indonesia in the 1890's was been described by Pramoedya Ananta Toer, in his book *This Earth of Mankind*. Parts of it ring true even today for Muslims in many countries. A letter written by the daughter of a senior Dutch colonial government official to a native friend stated:

...How they gave birth to hundreds and thousands of leaders and heroes in their struggle against the European oppression. One by one they fell, defeated, killed, surrendering, gone mad, dying in humiliation, forgotten in exile. Not one was ever victorious in war. We listened and were moved, and became angry also to hear how your rulers sold concessions to the Company, benefiting no one but themselves. Your

heroes, according to Papa's stories always emerged out of a background of selling concessions to the Company; and so it was over and over again, for centuries, and no one understood that it was all a repetition of what had gone before, and that as time went on the rebellions became smaller and more and more stunted. And such is the fate of people who have thrown all their body and soul and all their material wealth into saving a single abstract concept called honor.

According to Papa, the fate of humanity now and in the future is dependent on its mastery over science and learning. All humanity, both as individuals and as peoples, will come tumbling down without such mastery. To oppose those who have mastered science and learning is to surrender oneself to humiliation and death.

...He mustn't become like the general run of his people; when among themselves they feel as if they are from a race which has no equal on earth. But as soon as they are near a European, even just one, they shrivel up, lacking the courage even to lift up their eyes . . . [23]

122.   **Limited Freedom of the Press.** Freedom of the press is synonymous with freedom to speak out, which was fully practiced in the days of the Prophet and well-guided successors. Most Muslim governments try to curb press freedom for reasons of self-preservation, under the guise of "national security." Freedom of the press as practiced in some Western countries need not be imitated. Obscenity, violence and immorality have no part in Islamic society. In addition, gossip, rumors, and slander can become so common that citizens have difficulty distinguishing fact from fiction. In some Muslim countries, the ethnic press has advocated violence rather than peace. While almost all media in Muslim countries have condemned Rushdie's *Satanic Verses*, a Turkish newspaper published its excerpts, thereby infuriating local Muslims. Freedom of the press needs to be guaranteed in all cases with clear legal recourse for those who may be unjustifiably defamed, individually or collectively. True national interest, local sensitivities, and religious concerns can be protected by the law.

---

[23]   Pramoedya Ananta Toer, *This Earth of Mankind* (New York: Avon, 1975).

123. **Leadership Needs.** Today, Muslims need a different kind of leadership than that prevailing. Muslims need leaders who recognize the present weaknesses of the *Ummah*, leaders who can question the status quo and who believe in changing it for the benefit of all Muslims. As Muslim leaders they must affirm their beliefs and put them into practice. They must:

a. seek the support of Allah through prayer and study, acknowledging that all efforts are for seeking His blessing;
b. analyze the *Ummah's* problems honestly and with integrity; use authority effectively; set a good example;
c. learn from people who are closest to the problems at the local level, from scholars and from other religious leaders, experimenting with alternate approaches and taking appropriate risks;
d. enlist the help of others to get the task done, delegating and teaching others, thereby strengthening supporters and making all feel a part of the national effort; give recognition to people for the job well done;
e. plan victories, even if they are small, to provide the taste of success and re-energize the followers.

B. Conflicts.

124. **Party to Many Conflicts.** About thirty parts of the world were affected by serious armed conflicts during 1992. Muslims are directly affected in at least Bosnia, Afghanistan, Palestine, Kashmir, Sudan, Somalia, Morocco (on the issue of Western Sahara), Iraq, Tajikistan, Azerbaijan (against Armenia over Nagono-Karabakh), and Burma and most recently Chechnya. There are many other "civil wars."

These conflicts, regardless of the causes and responsibilities, have enormous human, military, economic, and political costs for Muslims. In each case, they further weaken already weak Muslims. It should be remembered that:

If two parties among the believers fall into a fight, make ye peace between them: but if one of them transgresses beyond bounds against the other, then fight ye (all) against the one that transgresses until it complies with the command of Allah; but if it complies, then make peace between them with justice,

and be fair; for Allah loves those who are fair (and just)
(Surah 49:9).

125. **Division Among Arabs.** The "religions of the book" have been
revealed to mankind through Semitic people; Arabs are Semites. Unity
among Arabs after the revelation of Islam, led all Muslims, Arab and non-
Arab, to great glory, power, knowledge, and civilization. But fratricidal
warfare has ravaged Muslims throughout their history.

Then came Lawrence of Arabia who convinced Arabs that they were
superior to other Muslims and ought to fight against Turkish Muslims and
be free. With the help of Arabs, the "family" of Lawrence succeeded in
breaking the last Muslim empire and *Khilaafah* (Caliphate). Instead of
being free as promised, Arabs came under Western colonial powers.

After regaining independence at the end of World War II, they
appeared to be united. The Arab League held some promise. Then came
descendants of Lawrence again, who whispered to each Arab ruler that he
was superior to anyone else. Each one has gone, more or less, his own
way since then. The descendants of Lawrence have picked them of, one at
a time. Egypt, Syria, Jordan, Iraq, Lebanon, Libya and Kuwait have all
tasted war and suffered casualties, from the attack on Suez to the latest
bombings of Lebanon. Today, they are the most ridiculed people in the
media owned by the descendants of Lawrence. They are not only divided,
but, according to the Western press, even privately urge Western powers
to punish their Arab enemy more severely than they themselves can. While
Muslims, and often Arabs bleed, reportedly their rivals rejoice in private.

God blessed Arab lands with oil wealth under the deserts. However,
according to some press reports, they have spent more on wars than then
they have earned from oil. As a result, even the rich ones among them are
in debt to the descendants of Lawrence.

The plight of Arabs is reflected in general among other Muslims.
They exhibit the same internal division that plagues Muslims throughout
the world, wherever they are fighting each other militarily, culturally,
politically, and ideologically.

126. **Disagreement Over Definition of Islamic Government.** Muslims
are not in agreement among themselves on what an Islamic government
should be in the world of today; there is continuing debate between the
various religious sects and rulers. Supporters of democracy argue that the
consultative process of succession, used after the passing of the Prophet

(PBUH) fourteen hundred years ago, dictates nothing less than one person one vote.

Supporters of existing unrepresentative governments point to the Qur'anic injunction requiring obedience to rulers and insist on continuity of current governments. Some Muslims advocate a hand picked assembly of elders for consultation, if and when deemed necessary by the ruler. Scholars and many religious leaders, from many Qur'anic verses, infer Allah's approval of various types of governments, so long as they are righteous. They point to the several types of institutions favorably described in the Qur'an, including the kingly rule of David and Solomon, and the authority exercised by Joseph under the pharaoh. In addition, they warn that the institutional framework is only as worthy as the spiritual and moral foundation upon which it is built. In other words, a democratically elected government can be despotic while a dictator can be benevolent. There is an urgent need for identifying the differences of opinion regarding the form and content of Islamic government, and working toward resolution of the issues and an agreement.

127. Experience of Christian Government. It must be remembered that Christians have tried religious forms of government in the past. In the Middle Ages, the most important and powerful institution in Europe was the Roman Catholic Church. In religious matters, it dominated the lives of people; in non-religious matters, it performed many functions which weak medieval governments were unable to accomplish.

Religious powers of the Church included: (a) provision of traditional religious services from birth to death; (b) religious courts dealing with heretics who held views different from those of the church (holy inquisitions); and (c) expulsion of serious violators of Church doctrines (excommunication), making them outcasts from society sentencing them to eternal damnation.

Economic powers of the Church included: (a) levying a special tax equal to 10 percent of the value of crops and other produce; (b) building and operating many schools, orphanages, hospitals, and asylums; (c) monks farming church lands advising the public on the best agricultural practices to follow; and (d) prohibiting Christians from taking interest on loans (usury).

Cultural powers of the Church included: (a) encouraging learning through church schools -- monks being among the best educated people in the society; (b) publishing literature resulting in large numbers of books on religious subjects; and (c) architecture and artistic projects, including construction of churches, church buildings and their adornment.

Political powers of the Church included: (a) religious and civil control over vast lands acquired through donations; (b) its own system of courts in which cases involving marriages, wills, clergymen, orphans, and widows were tried; (c) limitation of warfare by declaring a truce of God from Wednesday evening to Monday morning; and (d) asserting that its authority was superior to that of civil rulers. The assertion was challenged by many rulers and resulted in several wars. The Church and the papacy were generally victorious in such wars, further strengthening their position.

The Reformation was a revolt against some of the teachings of the Roman Catholic Church and the abusive powers of the Pope. It inaugurated religious diversity in Europe. Reformers, culminating in Martin Luther (1483-1546), John Calvin (1509-64), and John Knox ((1505-72), had been pushing for changes for a long time. These protestors against Rome's authority (known as Protestants) received much support from monarchs such as King Henry VIII of England for a variety of reasons, some personal and economic.

The Reformation ended religious unity in Europe, and was a cause of religious warfare including the Dutch war for independence from Spain, the English naval war against Spain, and civil wars in Germany and France. The Treaty of Westphalia, in 1648, recognized Protestant sects and their governments in Sweden, Holland, and Switzerland. Eventually, this ended religious warfare, increased religious tolerance, encouraged education, including study of the Bible by common people, and strengthened civil authority. Once the people succeeded in challenging the rule of the all-powerful Roman Catholic Church, they could think of challenging the absolute monarchs as well. The Reformation and the resulting religious tolerance proved to be a major step in the development of democratic theory.

It is interesting to note that Roman Catholics have tried combining religion and government. However, over centuries, nationalism prevailed over spiritual unity. They have gradually moved to religious diversity with nationalism based primarily on geographical boundaries. Eventually, church and government were constitutionally separated in order to assure protection of the diversity which had multiplied.

Today, most Western government leaders continue to give respect to Catholic and Protestant churches, and religious interests are rarely ignored. Christians, however, complain ardently that the secular character of today's government was never intended by the founding fathers. They accuse the secular humanist movement of controlling the educational establishment and advocating atheism as its own religion. They claim that removal of prayer from public schools has led to the degeneration of the educational system and destruction of social institutions. They lament the spiraling divorce rate, mounting crime, drug use, and overall laxity of values. They point to the arbitrary separation of church and state and the decline in spiritual affirmations as primary reasons. The November 1994 elections in the United States validated this public sentiment.

Many Muslims, conditioned by colonial forms of government have failed to find satisfactory alternatives. They seek to imitate the West while the West seeks solutions for its decaying social order. Others continue to long for combining government and religion as practiced by the Prophet (PBUH).

C. Human Rights Violations at Home.

128. Corrupt Police and Weak Judiciary. Despotic governments are often accused of human rights violations. In dictatorships throughout the world, it is reported that people are routinely put in jails without charges being filed, left in prisons for extended periods, and tortured. People living near police stations have often heard screams of people in custody being tortured. Severe beatings, pulling of nails, lying naked on blocks of ice in winter, hanging up side down, and electric shocks to genitals are just a few of the routine police interrogation methods. Whether this happens in Latin America, the Far East, or Eastern Europe, repression of political dissent and even of the common citizen is reprehensible.

In all such countries, including those whose rulers have Islamic names, common citizens do not enjoy the rule of law. Powerful individuals are able to carry out their will with brute force. The victim is left to seek redress through a corrupt police and weak judiciary. He is forced to pay off the police, lawyers, and sometimes even judges in order to start the process of "hearings." Ultimately the stronger one is able to thwart the process with more money and power. "Fight or shut up" is the basic rule. A general feeling prevails within the government and the general populace that (a) Muslim people are "bad" and cannot be controlled without threat and use of excessive force; and (b) the rule of law will not function in a Muslim country.

129. Need for Human Rights Protection. It was argued by some, including Muslim leaders at the June 1993 United Nations Conference, that "human rights" has become a Western concept applied according to Western standards; in reality, different regions, religions, and cultures interpret "human rights" according to substantially different standards. This assertion echoes the imperial, colonial approach namely, "Give them a full belly, a strong hand, and an occasional boot and they are happy; that is their nature and culture."

As the Muslim and the Asian blocks have argued, economic development is also a fundamental human right. However, this is tied to (a) general inefficiency and misuse of resources by the developing countries, and (b) control over the purse strings of the world by the few developed countries. Similarly, the rights of society as a whole are also important. However, violation of individual human rights cannot be a condition for economic development or the protection of society as a whole.

The Holy Qur'an has laid out the basic human rights for Muslims and others. There is little debate on substance among the followers of various religions. Accordingly, the United Nations Declaration on Human Rights is internationally acceptable. In principle, the United Nations charter on human rights ought to be implemented everywhere.

D. External Issues.

130. **Fear of Muslims in the West.** Some Western historians accuse early Muslims of persecuting non-Muslims and spreading Islam by the sword. Muslims have repeatedly defended their history. Recently even some Western experts are coming to the Muslims' defense. In discussing the issue of Muslim tolerance of non-Muslims, Bernard Lewis has stated in his book *Islam and the West*:

> **Persecution, on the other hand, though not unknown, was rare and atypical, and in Muslim history there are few excesses comparable to the massacres, the forced conversions, the expulsions, and the burnings that are frequently found in the history of Christendom before the rise of secularism.[24]**

After the defeat of communism, the world community is still divided along nationality, religion, race, economic position, etc. World power is however largely concentrated in the hands of the United States, Western

---

[24] Bernard Lewis, *Islam and the West* (Oxford: Oxford University Press, 1993), p. 182.

Europe, Japan, Russia, and China. None of the Muslim countries belongs to this elite group. Yet, some can see the large potential of Muslims if they were to unite or even cooperate in a meaningful way. Most Muslim governments are struggling to survive politically and economically moving from crisis to crisis.

Some Muslims appear willing to use the little force available to them in a personal or national capacity to vent their frustrations through acts of violence. Through Western media coverage, these personal acts of violence portray all Muslims as threats to the current stability of the world. There is a danger that Muslims are likely to be portrayed as the new threat to the existing world order. As in the past, this could result in massive forces being directed against Muslims, again.

> . . .and you shall certainly hear much that will grieve you, from those who received the Book before you and from those who worship many gods. But if you persevere patiently, and guard against evil -- then that will be a determining factor in all affairs *(Surah 3:186)*.

Muslims can ill afford such a confrontation. There is an urgent need to assure and demonstrate to the West that their fear of Muslims is not justified.

131. **Image Problem.** In spite of many weaknesses, Muslims have unfairly acquired an excessively negative image among non-Muslims. As portrayed by the Western press, a Muslim is the one with white robes, swarthy features, and wild eyes. He has a bomb factory in his basement, and four wives at home. He is tricky, unreliable, and a coward. Evil acts and crimes of Christians escape identification with their religion, while every evil act by a Muslim is identified by mentioning the religion. The non-Muslim world is quick to judge and fear all Muslims, even though Islam means peace, and extremism is uncommon and unpopular within Islam.

Many minorities continue to face image problems in the United States. Blacks, Japanese, Hindus, etc. face stereotyping. However, they face ignorance alone. However, Muslims face large, well organized, and well-funded lobbies, too. Those who have a quarrel with one or another Muslim group (i.e., Israel, India, Serbs, etc.) keep reinforcing a negative image of Islam. Friends of Israel ensure continued massive financial and military assistance to Israel from the United States by portraying Muslims, particularly Arabs, as the enemies of Western civilization and the United States, and Israel as the first line of defense. These groups have been politically active for many decades. Muslims in America have started to respond, and to explain their point of view, only recently. Organizations such as the American-Arab Antidiscrimination Committee (ADC) and the American Muslim Council (AMC) are presently no match for the pro-Israel groups. In the 1990's, when the West prides itself on being fair, the Western press is being very unfair to Muslims as a whole and to the religion of Islam.

132.   **Dajjal and the Media.** It may be noted that the appearance of the "Dajjal" is mentioned in *Hadith* as a sign of nearness of the end of the world. Ahmad Thompson has described some signs to recognize Dajjal in his book, *Dajjal (The King Who Has No Clothes)*. There can be three aspects of Dajjal, the individual, a worldwide social and cultural phenomenon, and an unforeseen force. According to some *ahadith*, Dajjal has one eye; it can be heard all over the world at the same time; it will show fire, but will not burn; it will show water which cannot be drunk.[25]

Some feel that television fits the description of Dajjal. Some feel it refers to the mass media as a group. Whether or not one assumes that Dajjal refers to the Western mass media, most Muslims agree on the need to develop mass media of their own to balance or counter the influence of their opponents. A start may have been the reported purchase of United Press International by a group headed by Muslims. While it is not likely that Muslims can soon establish institutions such as the New York Times and Washington Post newspapers, BBC radio, or CNN television, they have already started working to influence these institutions. Their coverage of Islamic issues is changing from total insensitivity to occasionally showing signs of some sensitivity to Islam.

133.   **Impact of the Arab-Israeli Conflict.** The Arab-Israeli conflict, which has its contemporary roots in the partition of Palestine, has been expensive for all Muslims. Jewish people around the world are committed to defend Israel. At first, it was a question of making it strong enough to defend the territory granted by the United Nations against possible attack from the neighboring Arabs. Victories in the 1948, 1967, and 1973 wars have made Israel strong enough to hold on to the original territories plus

---

[25] Ahmad Thompson, *Dajjal: The King Who Has No Clothes* (London: TaHa Publishers, 1986), p 2.

those conquered from Jordan, Syria, and Lebanon. The exchange of conquered territory with Egypt has effectively neutralized the largest potential Arab adversary.

The long Iran-Iraq War weakened both Muslim countries, and depleted their accumulated cash reserves. The subsequent defeat of Iraq at the hands of the U.S.-led coalition effectively destroyed another adversary of Israel and garnered huge stocks of the latest American equipment. One by one, the Arabs have been so weakened that Israel has become the master of the Middle East. It walks in Lebanon at will, and can do so in any other Arab country if so needed.

Israel has widened its horizon to non-Arab Muslim countries. With the efforts of Israeli supporters in the United States, it has already portrayed Iran as Western civilization's number one enemy. By providing technical and military advice, Israel has reportedly helped India to crush Kashmiri people.

E. Are Weaknesses Unique to Muslims?

Are Muslims being too harsh on themselves? Followers of many religions and members of many communities can identify with similar spiritual, economic, political, and military weaknesses. Economic issues of low per capita income, poor distribution of income, large unemployment, and dependence on foreign aid are common to all "less developed countries." Of course, such commiseration does not solve the problem for Muslims. The New World Order, dominated by secular nations, is presumed to be threatened by Muslims who have not accepted separation of religion and state. The enormous potential of Muslims is perceived as a menace.

In the New World Order, Muslims stand out as divided people lacking organized leadership and involved in many conflicts; they are experiencing widespread poverty, are easily manipulated and have poorly educated religious leaders. They are the subjects of rulers who govern despotically, violate human rights, control the media, and relegate women to second-class roles. They either practice Islam without conviction or fanatically; in addition, to the Western eye, they are unusual in appearance (even though orthodox Jews look similar in some ways). Muslims definitely have an image problem.

> Not all of them are alike: of the People of the Book are a
> portion that stand (for the right); they rehearse the Signs of
> Allah all night long, and they prostrate themselves in
> adoration. Thy believe in Allah and the Last Day; they enjoin
> what is right and forbid what is wrong; and they hasten (in
> emulation) in (all) good works; they are in the ranks of the
> righteous. Of the good they do, nothing will be rejected of
> them; for Allah knoweth well those what do right *(Surah
> 3:113-115).*

134. **Monotheistic Religions**. Islam is the last major revealed
monotheistic religion. While Muslims believe in the validity of Judaism and
Christianity, they believe that God has perfected His religion through His
last revealed book, the Qur'an. By contrast, in spite of references to
Prophet Muhammad in the Bible, Jews and Christians have historically
been antagonistic to Islam. Some Orientalist scholars actually still question
the authenticity of Islam. Accordingly, the relations among followers of the
three religions have been tense. There is also discord with followers of
other religions of the world, particularly Hindus and Bahá'ís.

> It is odd in many ways that misunderstandings between Islam
> and the West should persist. For that which binds our two
> worlds together is so much more powerful than that which
> divides us. Muslims, Christians and Jews are all "peoples of
> the book." Islam and Christianity share a common monotheis-
> tic vision: a belief in one Divine God, in transience of our
> earthly life, in our accountability of our actions, and in the
> assurance of life to come. We share many key values in
> common: respect for knowledge, for justice, compassion
> toward the poor and underprivileged, the importance of
> family life, respect for parents. "Honour thy father and thy
> mother" is a Qur'anic precept too . . .[26]

---

[26] Lecture by the Prince of Wales at Oxford University, England, October
27, 1993.

135.   **Common Characteristics of Religions.** As described in *Religions of the World,* almost all religions have the common characteristics:

a. believe in a supernatural, or another ultimate, reality beyond and yet basic to ordinary human existence and experience;
b. make some distinction between sacred and profane objects, territory and time;
c. encourage or require ritual acts around sacred objects;
d. promote a moral code or ethical principles and precepts;
e. possess a unique blend of fear and fascination about the Divine;
f. encourage prayer and communication with God;
g. provide a world view and a place for the individual in it;
h. require more or less total organization of life often entailing personal commitment and sacrifice;
i. promise inner harmony or psychological peace and well being;
j. teach of a new age to come and/or promise an afterlife; and
k. encourage propagation of its tenets.[27]

The Parliament of the World's Religions, held in Chicago in August 1993, recognized the many common features of all religions in a Declaration of Global Ethics. The religious leaders condemned violence, inequality, intolerance, and economic injustice. They felt that no religion had the right to hate, discriminate, or liquidate followers of any other religion. They advocated equal treatment of all human beings -- both men and women, and peaceful settlement of all disputes.

The "religions of the book," namely Judaism, Christianity, and Islam, have many common doctrines, as discussed earlier. Among them, their moral code, ethical principles and precepts of conscience are virtually the same. Some Muslims propose that these ethical principles are better manifested by the average Christian than the average Muslim. Many Muslims remember their former colonial masters with fondness, admiring their personal honesty and impartiality in giving justice to common people.

By contrast, other Muslims point to the degenerative customs introduced by Western governments into their colonies. They argue that the West is declining morally and spiritually and that it is the duty of Muslims to enjoin righteousness and fight iniquity. They quote religious leaders in the West who also see their own society threatened by a moral slide.

---

[27] Niels C. Nielson Jr. and others, *Religions of the World* (New York: St. Martin's Press, 1988), pp. 3-10.

Muslim often see themselves as the saviours of humanity, the last bastion against the rampaging debauchery of modern culture.

136. Religions and Qualities of the Non-Muslim World Powers.

The Western powers are predominantly Christians. The vast majority of Americans, Australians, British, French, Germans, and other Europeans are Christians by birth. Many devoutly practice their faith. However, many only nominally profess their religion and are not active in a church. While Christianity is practiced by many in China and parts of Russia and Japan, these other world powers are not Christian.

A 1992 Gallup poll in the United States indicated that 45 percent of Protestants and 51 percent of Catholics attended church once a week. However a 1993 study titled "What the Polls Don't Show: A Closer Look at Church Attendance" indicated that only about 20 percent of Protestants and 28 percent of Catholics attend church in any given week. Given these numbers, it is apparent that commitment to the requirements of Christianity is not as strong as population numbers suggest.

The governments of practically all non-Muslim world powers are secular in nature and separated from any religious affiliation. These governments and most of their citizens accept the principle of freedom of religion, while respecting the interests of the church in making relevant policy decisions. However, to the utter disappointment of church leaders, the government supports secular explanations of life rather than the scriptural one. There is ever-increasing polarization over religious issues, including homosexuality, abortion, prayers in school, ethics in the media, and even the idea of separation of church and state. Religious leaders have entered politics (e.g., Reverend Pat Robertson in the 1988 presidential campaign in the United States and Jerry Falwell's Moral Majority) and demonstrated considerable influence in the elections of 1994. The power and influence of the so-called Religious Right threaten to dramatically change the Republican party.

At a White House prayer meeting, President Clinton pointed out that "secular government" meant freedom of religion, but not freedom from religion. While Western governments are constitutionally not based on religion, most of their leaders believe in and follow traditional faiths. As Christians, they believe in Jesus as God, the Old and New Testaments as their divinely inspired scriptures, life after death, and the Christian moral code. As with all nations, there are good human beings among them who respect human rights and follow ethical principles not much different from those taught by Islam. Muslims have noted exemplary behavior of many westerners and have recognized qualities in them which they identify as Islamic. Some have even attributed the success of the West to the fact that they are following the teachings of Islam more closely than Muslims.

137.   **Islamic Approach to Relations with Non-Muslims.** The Islamic approach to relations with non-Muslims is based on a number of explicit instructions in the Qur'an. To start with, Allah has taught Muslims to be tolerant of others, and prohibited them from insulting other people's religions and objects of worship.

> **Revile not ye those whom they call upon besides Allah, lest they out of spite revile Allah in their ignorance...** (*Surah 6:108*).

Muslims believe that there is only one Allah (or God). Allah has sent a guide for every nation:

> **And the disbelievers say: "Why is not a sign sent down to him from his Lord?" You are only a warner, and to every people there is a guide** (*Surah 13:7*).

According to prophetic tradition, there were 124,000 to 200,000 prophets.

> **We did aforetime send Messengers before thee: of them there are some whose story We have related to thee, and some whose story we have not related to thee. . .** (*Surah 40:78*).

The Qur'an also mentioned the names of Adam, Noah, Aaron, David, Hud, Saleh, Abraham, Ismail, Lot, Jacob, Joseph, Moses, Solomon, Elisha, Job, John (Yahya), Jonah, Idris, Jesus, and Muhammad (Peace be upon them all). As explained by Maulana Fazlul Karim:

> **. . .Muslims can neither say nor deny that Krishna, Buddha, Zoroaster, Confucius and other religious luminaries of the world were not prophets. Not only that, it is an article of faith with Muslims to believe in all the religious personalities of the world.**[28]

---

[28] Maulana Fazlul Karim, *Al-Hadis of Mishkat-ul-Masabih* (Dacca: F. K. Mission, 1971), p. 200.

Allah (God) is He who created and sent Prophets Abraham, Ishmael, Isaac, Jacob, Jesus, and Muhammad (peace be upon them). Muslims believe that earlier prophets testified to the fact that Muhammad (PBUH) would come but the testimony has been concealed.

> **Say: Will ye dispute with us about Allah, seeing that He is our lord and your lord; that we are responsible for our doings and ye for yours; and that we are sincere (in our faith) in Him? Or do ye say that Abraham, Ismail, Isaac, Jacob and the Tribes were Jews or Christians? Say: "Do ye know better than Allah?" Ah! Who is more unjust than those who conceal the testimony they have from Allah? But Allah is not unmindful of what ye do!** *(Surah 2:139-140).*

Referring to Prophet Jesus (PBUH), it is stated in the Qur'an:

> **And remember, Jesus, the son of Mary, said: "Oh children of Israel! I am the messenger of Allah (sent) to you confirming the Law [Torah] (which came) before me, and giving glad tidings of a messenger to come after me, whose name shall be Ahmad." But when he came to them with clear signs, they said, "This is evident sorcery!"** *(Surah 61:6).*

> **From those, too, who call themselves Christians, We did take a Covenant, but they forgot a good part of the Message that was sent them: so We estranged them, with enmity and hatred between the one and the other, to the Day of Judgment. And soon will Allah show them what it is they have done** *(Surah 5:14).*

According to A. Yusuf Ali, the Christian covenant may refer to the charge which Jesus gave to his disciples, and under which they accepted to welcome Ahmad (which is another name for Prophet Muhammad (PBUH).[29] This is reflected in the Gospel of St. John, even in its modern form *(John* 15:26; 16:7). Islam looks at Christians with affection:

---

[29] *Holy Qur'an,* trans. Abdullah Yusuf Ali (Brentwood, MD: Amana Corp., 1989), p. 250, footnote 715.

...And nearest among them in love to the believers wilt thou find those who say, "We are Christians": Because amongst these are men devoted to learning and men who have renounced the world, and they are not arrogant *(Surah 5:82)*.

Not all of them are alike: of the People of the Book are a portion that stand (for the right); they rehearse the Signs of Allah all night long, and they prostrate themselves in adoration. Thy believe in Allah and the Last Day; they enjoin what is right and forbid what is wrong; and they hasten (in emulation) in (all) good works; they are in the ranks of the righteous. Of the good they do, nothing will be rejected of them; for Allah knoweth well those what do right *(Surah 3:113-115)*.

The Qur'an gives peace high priority. Make peace whenever possible is the charge to Muslims:

Do not mischief on the earth, after it hath been set in order, but call on Him with fear and longing (in your hearts) . . . *(Surah 7:56)*.

. . .For Persecution is worse than slaughter . . . *(Surah 2:191)*.

If necessary, formalize peace through treaties.

But if the enemy (unbelievers) incline towards peace, do thou (also) incline towards peace, and trust in Allah: for He is the one that heareth and knoweth (all things) *(Surah 8:61)*.

Should they intend to deceive thee -- verily Allah sufficeth thee: He it is that hath strengthened thee with His aid and with (the company of) believers *(Surah 8:62)*.

They are those with whom thou didst make a covenant, but they break their covenant every time, and they have not the fear (of Allah). If ye gain the mastery over them in war, disperse, with them, those who follow them, that they may remember *(Surah 8:56-57)*.

> **If thou fearest treachery from any group, throw back (their covenant) to them, (so as to be) on equal terms: for Allah loveth not the treacherous** *(Surah 8:58).*

If the peace and the treaties breakdown, and there is no alternative to war, Allah's help is assured for a just cause.

> **Oh Prophet! Rouse the believers to the fight. If there are twenty amongst you, patient and persevering, they will vanquish two hundred: if a hundred, they will vanquish a thousand of the unbelievers: for these are a people without understanding** *(Surah 8:65).*

The key points are that believers must be (a) patient and persevere in getting ready for the fight, and (b) must have understanding of their faith, a just cause for the fight, and expect rewards in this world and in the next.

138.   **Attitude of Non-Muslim Powers Toward Islam.** There exists (a) historical antagonism between Muslims and Christians dating back to the Crusades, and even back to Charles Martel, (b) generally negative portrayal of Muslims in the Western media and history books, and (c) distinct cultural, linguistic and ethnic differences. Therefore, it can be understood why Western peoples and their leaders are suspicious of Islam and Muslims. The secular governments and societies just do not understand or appreciate that Islam covers all aspects of life including government. They are much more at ease with Westernized Muslim leaders representing secular governments of Muslim people than with bearded religious leaders representing Islamic republics. The latter are threatening in appearance, hard to understand and deal with, and better kept at arms length.

Nevertheless, there may be some softening of hearts. According to Pope John Paul II:

> **The Council has also called for the Church to have a dialogue with the followers of the "Prophet" and the Church has proceeded to do so. We read in Nostra Aetate: "Even if over the course of centuries Christians and Muslims have had more than a few dissensions and quarrels, this sacred Council now urges all to forget the past and to work toward the preservation and promotion of social justice, moral welfare,**

peace, and freedom for the benefit of all mankind (*Nostra Aetate* 3)." [30]

139.   Cooperation with Non-Muslim Powers. Almost all Muslim countries have maintained cordial relations with the Western powers. Each former colony has tended to remain a client of its colonial master. In addition, Pakistan, Iran, and Turkey had defense treaties with the United States, under SEATO (South East Asia Treaty Organization), and CENTO (Central Treaty Organization). Even Iraq was a party to CENTO at one time. Pakistan befriended the United States but the latter failed to honor its obligations during the 1965 India-Pakistan War. Nevertheless, Pakistan has continued to side with the United States on most issues.

The Gulf War and UN action in Somalia are two recent examples of cooperation. The war in Afghanistan also saw close collaboration between the United States and virtually all Muslim countries. The Gulf kingdoms continue to enjoy close relations with the U.S., the U.K., and other Western countries. Egypt has been firmly in the Western camp since the Camp David accords and treaty with Israel. Indonesia and Malaysia have maintained cordial relations with the West for at least 25 years. Turkey has been the closest ally of the West among all Muslims. It belongs to NATO and is an associate member of the European Economic Community. In light of this, Muslim leaders are surprised at the West's anti-Muslim behavior after a long and relatively harmonious relationship. The Revolution in Iran, the Iraqi attack on Kuwait, and the rise of Muslim countries from the dissolved Soviet Union has changed the nature of the relationship.

Developing countries, and Muslims in particular, do not seriously consider confrontation with the world powers. However, some Muslims view the West as the ultimate "Dajjal," whose rise before the Day of Judgment has been predicted in the saying of the Prophet (PBUH). Given the current power structure and the common heritage and values shared with the West, Muslim leaders are averse to such a confrontation. Similarly, there is increasing awareness of and respect for the Islamic faith and way of life. Much of the rest of this book deals with an approach for coexisting with the West.

140.   Improving Ties with Followers of Other Religions. There are historic "misunderstandings " between Muslims on the one hand, and Jews, Christians, and Hindus, respectively, on the other. Mistrust exists on all

---

[30] Pope John Paul II, *Crossing the Threshold of Hope*, page 93.

sides and it has been exploited by special interest groups and by governments. There is an urgent need to build bridges across different religions. Time can heal. Christians have largely forgiven Jews whom they blamed for the crucifixion of Jesus. The Vatican has normalized relations with Israel. The U.S. today is the main protector of Israel, and there is cooperation between the two religions. With patience and effort, it should be possible also to increase cooperation between Islam and other religions.

Pope John Paul II has repeatedly called for improved relations with Muslims. Bosnia and Chechnya have shown many in the West that injustices are being done to Muslims. The Clinton administration in the U.S. is eager to show that there is no religious animosity. The process of reconciliation needs to move forward. The media can play a useful role on each side. Muslims must work closely with the media in the West.

141. Vital Interests of the West. Non-Muslim states, including Japan and Russia, are united in feeling threatened by any Muslim power that can adversely affect them in terms of:

a. nuclear or other weapons of mass destruction which can be used to threaten non-Muslims, particularly Israel;
b. denying them the supply of energy resources;
c. threatening Muslim states who are especially friendly to them (e.g., Saudi Arabia and Kuwait).

Iran, Iraq, Libya, and to some extent, the Sudan, are the Muslim states most often mentioned as threats to one or more of the interests of the West. Iran, in particular, is assumed to be poised to challenge Western influence in several spheres, and is cited for its hostility to Saudi Arabian government policies.

142. Protection of Non-Muslims in Muslim Countries. Muslim leaders are obligated by their religion to protect the life and property of non-Muslim minorities in their countries. While the rights of Muslims in India are being violated, Christian minorities in the Sudan and Hindu minorities in Pakistan are themselves complaining of persecution at the hands of Muslims. Frequently, it is not government policy to persecute minorities but the acts of zealous religious groups. The media however rarely distinguish between official and personal inhumanity, nor do the victims. Muslims personally and governments officially must take effective measures to protect minorities.

143.   **Fundamentalism vs. Political Issues.** Many events in recent Islamic history have been viewed with alarm in the West. These include the formation of the Muslim Brotherhood by Hassan al-Banna in Egypt in 1928; the triumphant return of Imam Khomeini to Iran to set up an Islamic Republic in 1979; the assassination of Egyptian President Sadat in 1981; the suicide bombings of American and French barracks in Lebanon in 1983; the taking of Western hostages in Iran and Lebanon; the conflict between Iranian pilgrims and Saudi authorities in Mecca in 1987; the verdict authorizing the death of Salman Rushdie in Iran in 1989; the formation of an Islamic government in Sudan in 1989; the success of Islamic parties in elections in Jordan in 1989; the victory of an Islamic party in local elections in Algeria in 1990 and in first-round national elections in 1991; the defeat of the communist regime in Afghanistan at the hands of Muslim fighters in 1992; and the World Trade Center bombing in New York in 1993.

All these events represent a mixture of issues and a variety of responses by different people at different times. Much has been written explaining these events. However, they are often lumped together as Islamic fundamentalism in the minds of the Western public. They are viewed as a threat to the West, as a whole, regardless of the specific political, diplomatic, and even economic circumstances of each event.

The antagonistic element of the Western media has a valuable commodity in "Islamic fundamentalism." Its appeal as the subject of news reports, television and movie drama, and political debate is almost universal. It is well suited for yellow journalism techniques and espionage thrillers. The Western public's response has been to be suitably alarmed and suspicious. Islamic appearance and clothing (beard, head cover or full-body clothing) are suspected and discouraged in the work place.

For many Muslims, fundamentalism means giving at least lip service to the basics of Islam -- belief in one Allah (God); authenticity of the Prophet Muhammad (PBUH) as the messenger of Allah; regularity in prayers, at least five times a day; charity (*zakat*); pilgrimage to Mecca once in a life time if affordable; and belief in the Day of Judgment. To active Muslims, fundamentalism has come to represent a return to Islamic values in all aspects of daily life, including caring for all members of the brotherhood, and providing charity for the less fortunate. To some, it has taken the form of rejection of Western values and customs. In general, fundamentalists seek to follow the model established by the Prophet in the way life is led and in the manner one serves his Creator.

Muslims and the West are not always on the war path. They do agree on several issues. The purpose of this chapter is to point out some areas of agreement, and how to build on these. The chapter also points out (a) the common heritage of Muslims, Christians, and Jews, (b) the common history and culture between Muslims and Hindus of the Indian subcontinent, and (c) the common interests of all minorities.

A. Convergence of Views with the West.

144. **Measures Supported by the West.** In theory, the Western powers are less threatened by governments in Muslim majority countries which are, *inter alia,* capitalistic in philosophy, support privatization, are sensitive to ecological issues, fight drugs, and support improved governance, particularly with regards to human rights. The West's diplomatic posture supports countries whose philosophy and principal objectives are to:

    a. practice democracy on a continuing basis, at national, provincial, and local government levels;

    b. practice decentralization by delegating authority and responsibility downwards to the citizenry;

    c. maximize their economic growth by focusing national energies and attention on economic development;

    d. allow the private sector to play a significant role in the economy;

    e. improve the economic well-being of their people through increased attention to and expenditure on education, food, and shelter;

    f. improve their judiciary, with impartial and prompt justice, and emphasize human rights for their citizens, and particularly women;

    g. settle domestic and international disputes peacefully leading to reduced expenditure on the military;

    h. treat religion as a personal matter even if the ministries of religious affairs and private organizations are active in supporting Islamic education, construction of mosques, performance of Hajj, payment of *zakat,* fasting, offering of prayers, and missionary activities based on freedom of choice;

    i. eliminate corrupt practices (e.g., bribery, food and drug adulteration, thievery);

   j. devote national resources to eliminating poverty, eliminating illiteracy, raising education and health standards, improving environmental conditions, and developing infrastructure; and

   k. fight illegal drug production, distribution, and consumption.

In practice, international relations are a complex mosaic of political, economic, and military interests. Often, the West is seen supporting some governments totally opposed to their declared policies while opposing other governments whose ideals and purposes are much closer to their own.

145.   Additional Measures Supported. As one goes deeper, there are many additional non-controversial points. For example, the World Bank's *World Development Report, 1992* mentioned:

   a. removing subsidies that encourage excessive use of fossil fuels, pesticides, and excessive logging;

   b. clarifying rights to manage and own land, forests, and fisheries;

   c. accelerating provision of water, sanitation facilities, agricultural extension, and research;

   d. accelerating measures that will improve life for millions of women and children who suffer from indoor air pollution caused by cooking fires;

   e. empowering, educating, and involving farmers, local communities, indigenous people, and women so that they can make decisions concerning their long-term future;

   f. taking the long-term impact of all costs and benefits into account (including environmental ones) in making investment decisions; and

   g. building constituencies for change to curb vested interests, to hold institutions accountable, and to increase willingness to pay the cost of protection.

The policies which are non-threatening to the world powers also happen to be consistent with Islamic behavior, and are important for improving the life of common Muslims. Malaysia and Indonesia have been mentioned as examples of "good, non-threatening" Muslim countries.

146.   The Case of Malaysia. Malaysia is one of the fastest growing Muslim countries with a population of about 18 million and annual per capita income of about $3,000. Muslims comprise more than 80 percent of the population. After initial turbulence, it has shown tolerance for its minority religions and ethnic groups. The society is modern and yet facilitates the practice of Islam. A majority of the people pray, fast during *Ramadhan*, and show signs of being good Muslims, women cover their heads, etc., all without the country being declared an Islamic republic. The penalty for use of drugs is death and is regularly carried out regardless of nationality or religion of the convict. The literacy rate is reasonably high at about 78 percent. Islamic education is part of the official school curriculum. Religious leaders are regularly exposed to modernization and consulted on developmental needs. It is one of very few Muslim countries where elections are held regularly.

147.   **The Case of Indonesia.** Indonesia is the largest Muslim country in the world with a population of about 184 million; about 90 percent people are Muslims. It is not as democratic and as rich in terms of per capita income as Malaysia. Widespread bribery and powerful monopolies are rumored. However, most Muslims practice Islam seriously. Senior government officials have prayer rugs in their offices and use them regularly. Each floor in each government office building has a simple room labelled *"Mushola"* for prayers. Even young office girls pray five times a day and fast during *Ramadhan*.

In order to keep peace among the different religious groups, Indonesia has proclaimed five basic guiding principles -- faith in one God, respect and justice for each individual, unity of all groups within one country, representation of all important groups within the legislature, and balanced development for all people.

Many feel that Indonesia has the potential to be a great power. It has the land, natural resources, the fourth largest population in the world, and one of the largest economies in the world. Economic development for the last 25 years has been impressive while the percentage of the population below the poverty line has been drastically reduced. In spite of many challenges, schools, health services, and basic infrastructure have come to virtually every village. Corruption, in the private and public sectors, is one of the remaining serious problems to be solved.

After completing the first 25 years of economic development, Indonesia is about to launch the second 25-year, long-term development plan. Four national objectives have been identified by the planners: protection of the land and people of Indonesia; advancement of the general welfare of the people; development of the intellectual life of the nation; and contribution to a world order based on freedom, peace, and social justice. The development will focus on material as well as spiritual aspects and aim to serve the people rather than exploit them. Emphasis is being placed on science and technology, equitable distribution of advancement, wealth, and benefits, and industrialization without harming the environment. Words are cheap and anyone can prepare a wonderful sounding plan. However, Indonesia's record for the last 25 years shows that the words have some meaning.

Political stability has been a critical factor in the past and will remain so in the future. There is some concern about stability in the post-Suharto era. The West has become accustomed to the Islamic practices of Indonesians in private life and their secular policies in government. The West is likely to react nervously at a substantial reorientation of public policies based on religion. However, barring unforeseen developments, it will continue to support Indonesia's development.

In short, without proclaiming themselves Islamic republics, both countries (Indonesia and Malaysia) achieved impressive accomplishments. They have focused on the economic well-being of their people, improving human rights, settling domestic and international disputes reasonably peacefully during the last 20 years. Religion has been treated as a personal matter without it being ignored. Also, some of harmful practices such as food and legal drug adulteration, and the use of illegal drugs have been reduced. As a result, both countries have good relations with Western countries, Japan, and their neighbors. Both countries have benefitted from large investments and resulting employment, from developed countries as well as domestic minorities. Malaysia, in particular, presents a successful model for modern Muslim leaders.

Some Muslim skeptics feel that as soon as Muslim countries such as Malaysia and Indonesia become strong, the interests of the West will somehow be "threatened" and Western policies will become obstructive. They cite Japan as an example of the United States changing policies toward trade rivals. However, many common bonds are established with the West during the process of development which continue serving as links to cooperation.

B. Allies Among Non-Muslims.

148.   **Alliances Based on Single Issues.** There are political, institutional and individual forces in the world which support human development and progress for all people, including Muslims. These forces oppose human rights violations everywhere (including in Bosnia, Kashmir, Palestine, etc.) and wish to eliminate hunger everywhere (including in Somalia, Sudan,

Bangladesh, etc.). The Western media have done a remarkable job of keeping the world's attention focussed on Bosnia. Similarly, a large number of Jewish people and organizations have supported the Muslims' cause in Bosnia. Such are the origins and bases for lasting alliances which eventually transcend single issues.

149. Internationalists. International organizations such as the United Nations, World Bank, Asian Development Bank, and African Development Bank have helped many Muslim countries in entering the modern era. In spite of weaknesses, these organizations have provided considerable assistance to Muslim countries for many years. These organizations can be of much further benefit to Muslim countries under proper conditions. Similarly, "internationalists" and peace groups everywhere can be helpful allies on certain issues.

150. Common Heritage with Christianity and Judaism. Most people in the West do not seem to realize that there are many common features among Islam, Christianity, and Judaism. Faith in one God, the Day of Judgment, the Divine origin of scriptures, the prophets of God, regulations on food, clothing, and rules of behavior are just a few of the common areas. The commandments given in *Exodus* 20:2-17 and *Deuteronomy* 5:6-21, the second and fifth books of Prophet Moses (PBUH), are fully supported by Islam:

1. **I am the Lord, thy God. Thou shalt have no other gods before me.**
2. **Thou shalt not make unto thee any graven images.**
3. **Thou shalt not take the name of the Lord thy God in vain. . .**
4. **Remember the Sabbath day, to keep it holy. . .**
5. **Honor thy father and thy mother.**
6. **Thou shalt not kill.**
7. **Thou shalt not commit adultery.**
8. **Thou shalt not steal.**
9. **Thou shalt not bear false witness against thy neighbor.**
10. **Thou shalt not desire thy neighbor's wife, neither shalt thou covet thy neighbor's house, his field, or his manservant, or his maidservant, his ox, his ass, or anything that is thy neighbor's.**

Indeed, there is a consensus among many scholars that if the Jews, Christians, and Muslims practiced what is taught by their respective religions, there would be a great deal of harmony among them. While some differences would obviously remain, many misunderstandings would be removed. Public relations can educate people in Western countries about the heritage and beliefs they have in common with Muslims.

151.   Common Heritage of Hindus and Muslims. The common Muslim in the Asian subcontinent feels that Hindus have many gods in the form of statues and cows. Hindus are thought to worship them all. However, study of the Hindu religion suggests that there is only one supreme God known as Permatma. He has been manifested to the followers in three forms, Brahma (the Creator), Vishnu (the Preserver), and Shiva (the Destroyer). The Preserver is to reappear from time to time to show the right way to the followers. Rama is said to have been one of the appearances of Vishnu. Hindus explain that they make statues of all physical appearances of God as well as other important characters in their history and mythology. They show respect to all such manifestations including cows, but they worship only one God. Hindus feel that it is as unfair to think of destroying their statues, as it would be to destroy graves or shrines of holy men of Islam.

Just as Muslims await the coming of the Mahdi and/or Prophet Jesus (Isa, son of Maryam), and Christians await the second coming of Jesus, Hindus await the final appearance of Vishnu, the Preserver. On the Day of Judgment for Hindus, Shiva will destroy it all. Under different names, Hindus believe in one God and a Day of Judgment.

Hindus and Muslims have noted their differences (e.g., Muslims believe in the equality of humans while Hindus have an elaborate caste system; Muslims pray relatively quietly, while Hindus sing and play music in their temples; Hindus do not eat beef, while Muslims do not touch pork). However, they have either failed to see, or chosen to ignore the common features of their faiths, as well as their similar codes of good human behavior.

After centuries of misunderstandings and conflict in the name of religion, economics, and national aspirations, Hindus and Muslims of the subcontinent (about 700 million Hindus and 350 million Muslims) still fail to acknowledge their numerous common beliefs, culture, history, and languages. These are recognized more clearly by Hindus and Muslims living abroad than those living in the subcontinent. Horrors and tragedies at the time of the partition in 1947 reflected the differences. With three major wars between them in the last 50 years alone, and the current possibility of a nuclear war between India and Pakistan, they can only benefit from research, understanding, and emphasis on their common heritage. The welfare of over the 1,000 million people of India, Pakistan, and Bangladesh depends on it.

152.   Common Features with Buddhists. Buddhist life is divided in three phases. Kamadhatu is the world of desires, in which humans are controlled by lust for sex, money, power, and worldly possessions. With much self-control, meditation and self-sacrifice, one reaches the second phase or Rapadhatu. It is a transitional sphere where one is released from worldly concerns and actively seeks the pleasure of God. In the final stage of Arupadhatu, one reaches the stage of perfection and enlightenment. Buddhists are asked to renounce worldly needs in order to reach enlightenment and closeness to God. As with Muslims, the main purpose of life for a Buddhist is to worship God and seek His pleasure.

> **I have only created jinn and men, that they may serve Me**
> *(Surah 51:56).*

The Buddha, the founder of the religion, was born as a prince. He renounced his palace and the kingdom. He wandered through the land and meditated for years before reaching enlightenment.

While the Buddha is not specifically mentioned in the Qur'an, he may be one of the unnamed prophets. In many ways, the life of a practicing Buddhist is not much different from the life of a Sufi in Islam and a Sadhu among Hindus. With many followers in Japan, China, Thailand, as well as in many Western countries, Buddhism is one of the most important religions of the world. Muslims have a good basis for coexistence with Buddhists as well as with the followers of other great religions such as Christianity, Judaism, and Hinduism.

153.   Common Interests with Minorities. Minorities everywhere tend to have much in common. For example, all non-Christians in the United States have a common interest in the preservation of religious freedoms and preventing the establishment of a state religion. This has helped to keep any single religion from being taught in public schools in the United States. Jews are allied with Muslims, Hindus, Buddhists, and others in this regard. At the same time, Muslims work closely with Christian religious groups in fighting homosexuality, abortion, and immorality.

154.   Reliance on China. China is the only world power of some significance that continues to provide military and political help to some

Muslim countries, in spite of threats from the West. China's special friendship with Pakistan (which is partly a function of mutual distrust of India) and reported help to Iran and Syria are examples. Muslims continue to be appreciative of China's support and are making efforts to build on that relationship.

Long-term reliance on China as a friend of Muslims is, however, questionable. First, China is still a low-income, developing country with 1992 per capita income of only $470, which is significantly less than that of Muslims as a group. However, with cooperation from the West, it is developing fast. The leaders of China's more than 1,100 million people wish to continue economic development. It is unrealistic for Muslims to expect China to defy the West in defense of the interests of Muslims, who have little ideological or cultural compatibility, and who offer little financial rewards to China in return. China has become increasingly pragmatic in its foreign policy in recent times. On major international issues, China has been content to support the majority in the UN Security Council. The Gulf War was a prime example.

Second, China is a communist power. Its leadership does not support any religion. China continues to take action against the followers of all religions within its borders, including Chinese Muslims. Under current conditions, long-term reliance on China as a major international shield for Muslims does not appear probable.

> . . .When (at length) the order for fighting was issued to them, Behold! a section of them feared men as -- or even more than -- they should have feared Allah: They said: "Our Lord! Why has Thou ordered us to fight? Wouldst Thou not grant us respite to our (natural) term, near (enough)?" Say: "Short is the enjoyment of this world: the hereafter is the best for those who do right; never will ye be dealt with unjustly in the very least!" *(Surah 4:77).*

Muslims have faith in Allah. Nevertheless, Muslims as a group are worried. As literacy data suggest, a vast majority cannot read or write. As per capita income data indicates, most belong to low-income countries. As distribution of available income indicates, a very large number must worry about finding food and meeting other basic needs each day. It is apparent that things are not going well for Muslims within their own countries or abroad. They have worries on economic, political, spiritual, and military fronts. However, the real causes for their problems and worries are not yet well identified, analyzed, or diagnosed.

On the international front, Muslim countries face threats from individual as well as collective adversaries. Pakistan feels threatened by India. Iran and the Gulf countries face threat from Iraq. Arabs feel threatened by Israel and Iran. Muslim countries as a group feel apprehensive about policies of England, the United States, and the West. Muslims are taught not to fear anyone but Allah. However, there are historic reasons for the apprehension, and the concerns need to be studied and addressed.

A. Major Concerns of Muslims.

155. **United States Policy.** Since the United States is the only superpower left in the world, many Muslims are particularly sensitive to its policy. Even though the Bush administration led the alliance which defeated Muslim Iraq, Muslim leaders sensed a movement toward even handedness when it came to (a) dealings with Israel after the Gulf War, and (b) resolution of the Palestine issue. The Clinton administration appears to have resumed the previous policy of unconditional support for Israel.

Muslim leaders assert that President Clinton and Congress have promised Israel to: (a) continue annual aid of at least $3 billion a year disregarding a large deficit at home; (b) maintain its qualitative military edge over the combined forces of all Arabs; (c) insist on nuclear non-proliferation among all Arabs, and even all Muslims, regardless of Israeli nuclear weapons; (d) continue to reward or punish Arabs based on their attitude toward Israel; and (e) treat all present and potential enemies of Israel as enemies of the United States. They argue that this has emboldened Israel to continue its military attacks on Lebanon, destroying towns and villages and depopulating areas. This type of policy toward Israel worries many Muslims and makes the United States's claim of neutrality in resolving Middle East issues less credible.

156.   **Physical Force.** Israeli aerial and artillery attacks in Lebanon, Serbian aggression against Muslims in European Bosnia, Indian military action against Muslims in Kashmir, the United Nations police action in Somalia, and the United States air war on Iraq are just some of the recent reports that make Muslim leaders worry about the escalating use of force against them by the West. In addition, there is fear of military action against Iran for its support of "militant" Muslims, against Libya for refusal to hand over those accused of the PAN AM bombing, against Iraq for menacing action against Kuwait, and against Sudan for its aggressive stance against Western influence. These are some of the recent reports that make Muslims worry about the escalating use of force against them by the West.

Muslim leaders everywhere are alarmed at the growing threat of military assault against them in many parts of the world. The West claims it is merely reacting to aggression. Any action by Muslims or even a belligerent statement can be enough to provoke use of massive force against whole populations. Some Western observers argue that the United States should take additional preemptive military action against Iran and Libya. Preemptive strikes are viewed by Muslims as rhetoric to excuse aggression against them. The new word, "collateral damage" also glosses over and justifies casualties of innocent civilians. Some military actions against Muslims have been so blatantly unjust that even the Western media have criticized them on humanitarian grounds.

157.   **Genocide in Yugoslavia.** The breakup of Yugoslavia into several states has meant tragedy for many people. It has reignited conflicts of centuries ago. Serbian leaders are determined to unite all Serbs into a greater Serbia. If a Serbian population happened to be outside Serbia (e.g.,

in Croatia, Sylvania, or in Bosnia), they seek to extend Serbia to them. The arms embargo imposed by the United Nations against all Yugoslavia has had little impact on the Serbs who, with access to the weapons of the preexisting Yugoslav army, have had no problem in conquering desirable parts of Croatia and about 70 percent of Bosnia. The whole world, including Europe and the United States, has been shocked by the "ethnic cleansing" of hundreds of thousands of innocent Europeans through murder, concentration camps, torture, and rape.

The largest number of victims happens to be Muslims. Other Muslims all over the world have appealed to the world powers and were repeatedly assured that the European and American governments were doing all that was possible. However, the arms embargo, with its primary impact being felt by the Bosnian Muslims, has not been lifted, on the pretext that it is necessary for the protection of British, French and other European soldiers in Bosnia.

158.   **Bosnia.** While the United States claims to have taken a high moral position regarding the Bosnian conflict, it has not been willing to commit the necessary force to bring about an equitable solution nor to lift unilaterally the arms embargo. France and Britain have provided ground personnel to the UN, but many have doubted their commitment to an equitable solution. While NATO has pointed fingers at the UN for not allowing the required air strikes against Serbs, in fact, both institutions are controlled by the same major powers. If the world powers really wanted to, they could have agreed on a resolution in NATO and the UN.

Humanitarian concerns of candidate, and subsequently, President Clinton and Senate Minority, and subsequently Majority, Leader Dole have been welcomed, but have not been sufficient to mobilize the powers into adequate action. Many have noted that if the principal victims were non-Muslims, there would have been stronger action.

Muslim governments around the world could have and should have done more to help their fellow Muslims in Yugoslavia. The results have given ammunition to Muslim critics who claim that, to the West, the life of a Muslim is expendable, even if the Muslims happen to be Europeans, White, and secular. It has also advanced the image of Iran as the only Muslim country willing to affirm Islamic ideals in aid of persecuted Muslims around the world.

159.   **Hindu Parties in India.** In the late 1930's, the Bharatiya Jauta Party (BJP) and RSS founder, Gavalkar, wrote about the superiority of

Hindus and the need to purify India of all non-Hindus. He openly admired the example of ethnic purification being followed by Nazi Germany against Jews at that time. His followers are essentially pursuing the same objective, even though the first step is to gain political power through public service at the community level. Simultaneously, Hindus have laid claim to several mosques arguing that they were sites of Hindu temples several hundred years ago. The famous mosque in Ayodhia was first locked for several years and then demolished in December 1992, against the order of the Supreme Court of India and while law enforcement officials looked on. In subsequent riots, thousands of lives, primarily Muslims, were lost and much property was burnt.

Approximately 150 million Muslims in India already feel like second class citizens under Hindu rule. They are anxious about their future in terms of freedom to practice Islam and their ability to live in security and progress economically. They dread the day when BJP might gain power at the national level.

Press reports indicate that the Indian Muslims have begun to react. For example, a letter published in *Saudi Gazette* (Riyadh) of February 26, 1993 indicated that among Indian Muslims working in Saudi Arabia "unskilled and semiskilled workers wished to hit back, and die the death of martyrs rather than dying in rat holes." Militancy was freely advocated without any thought of consequences. Skilled labor and non-executive office workers were advocating training in self-defense for men and women, and creation of "lookout squads." Disillusionment with current Muslim leadership was also mentioned. Senior executives were also worried but put more emphasis on prevention as a remedy. They advocated: (a) educating and reminding Hindus that Muslims are as much Indians as they are; (b) cultivating closer relationships with uneducated Hindus and emphasizing the classless nature of Islam and Muslim society; (c) patronizing the secular media to clarify questions about Muslim laws which have been attacked in the Hindu press; (d) greater Muslim activity in politics through support of secular parties, as well as personal participation in elections at various levels; and (e) help for needy Muslims in re-starting their lives, and providing education (English and religious) for their children.

The results of regional elections in several Indian states in November 1993 punched a hole in the efforts of BJP to advance its power and its platform of Hindu nationalism. BJP performed much worse than expected in Himachal Pardesh, and Uttar Pardesh. Political analysts have interpreted these and other results to date to mean that the voters were not swayed by appeals to their religious emotions. They expressed hope that Muslims and Hindus can peacefully coexist in India.

160. **Repression in Kashmir.** In 1947, when the British were leaving India, each province and princely state was given a right to choose whether they wanted to join India or Pakistan. The areas with Muslim majorities chose Pakistan. There were many injustices in the partitioning of Punjab and Bengal, and in the states of Hyderabad and Junagarh. However, the case of Kashmir was the most poignant. The overwhelming majority of the people wanted to join Pakistan. However, the ruler, a Sikh, was ambivalent and invited Indian troops for protection. The Indians never left. Subsequently, India promised the United Nations that a plebiscite would be held to determine the views and the fate of Kashmir and its people. That was in 1949. The promise was never kept.

For the past few years, Kashmiris have been in open rebellion. The Indian army is there in full force with Western and Israeli advisors. Based on press and Amnesty International reports, thousands have been killed, permanently injured and raped. Many more thousands remain in Indian jails. The beautiful valleys have been devastated and its inhabitants face constant suffering. In spite of sympathetic international media coverage, the world powers have shown little desire to become entangled or to enforce this particular United Nations resolution. Kashmiris are demanding an explicit opportunity to decide whether they wish to remain with India, join Pakistan, or become independent.

161. **Relations Between India and Pakistan.** Pakistan and India warred over Kashmir in 1948 and 1965. They fought again over East Pakistan and Kashmir in 1970-71. Past agreements at the United Nations, Tashkent, and Simla have failed to bring peace. It is widely recognized that both countries either have nuclear weapons or can assemble them with ease. Reportedly, the two countries came close to a nuclear confrontation in the early 1990. Recognition of this fact may prevent both from starting a major war.

There have been proposals for peace. Under one proposal, Pakistan and India may be allowed to keep an agreed number of nuclear weapons each. However, India may also be allowed to keep additional weapons for protection from China. Each side will then be given full inspection rights over the facilities of the other.

The United States and Europe seek to ensure that (a) there will be no nuclear war in the subcontinent and (b) Pakistan will not pass on any nuclear weapons to any Middle Eastern country which can threaten Israel.

Presumably, India would want China to be a part of the agreement. This, however, would not solve the problems of Kashmir and the threat felt by Indian Muslims.

162.   **Attacks by Western Powers.** For three centuries or so, Western powers colonized and directly ruled most Muslim countries. Following the independence of many of the former colonies, when diplomatic efforts failed, Western countries often used surrogates and covert operations to achieve their objectives.

It is clear in the eyes of the Western public that terrorist activities deserve the strong reaction that has recently characterized their government's policies toward "terrorist nations." On the other side, there are those who worry that, since the start of rapprochement with Soviet Union and its subsequent breakup, the West has been destabilizing and physically attacking selected Muslim countries. They complain that killings of Muslims by Israeli, Serbian or pro-western regimes evoke mild statements from Washington urging all parties to "resolve their disputes peacefully." However, action by Muslims justifies full state-sponsored reprimands, embargoes and violent physical attack. They assert that, in the past few years, Western powers, and the United States in particular, have become increasingly bold in physically attacking Muslim countries regardless of world opinion, reaction of other Muslims, military consequences, or killing of innocent civilians.

Attacks against a civilian passenger airliner in Iran resulted in the deaths of over 300 innocent victims. Under President Reagan, air strikes against Libya were conducted in retaliation for the bombing of a night club in Europe. Subsequent press reports that Libya was not involved went unnoticed. Massive attacks on Iraq have resulted in an unknown number of civilian casualties. Since the Gulf War, additional air strikes have been made against Iraq for assorted reasons.

It is generally acknowledged that Iran and its Islamic Revolution represent the vanguard of the revived Islamic activism. In the opinion of many commentators, Iran will be the next target of Western "retaliation." Since destruction of Iraq, the Israeli government has portrayed Iran as the biggest security threat to the West, to moderate Arabs, and, of course, to Israel itself. Like Pakistan, Iran is supposed to be on the verge of making an "Islamic bomb."

The Egyptian government, which has been unable to remedy its domestic economic and social problems, is beginning to subscribe to the Israeli view. Both countries need to justify a threat to the West in the

Middle East in order to keep the major portion of the United States's worldwide aid flowing to them. Some worry that even Saudi Arabia may be urging the United States to take action against Iran. All that is needed, they fear, is an anti-American incident linked to Iran. The bomb blast at a Jewish center in Buenos Aires, Argentina in mid 1994 could have been the incident. However, Argentinean officials failed to link the bombing to Iran.

163. Spiritual Threats (Temptations). Pious Muslims are worried about the enormous temptations presented by Western societies. Humans, especially the young, prefer living free, without restrictions. They are lured by imagined freedoms: unregulated dating and casual sex, without constraints of marriage; easy access to liquor; sensual dancing; freedom from modest clothing in hot weather; irreverent speech and actions; and freedom from established religious rituals. All these are seductive to almost any immature Muslim. They are all common practices in Western society and regularly depicted in its entertainment media.

A number of Muslims visiting the West or living in the West have fallen prey. Affluent Muslims in other parts of the world, including Muslim majority countries, are following suit. Others are merely observing this life style personally or through TV, and though not participating are greatly tempted. How to resist and protect themselves and their families is of concern to many Muslims.

Ironically, in the United States politically active Christians are asserting that this plague in their society can be counteracted only by a return to the fundamentals of religion. So, too, do many Muslims believe. In Muslim countries, the situation has provoked a profound reaction against modern Western values and inspired many again to don *hijab*, leave off liquor, and visit the mosques on Friday. As in the recent elections in the United States demonstrated, such a religiously-based political movement can have profound implications for the ruling party.

164. Anti-God Behavior. Karen Armstrong, a former Catholic nun, in her best-selling book, *A History of God*, explores the traditional belief that God has created man and contrasts it to the modern Western idea that man has created God. Even though the three monotheistic religions, Judaism, Christianity, and Islam, believe in the idea of a God who sees, hears, rewards, and punishes, many in the world are turning away from this basic belief.

The power and attraction of secularism are growing. Similarly, fundamental religious principles are being passionately affirmed by increasing numbers of Christians, Muslims and Jews, among others. Conditions appear to be developing where a violent clash will become inevitable. Many have predicted that such a polarization would take place, a separation along the most basic of human thoughts, belief versus unbelief.

165. Secular Behavior of Muslim Governments. Many Muslim governments have secular constitutions requiring separation of religion and government. Some, like Egypt, have banned formation of religious parties. Turkey has sought to be recognized as a member of the European Economic Community and has been willing to compromise religious doctrine. The military regime in Algeria is openly persecuting members and supporters of its Islamic parties. Pakistan, fearing sectarian violence at home and the "fundamentalist" label abroad, is eager to practice separation of religion from the government.

B. Anti-Religious Behavior of Non-Muslim Governments.

166.   Anti-Christian Behavior. The West and its press, particularly the United States, have portrayed themselves as secular, in spite of a deep religious heritage and a population overwhelmingly Christian in belief. This secular affirmation is not well received by evangelical and other serious Christians in the United States. They see their government and the mainstream media as having moved away from God and having become hostile to religion. These Christians reject their government's position on abortion, homosexuality, exclusion of religion from schools, etc.

The government sees itself as neutral to all religions and a proponent of secularism. The neutrality, however, appears to be weighed against Christians. They argue that enforcing the separation of church and state results in excluding traditional Christian principles from the society while permitting the practice of every new and deviant kind of antireligious behavior that can be imagined. They have tried to document that this was not the original intent of the Constitution or of the founders of the United States.

167.   Anti-Judaism Among Jews. Jews are well-organized and exert considerable political influence in the United States. Most Jews are very nationalistic when it comes to protecting and strengthening Israel. Also, they take pride in their culture and traditions. However, many Jews have fallen prey to the modern secular society and have distanced themselves from the obligations of their religion. Many modern Jews have much more faith in science than in Judaism. They reflect the same movement toward secularism that European and American societies have manifested in the twentieth century.

In Israel, religious parties play a pivotal role in the balance of political power. Nevertheless, they represent a minority in actual number of votes. Israel itself is a secular state. While there is overwhelming support for the defense and protection of Israel as a political state, very few are advocating the return of the Torah and the Talmud as the law of the land.

The controversy over the Dome of the Rock, sacred to both Muslims and Jews, illustrates the nature of the Jewish paradox. As the site of the Temple of Solomon, it is claimed by Jews who wish to demolish it to rebuild Solomon's Temple on its site. As a political/military issue, Jews are united against Muslims. However, with regards to the religious issue involved in rebuilding the Temple, such as ritualistic practices to be observed, administration, and even the role of the expected Messiah in its reestablishment, there is deep division. As in the controversies in India over Hindu sites, the issues are more political than the religious. For many, the Jewish religion has similarly become a secular, political, military and even ethnic matter; Zionism has displaced Judaism. This is a matter which seriously worries devout Jews.

168.   Anti-Islamic Behavior. Muslims are envisioned as enemies of fundamental rights asserted by secular Western humanists. While respect for the Islamic religion is nominally expressed, the attitude toward those who seriously practice Islam often reflects either ignorance or premeditated bias.

Muslims protest that the United States government and the media display their general anti-religion bias most explicitly when it comes to Islam. Muslim leaders in Iran and Sudan who wish to promote the religion are strongly opposed. Countries, such as Turkey and Indonesia, who keep religion separate are embraced and encouraged. For years, Turkey has been seen and promoted as a model of secularism to be followed by all Middle East and Central Asian countries. However, as the United States has become more secure in its role as the sole superpower, even Turkey is criticized. Leaders challenging secularism and injecting religion into political life are noticed and censured.

As an example, on July 24, 1993, when the slaughter of Muslims in Bosnia was progressing and Muslims were near total defeat, the

Washington Post saw fit to question editorially the "health of secularism" in Turkey, citing violence against an author who had translated and published parts of Rushdie's *Satanic Verses*. Apparently, to the editors of this influential newspaper, the ideals endangered by the *fatwah* against Rushdie were closer to home than those transgressed by the ethnic cleansing in Bosnia.

169.   **Russia.** During the 1993 United Nations Conference on Human Rights, there was an 88 to one vote in favor of lifting the arms embargo against Bosnia. Only Russia voted against the resolution sponsored by Muslims. Why is Russia so anti-Muslim? Some explanations may lie in (a) communist antagonism to all religions, including Islam; (b) the humiliating defeat at the hands of Muslim *mujahiddeen* in Afghanistan; (c) the uneasy relations with the new Muslim republics carved out of the Soviet Union; (d) Russian military officials' sympathy for the Serbian military, whom they trained and equipped; and (e) the threat of increasing Iranian influence in the region. Whatever the reasons, the Russians are the main opponents to arming Muslims in Bosnia. In addition, they supported India against Pakistan in two significant conflicts and have always supported India on the Kashmir issue.

170.   **Fear of Islamic Form of Government.** The Islamic form of government, its constitution, and experience to date are discussed elsewhere in this book. It should be mentioned here, however, that many within and outside Muslim countries are vehemently opposed to such a form of government. Many Muslims fear the rule of "irrational and poorly educated *mullahs*," envisioning a highly restrictive society in which modern technology and progress are stunted while religious rituals are imposed on all.

While the Western countries often appear to be unified in dealing with Muslims, they have individual as well as collective agendas. It is worth studying the worries of Americans and Europeans separately, as well as noting their common concerns.

171. American Worries. The *Los Angeles Times* of November 2, 1993, contained a special piece on America's World Role: "Divided We Stand." It published the results of a survey about worries of more than 600 U.S. opinion makers drawn from the top ranks of business, government, the news media, foreign affairs, security, academics, arts, religion, science and engineering, and the public. It listed the following immediate problems as requiring top priority from the U.S. government:

a. insuring that democracy succeeds in Russia and other former Soviet states;
b. strengthening the domestic economy to improve the U.S. international position;
c. better management of trade and economic disputes with Japan;
d. ending warfare in the Balkans;
e. bringing about a permanent settlement between Israel and the Arabs;
f. stopping the flood of illegal aliens into the United States;
g. adopting a North American Free Trade Agreement;
h. guarding against a resurgent Germany;
i. protecting the global environment;
j. getting Saddam Hussain out of Iraq;
k. stopping the international drug trafficking;
l. countering North Korean militarism; and
m. keeping a careful watch on the emergence of China as a world

172. Long-Range Policies. The results of the survey indicated the following long-range foreign policy goals as requiring top priority:

a. preventing the spread of weapons of mass destruction;
b. improving the global environment;
c. helping improve the living standards in developing nations;

    d. insuring adequate energy supplies for the United States;
    e. promoting democracy in other nations;
    f. aiding the interests of U.S. business abroad;
    g. protecting jobs of American workers;
    h. strengthening the United Nations;
    i. reducing the U.S. trade deficit;
    j. promoting and defending human rights abroad; and
    k. protecting weaker nations against foreign aggression even if U.S. vital interests are not at stake.

173.   **Threats to Stability.** Each issue received a score from influential leaders and the general public indicating whether it was a top priority or not. Some received scores in the eighties, while others were in the teens. Nevertheless, all of the above reflected worries of the U.S. public and policy-makers.

The survey sighted the following threats to world stability:

    a. nationalism and ethnic hatred;
    b. proliferation of weapons of mass destruction;
    c. international trade conflicts;
    d. religious fanaticism;
    e. environmental pollution; and
    f. population growth.

174.   **Criteria for Use of Force.** It sighted threats to the United States from China, Japan, and North Korea in Asia; Iran, and Iraq in the Middle East; and Russia. It sighted Europe and the Pacific Rim as being the most important regions to the United States. A large number of those surveyed were prepared to send American troops abroad under the following circumstances:

    a. Iraq invades Saudi Arabia;
    b. North Korea invades South Korea;
    c. Mexico is threatened by revolution or civil war; and
    d. the Arabs invade Israel.

Islam or Muslims were not sighted as threats directly. Nevertheless, the threat of religious fanaticism among Muslims, the militancy of Iran and Iraq, and the proliferation of nuclear weapons are implicitly connected with

Islam and Muslims. Both Iraq and Iran represent a threat that is generally identified as "Islamic," and both, plus Pakistan, are among the Muslim nations which may develop nuclear weapons. Some of the worries of the West are discussed in more detail below.

175. **Security of Oil Supplies.** Most of the oil rich kingdoms in the Middle East were created by the U.K. less than fifty years ago. Kings were supported and even installed based on their loyalty to the U.K. Some Arabs have not fully accepted their domination and many consider the oil wealth to be a collective Arab heritage to be used for the common good and not for the benefit of a few families. The kings have always felt threatened by larger Arab countries and their fiery leaders. They have given financial assistance to such leaders as Gamal Abdul Nasser and Saddam Hussain to secure their continued authority.

By walking into Kuwait overnight, Saddam showed how vulnerable these kingdoms are. The Gulf War clearly illustrated the intimate relationship between the oil kingdoms and the West. Once again, the Gulf kingdoms, who control much of the region's oil, owe their existence to the United States and the West. The security of the oil supplies is assured for now, but it remains the single most important issue and the only one that truly causes the West to worry about Muslims.

176. **Price of Oil.** After decades of extremely low prices of oil, Iran and Arab members of OPEC demanded and obtained higher price for oil following the 1973 Arab-Israeli War. It caused major difficulties and hardships to oil-importing countries. The West was particularly worried due to the large volume it imported. However, the threat of a major increase in price has been significantly reduced since the Gulf War due to the debt of gratitude owed by the oil-exporting kingdoms to the West. Nevertheless, the threat of higher oil prices over the long, and even, medium term remains.

177. **Security of Israel.** Next to the continued supply of oil at a cheap price, the security of Israel has been the most important objective of the West in the Middle East. While the Soviet Union posed a threat, Israel was strategically important. The argument was made that the United States needed such a stable ally as Israel in the region, particularly in light of the support received from the Soviet Union by Iraq, Syria and even Libya.

Since the dissolution of the Soviet Union, Israel's importance to the security interests of the United States has diminished. In addition, the Gulf

War exposed some liabilities in being too closely aligned with Israel. Saddam Hussein tried to use Arab enmity toward Israel to drum up support for his cause and weaken the alliance of Arabs fighting against him. During the Gulf War it became quite apparent to the world that the security of Saudi Arabia was as important as that of Israel. Any major shift in regimes in the region can threaten Israel. Israel and their guardians have kept Arabs divided in the Middle East. However, the Arabs themselves have made the job easy. Israel and the United States are able to bomb many Arabs at will, and both have the ability to use nuclear weapons.

Nevertheless, the commitment to Israel's security remains high among Western leaders for religious, political and economic reasons. Also, many influential Christian leaders have come to the support of the state of Israel for various reasons, including eschatological ones. All eyes are currently on implementation of the peace process between Israel and the Palestine Liberation Organization (PLO). This treaty with the Palestinians has made many friends for Israel, even among the Arabs. Genuine peace can make many more friends and go a long way in removing Western worries about the security of Israel.

178.   Problem of North Korea. North Korea has been a threat to South Korea since the late forties when it received support from the Soviet Union and China. It attacked the South which resulted in the United Nations intervention led by the United States. Reportedly, it is proceeding with development of nuclear technology. It refuses to permit international inspections of its nuclear facilities; sells conventional arms, including missiles to some of the "renegade" Middle Eastern states; and is a threat to South Korea. If North Korea develops nuclear weapons, Japan may reconsider its own renunciation of nuclear weapons. The United States is maintaining a large force in South Korea and has repeatedly warned the North. Even China, which supported the North in the Korean war, is cooperating with the United States in trying to find a solution. All eyes are on the implementation of agreements reached between the United States and North Korea, following former President Carter's visit.

179.   World Control Without Casualties. The West has been fortunate in recent years. The conflicts with Libya, Iraq, Grenada, Panama, and Haiti have resulted in relatively few casualties. Each U.S. government has known that significant American casualties could quickly result in loss of American voters' support. In any case, maintaining public approval of costly, whether in economic or human terms, international policies is a great challenge for the West's leaders. At times, threats are imagined or exaggerated in order to enhance support for a particular policy. Islam and Muslims become scapegoats.

180. Debt and Deficits. The West and the United States are worried about the long-run impact of large budgetary deficits year after year. Since the beginning of President Reagan's administration, the U.S. debt has increased fourfold, with no decrease in sight. At the same time, foreign aid to Egypt and Israel is in excess of six billion dollars a year, with no reduction in sight. These financial and economic considerations coupled with domestic disapproval of excessive government spending are sources of pressure on U.S. foreign policy in the Middle East.

The worry remains that militant Muslim leaders will destabilize the region necessitating additional commitment of military support and foreign aid. For example, when Saddam Hussein appears to be moving troops in a threatening manner, a military response is made that costs billions of dollars. The oil rich kingdoms can share the costs if they have money. With low oil prices, large levels of military expenditures, increasing national debts and budget deficits, they may not be able to be as generous in the future as they were in the past.

181. Unemployment. Elected leaders responsible to their citizens worry about unemployment. The recent end of the Cold War and the resulting "dawn of peace" has brought about massive job losses. Armed forces in the United States, Western Europe, Eastern Europe, and the former Soviet Union have been trimmed. The armament industry has lost much business and is in fear of losing more. The loss has a ripple effect on the steel industry, transportation, and many other sectors of the economy. It all means job losses. It all has come at a time when technological advances and recessions in many countries has already resulted in loss of many jobs. President Bush lost his reelection bid largely over economic issues.

182. Unity Among Enemies of World Wars I and II. Following the end of the Cold War, all major powers involved in the two World Wars -- the United States, the U.K., Germany, France, Italy, Japan, and Russia -- are now united, in a formal or an informal alliance. For the first time in history, all the major powers in the world are on the same side. Existing world trading blocks are shown on the next page. Even most of the smaller powers are anxious to be included. The Gulf War tested the alliance; the success has made the alliance even stronger.

WORLD TRADING BLOCKS

G-7 (Group of 7) - United States of America, United Kingdom Canada, Japan, Germany, Italy, France. Russia has been admitted to this group as a discussant on security issues.

EU (European Union) - England, France, Italy, Spain, Germany, Greece Portugal, Denmark, Luxembourg, Belgium, Ireland.

EFTA (European Free Trade Association) - Austria, Liechtenstein, Iceland, Finland, Norway, Sweden, Switzerland

EEA (European Economic Area) - European Community and European Free Trade Association.

NAFTA (North American Free Trade Area) - Canada, United States of America and Mexico.

CIS (Commonwealth of Independent States) - Russia, Kazakhstan, Kyrgyzstan, Tajikistan, Turkmenistan, Uzbekistan, Azerbaijan, Armenia, Ukraine, Moldova, Belarus.

ASEAN (Association of South East Asian Nations) - Philippines, Thailand, Malaysia, Singapore, Indonesia and Brunei.

EAEG (East Asian Economic Group) - ASEAN, Japan, China, South Korea, Hong Kong, Taiwan and Viet Nam.

Southern Africa - Namibia, Botswana, Zimbabwe, Lesotho, Mozambique, South Africa.

Caricom - Antigua and Barbuda, the Bahamas, Barbados, Dominica, Grenada, Jamaica, Montserrat, Saint Christopher Nevis, Saint Lucia, Saint Vincent and the Grenadines, Trinidad and Tobago, Belize and Guyana.

Central American Market - Guatemala, El Salvador, Honduras, Costa Rica and Nicaragua.

Andean Pact - Venezuela, Colombia, Ecuador, Peru and Bolivia.

G-3 (Group of 3) - Colombia, Venezuela and Mexico. (Southern Colombia Zone): Brazil, Paraguay, Argentina, Uruguay.

Mercosur (Southern Cone Zone) - Brazil, Paraguay, Argentina and Uruguay.

Figure 4. World Trading Blocks. 138

The formation of the European Economic Union initiated an era of reduction of trade barriers. The United States, Canada and Mexico signed NAFTA; additional treaties were signed by other Latin American states and the United States, excluding Cuba. Similar regional trade agreements are being proposed throughout the world. As the world shrinks, national boundaries have become blurred and the influx of immigrant labor is threatening the indigenous citizenry. Nationalistic sentiment often becomes a tool used by politicians to gain voter support. Germany and Russia, key players in the New World Order, have shown signs of such nationalistic sentiment. There is always the threat of a new Hitler or a new Stalin.

183. **Russia.** The breakup of the Soviet Union removed the largest single worry of the West. Several states within the former Soviet Union have declared their independence; Eastern Europe is eager to join the European Union. Poland, the Czech Republic, Hungary, Romania and Bulgaria have already established closer ties and are exploring membership in the EU by the early 21st century.

Russia, the largest single new country, under the leadership of President Boris Yeltsin, has been as cooperative as political wisdom can allow. A brief revolt by the old guard in the parliament was successfully crushed, and new parliamentary elections were held in December 1993. The results of the first free elections in more than seventy years were shocking for the West. Over 40 percent of the seats were won by nationalists and communists firmly opposed to the Yeltsin reforms.

The Russian people have already experienced significant lowering of their standard of living. They are now facing increasing levels of poverty and lawlessness. The West is particularly worried about the anti-West rhetoric of the opposition leader Vladimir Zhirinovsky. Germany, Poland, the Baltic states, Ukraine, and the United States all feel threatened, and have openly voiced their concerns. As a result, Yeltsin's government is cautious in implementing capitalistic reforms.

Bosnia and the proposed expansion of NATO have exposed major diplomatic disagreements between Washington and Moscow. In addition, as domestic economic problems increase and popular support wanes, Yeltsin finds cooperation with the West increasingly more difficult.

184. **Japan.** World War II saw a great conflict between Japan and the Allies, led by the United States. Japan is the only country which has attacked the United States in modern times. In return, the United States dropped nuclear bombs over Hiroshima and Nagasaki. In the postwar

period, the Japanese Constitution was rewritten to denounce force. Since then, Japan has focused on economic development, but has become "too powerful in economic terms" from the perspective of the West. Japan has a huge ($50 to $60 billion) annual balance of payments surplus with the United States alone. It has given rise to serious economic and trade conflicts with the West, in particular the United States. During the Gulf War, the United States encouraged Japan to begin participating in future military actions by the United Nations. Grudgingly, Japan has acquiesced. Though Japan is one of the group of seven dominant world economic powers, observers note that the West has not fully accepted Japan as one of its own.

In spite of its many achievements in technological fields and heavy reliance on nuclear energy, Japan has stayed clear of nuclear weapon development. It could all change under provocation. Nuclear weapon development by North Korea is an example. With a range of 1,000 kilometers, North Korean rockets are already capable of reaching Japan. *Asia Week* reported, in the October 6, 1993 issue, that it may take Japan only one month to produce a reliable nuclear weapon. With its enormous economic power, and possible nuclear development, future disagreements with the West, though unlikely, are not out of the question.

185. **China.** Enjoying significant economic growth, China is also expanding its military power. It is modernizing its armed forces, developing an armament industry including long range missiles, buying weapons from Russia and eastern European countries, and testing newer nuclear weapons. In spite of Western pressure, it continues to sell weapons to Pakistan, Iran, and other Middle Eastern countries. It views Western pressure for nuclear non-proliferation as an attempt to perpetuate Western superiority, and accordingly does not want any part of it. China would like to focus on its development and avoid direct confrontation with the West.

Following a protracted debate, the United States has separated trade from human rights issues, and is pursuing a strategy of economic cooperation and development. Immediate confrontation has been avoided. Nevertheless, communism still poses a major ideological challenge and the West continues to worry about China.

186. **Germany.** Germans are among the hardest working, mechanically minded, and disciplined people in the world. It is no wonder that they have remained strong. They were the main combatants in World Wars I and II. Following their defeat in World War II, the allies rewrote the German

constitution, divided the country into capitalist and communist governments, and ensured that Germans would not again be armed. In forty years, West Germany became the economic engine of Western Europe. The Germans were glad to reunite with their eastern part after breakup of the Soviet Union. While mobilizing for the Gulf War in 1991, the allies encouraged Germans to re-arm, so that they, too, could share the cost of playing world policemen.

Many are becoming alarmed by the growing German nationalistic fervor. Many who saw the horrors of World War II are either dead or retired. The younger generation neither suffered defeat nor feels strong guilt over war crimes.

Prominent politicians including the Prime Minister of Bavaria, have spoken out in favor of maintaining the national identity. Anti-foreigner violence is on the rise. According to the *Washington Post* (June 28, 1993) in 1990, there were 270 reported violent incidents involving right wing neo-Nazis. In 1991, the number increased to 1483. In 1992, it was 2584. The most violent year was 1993. As in the 1930's, there are reports of book burnings at German universities of books written by Jews and foreigners.

187. Anti-United States Feelings in Europe. Europeans have many concerns about the policies and actions of the United States. Many feel that:

a. The United States is turning inward, and retreating from global responsibilities.
b. The United States is not willing to commit troops to foreign crises, worries more about "body bags," and is lacking moral courage to take a stand. Many Germans mention the example of Bosnia.
c. The United States may not be a reliable partner in crucial situations, unless its own direct interests are involved.
d. The United States has not done enough to help East European countries.
e. Following the fall of communism, the United States is paying much more attention to East Asia than to Europe.

188. Anti-Continent Feeling in Britain. Britain and the continent are clearly not comfortable with each other. The British are not ready for political union with the rest of Europe. They are even unhappy with the speed of the economic side of the union. They feel that (a) they are denied a fair share of positions and promotions within EU, and (b) EU is overly influenced by the continent's farmers. Anti-continent reports are prominent in the British press. While the EU has made remarkable progress in bringing the historical enemies together, unity is not yet at hand.

189.   **Fear of Islam in Government.** Since their independence after World War II, new Muslim states have been largely ruled by the Western educated class. It has been easy for the West to work with them, and keep them on "the right track." Following the Revolution in Iran, the westernized Iranians were almost entirely replaced by locally trained Islamic activists. To some extent, Sudan has experienced the same phenomenon. With the rising tide of Islam, there is fear that the westernized Muslims will also be replaced in other Muslim countries.

There is a fear that if Islam and practicing Muslims gain control of political power and become full or partial rulers, the interests of the West and Western-educated officials would suffer. It is often ignored that the Saudi Arabian government, one of the West's closest allies, was founded and is run on the basis of fundamentalist Islamic principles. Saudis have not inflicted any economic loss to the interests of the West.

Similarly, Pakistan adapted an Islamic Constitution and became an Islamic republic as early as 1956. Since then, it has gradually moved toward adaption of Islamic laws. The movement toward Islamic laws was intensified during the 11-year rule of President Zia, however he had to temper his actions with the mood of people. Throughout the period, Pakistan maintained good relations with the United States and the West. The Pakistani nuclear program which is a bone of contention between the two countries was initiated by the secular government of Zulfiqar Ali Bhutto for reasons of gaining parity with neighboring India.

Bangladesh declared itself an Islamic republic in 1988. Jordan has a major block of Islamic parties in its parliament yet continues to maintain good relations with the West and even with Israel. Accordingly, it is wrong to label all Islamic governments as incompatible with modern politics and government.

The Iranian threat, always cited by the West, has its own unique history. The controversial role of the United States in Iran and the late Shah's cruel suppression of Iranian people has much to do with the reaction of the Islamic government. While issues of religion, ideology and values are very important in the controversy between Iran and the West, there are deep political, economic and financial issues which cloud the picture.

Given the economic hardships in many Muslim countries, Islamic parties can genuinely criticize their governments. These are often unrepresentative and oblivious to the needs of common people. Western support for such governments causes dissatisfied citizens to blame the West as well as their own officials for their miseries. However, when Islamic parties participate in the political process, they soon learn about the practical constraints facing all governments. As shown in Saudi Arabia, Pakistan, Bangladesh, and Jordan, they cooperate peacefully in the political process.

Western policies toward Islamic parties exhibit relics of the Cold War strategy towards communism. Islam is presented in terms of Marxism, as if its goal were social revolution, expropriation of wealth and the means of production, and destruction of the existing economic order. This, of course, is not true. Whether out of ignorance, desire to maintain a high military profile, or international intrigue, Islamic parties are being portrayed in a manner designed to create an atmosphere of hatred and fear in the West.

190.   Fear of Muslim Countries Uniting. The West has pursued a strategy of keeping Islamic leaders disunited and unable to form alliances. Iran, Libya and Iraq have been targeted one at a time. Arab countries have supported the attacks tacitly or explicitly. Iraq and almost all Arab countries joined the war against Iran. Again, most of the Arabs, Pakistan, Bangladesh, etc. joined the war against Iraq. Few if any voices were heard when Libya was attacked. Surprisingly, only Kuwait supported the United States's missile attack on Iraq in June 1993. Even westernized and secular Turkey raised objections. Nevertheless, the West appears concerned that Muslim countries may join forces.

191.   Fear of Cooperation Among Non-Western Peoples. Some observers have described the coming world alignment in terms of North versus South, pitting Africans, Asians and Latin Americans against Eastern and Western Europeans and North Americans. Such an alliance for economic and development policy has existed, to some extent, for some decades. It has resulted in some moral pressure being brought to bear on the West. While it may not have resulted in the improved terms of trade sought by the South, it has prevented further decline in aid flows. A military alliance among members of the South is unlikely because of the diversity of countries, the lack of a unifying ideology or traditional ties, and the existence of a strong desire to protect their economic self-interests.

However, close relations among China, North Korea, Russia, and some Muslim countries have existed in the past. Circumstances can bring them closer again.

Nevertheless, intense poverty, brutal oppression, and inhuman exploitation can bring divergent interests together against a common enemy. In their quest for international union and economic development, the highly-developed countries with technologically-advanced societies may inadvertently create an unforeseen antagonist.

192. **In Summary.** Just as Muslims have many worries, so too has the West. In dealing with a large number of people and nation states, worries are to be expected and normal. The challenge for Muslims and non-Muslims is to translate common spiritual affirmations into international political realities. They all must become as familiar with Islam and their own religions as they are with international politics, economics and technology.

This is one of the most difficult chapters to write. The purpose is to examine (a) the historical and (b) the current experience of Islamic governments. The last section points out some of the many issues which need to be addressed.

A. The Islamic State.

193.   **The Madinah Model**. The government established by the Prophet (PBUH) in Madinah is accepted by all Muslims to be a model one. *The Prophet and the Islamic State,* by Qutubuddin Aziz, treats this subject at length and provides valuable insight.

The Qur'an was accepted as the eternal Constitution. *Shari'ah,* based on the teachings and practice of the Prophet (PBUH), was the law of the state. The government used the Prophet's mosque as the state's secretariat. Education of the people was considered a duty to God. Science and discovery were highly valued and played a key role in advancement of Muslims.

As a ruler, the Prophet (PBUH) demonstrated qualities of honesty, patience, tolerance, humility, diplomacy, and sacrifice. He received complete allegiance and dedication from his followers. In war, he called upon the entire community to sacrifice; in peace, all enjoyed the protection and security of the state.

The new Muslim state paid special attention to the well-being of non-Muslims with emphasis on religious tolerance, persuasion, and dialogue. The Prophet (PBUH) was opposed to racism and slavery and emphasized brotherhood. Human rights were highly valued under the new state, exploitation was condemned, and respect for the dignity of human beings was observed. The rights of women were recognized and their status greatly enhanced. Under the new state, high priority was accorded to interfaith dialogue with emphasis on increasing mutual understanding and communication. Taxation provided welfare, economic justice, and care for all in need. The administration was based on full accountability, with no corruption or bribes.

194.   *The Khilaafah* **(Caliphate)**. *Shi'ah* Muslims believe that the state ceased to be Islamic after the passing of the Prophet (PBUH). To them, Ali ibn Abi Talib (RA), cousin and son-in-law of the Prophet, and the fourth *Khalifah* (Caliph), had exclusive, Divine right to the Caliphate upon the Prophet's death. Instead, Abu Bakr (RA) was elected to succeed the Prophet. He, in turn, was followed by Umar (RA); Uthman (RA) was elected as the third *Khalifah* (Caliph); Ali (RA) was elected the fourth. After Ali's death, the *Shi'ites* continued to advocate that the Prophet's family rule; from that demand developed the *Shi'ah* legitimism, or the Divine right of the holy family to rule.

Sunnis feel that the first four Caliphs, the Rightly Guided *Khulafa'*, did their best to maintain the ideal government. In any event, the office soon became hereditary, though not in accordance with *Shi'ah* doctrine. For a time, elections by religious authorities, *ulema,* continued to nominally legitimize rulers.

Both groups, *Shi'ites* and *Sunnis*, feel that the Islamic state ceased to exist in year 650 A. D., when the Umayyad dynasty came into power. While the monarchs followed many teachings of Islam, Muslims assert that the primary objective of the rulers was preservation of their own dynasty. Muslim *ulema* and the *Ummah* accepted these monarchs largely because they had no choice. At a minimum, Muslims expected justice and fair play from their rulers. Sometimes they got it, sometimes they did not.

History acknowledges that many Muslim rulers, including monarchs and despots, advanced architecture, higher education, science and technology, literature, etc. However, few Muslims wish to replicate these monarchies. The ideal throughout the Islamic world is recognized to be the model government established up by the Prophet (PBUH) in Madinah. Ironically, the Islamic government established more than fourteen hundred years ago contained features which modern Western governments have adopted but which sadly are lacking in many Muslim governments of today.

Fourteen hundred years ago, at the commencement of the Islamic government, Muslims were weak and almost entirely confined to Madinah. They were surrounded by powerful enemies, in Mecca and elsewhere in Arabia; powerful empires controlled all neighboring lands. Today, Muslims are stronger in terms of the numbers of followers, size of territory, financial and material resources, etc., than in Madinah. However, they lack the unity to establish an Islamic government.

195.   **Characteristics of Islamic Leadership.** The distinguishing qualities of Islamic leadership appear to have been forgotten. Maulana Fazalul Karim, who has translated *Al-Hadis of Mishkat-ul-Masabih*, has

summarized some characteristics of a good ruler in the following manner. He shall:

a. take the world as a temporary resting place for preparation for the everlasting next world;
b. try by just administration to acquire as much religious merits as possible;
c. take himself as a servant of the people and their trustee;
d. love for his subjects what he loves for himself;
e. keep his door open for hearing grievances and for redress of wrongs;
f. make justice coupled with mercy, the key of his administrative policies;
g. observe the religious rites;
h. appoint pious, truthful and sincere ministers and staff;
i. keep a strict eye on the government's affairs;
j. conduct speedy and prompt trials;
k. look to every community with an eye of equality as far as justice is concerned; and
l. govern people according to their respective laws.[31]

This does not mean that Muslim governments should be entirely run by religious scholars. There are a large numbers of Muslims in each Muslim country who know, understand, and practice basic rules of Islam. They refer to the Qur'an and *Hadith* on their own, as permitted in Islam. As long as they meet the required technical and other qualification of a job, they can be appointed.

196.   The Modern Islamic State and Democracy. In the context of the modern world, the question is often asked whether Islam embraces democratic governance. The word "democracy" as defined in the West remains one of politics and semantics. During the Cold War, it was used in contrast to communism, when often capitalism was meant. As most Western political scientists agree, the concepts of representative government are not limited to pure democracies or to capitalistic societies. In practice, the term democracy has as much, or as little, definitive meaning as the word fundamentalist, both being used in widely ranging contexts to describe innumerable situations.

---

[31] Maulana Fazlul Karim, *Al-Hadis of Mishkat-ul-Masabih*, pp. 580-581.

The point to be noted is that an Islamic government cannot be judged on the basis of whether or not it meets the Western nomenclature for representative government. The issue should not be posed in terms of democracy versus Islamic fundamentalism since, for Muslims, the political ideology of a leader is not the definitive quality by which he is judged. In reality, the most important qualities in both public and private life, from a Muslim perspective, are awareness of God and a desire to be in harmony with His will. Any government based on such a perspective would never have to worry about how it is classified by political scientists. In the opinion of Dr. Chapra, Islam has set out four basic criteria for legitimate government:

a. The government should be accountable to Allah, who is the Sovereign and the Source of *shari'ah*. The government must ensure the well-being of the people through "the adoption of all necessary measures, including the efficient and equitable use of the resources" since that is one of the primary objectives of *shari'ah*.

b. The government is a trust and must be accountable to people for meeting the terms of the trust. It must be open to people's suggestions and criticisms.

c. There must be a general atmosphere of consultation, which demands the widest possible participation of people either directly or indirectly.

d. There must be justice and equality of all before the law.

These four criteria for legitimacy may not be satisfied unless those who wield political power derive their authority from the people and are answerable to the people for the quality of their performance. This demands a system of free and fair elections. Without such elections, people cannot fulfill the Qur'anic imperative of giving "**the trust to those who deserve it**" (*Surah 4:58*).[32]

In recent times, Muslim scholars such as Hassan al-Banna and Maulana Maududi have come to similar conclusions. Accordingly, the democratic approach has been accepted by religious parties in Iran, Pakistan, Egypt, Jordan, Tunisia, Indonesia, and others.

---

[32] M. Umar Chapra, *Islam and the Economic Challenge* (Herndon: The Islamic Foundation, The International Institute of Islamic Thought, 1992) p. 244.

However, practical difficulties in the way of the ideal model remain. Most of these relate to human feelings, primarily the unwillingness to make the required sacrifice. Retired Air Marshal Asghar Khan of Pakistan has stated in his book, *Islam, Politics and the State -- The Pakistan Experience*:

> **A fusion of religion and political power was and remains an ideal in the Muslim tradition. But the absence of such a fusion is a historically experienced and recognized reality. The tradition of statecraft and the history of Muslim peoples have been shaped by this fact.**[33]

He has pointed out that, in practice, separation of religion and state has existed for at least eleven out of the last fourteen centuries. Nevertheless, attempts have been made at replicating the ideal model.

B. Experience of Proclaimed Islamic Governments.

Iran, Saudi Arabia, Pakistan, Sudan, and Bangladesh claim to have Islamic governments. Their experiences are different, and worthy of study.

197. **Iran.** The Islamic Revolution in Iran sought to attain four main goals: (a) the establishment of an ideal Divine rule; (b) the establishing of a true Islamic society; (c) restoration of an Islamic economic system; and (d) the restoration of independence to Iran and other Muslim nations.[34] Following the Revolution, Iran started as the most promising Islamic government in modern times. It enjoyed support of virtually 99 percent of its people, many of whom had lived under poverty, had suffered much under the Shah, and sacrificed for the success of the Revolution. As expected, differences with the West emerged quickly, leading to the taking of American hostages by Iran, countless attempts at sabotage, freezing of Iranian assets, and a virtual economic boycott by the West. This was followed by eight years of a very destructive war with Iraq resulting in a million or more Muslim casualties on both sides. Even though Iraq was

---

[33] M. Asghar Khan, *Islam, Politics and the State: The Pakistan Experience* (London: Zed Books, 1985), p. 19.

[34] Samir K. Farsoun and Mehrdad Mashayekhi, *Iran: Political Culture in the Islamic Republic* (London: Routledge, 1992) p. 116.

generally considered to be the aggressor, all efforts by other Muslims to restore peace came to naught for eight long years. The war ended in 1988.

In the June 1993 presidential elections, President Rafsanjani won a second term with 63 percent vote against two other relatively unknown but "approved" candidates. According to Reuters reports, a journalist candidate, who had attacked economic mismanagement of the regime, received a surprising 24 percent of the vote. Voters questioned complained about housing, low wages, and a high inflation rate of 20 to 40 percent per year. Criticism about declining living standards and the isolation of the ruling clergy from the common people was also voiced. The complaints reflected economic, material concerns to which Western opposition had undoubtedly contributed. On the other hand, it reflected a degree of freedom of expression and debate.

An Islamic constitution and Islamic laws have been passed which, in the long-term, may dramatically alter the society and its institutions. It is too early to draw meaningful conclusions about the permanent realization of the four main goals listed above, or about the Iranian form of Islamic government. What is already apparent, however, is that Iran, as an Islamic republic, has inspired numerous Muslims to advocate changes in their own governments. The Iranian Revolution has become a symbol of defiance against the West. Iran has superseded Saudi Arabia as the leading voice among many Muslims seeking an alternative to Western culture. Iran has also produced a reasonably democratic parliament which is willing and able to question government action. The experience of Iran is worthy of study by all Muslims.

198.   **Saudi Arabia.** As the custodian of Islam's holy sites and provider of aid to many Muslim countries, Saudi Arabia is admired and praised by many Muslims around the world. The government has established and enforces Islamic laws for citizens and visitors. With great oil wealth, the Kingdom has spent much on the economic well-being of its citizens and on the development of numerous poor Muslim countries. Ironically, the Saudi government was shocked that Sudan's new government could be so critical of its policies after receiving extensive aid for a number of years.

Critics, however, question the excessive dependence on Western powers for protection, especially during the Gulf War against Iraq, and the inordinate influence westerners have in forming foreign policy. Others denounce the repression of religious debate, the limited participation allowed common people in government, and the royal regime's measures to assure continued rule. Complaints are also heard about the "modern life style" of many powerful individuals who appear exempted from Islamic laws.

Undoubtedly, the Gulf War undermined Saudi influence in the Middle East and among Muslims throughout the world. Few Muslims could condone the killing of fellow Muslims by Western troops in order to safeguard foreign interests. By contrast, Saudi Arabia has solidly entrenched itself in the Western economic community. It uses effectively modern technology, financial and economic planning, and even pubic relations. Its oil dollars are intertwined in the West's most important industries, giving it, and by definition Muslims, a voice in international politics. Muslims wish that the Saudi influence could be used more effectively for the welfare of Muslims in general.

The Saudi experience also needs to be studied in the process of reestablishing an Islamic model of government.

199.   Pakistan. Islam is the reason Pakistan was created. Pakistan has been called an Islamic republic for some thirty years. It was cut out from India to provide a homeland for Muslims of the sub-continent who wished to live according to the laws of Islam.

Islamization of the society has received much attention. High level religious councils have been created; many Islamic conferences have been held to discuss various topics; some Islamic laws have been introduced which focus on punishment of criminals and regulation of social acts; and a parallel system of Islamic courts has been established to enforce the Islamic laws. Islam is visible throughout Pakistan: mosques are found throughout the country; large numbers of people observe Friday religious services and *'Eid* celebrations; women cover their faces, particularly in small towns and rural areas; and an official ban on the sale of alcoholic drinks to Muslims is enforced. Pakistani Muslims show strong compassion for Muslim struggles in the world and frequent calls for Muslim unity are made. Yet, Islam is rarely visible in the day to day performance of government and in business activities.

Pakistan has many Islamic political parties with many dedicated workers who regularly call for full Islamization. At least one ruler, President Zia, fully supported their cause. However, Pakistani voters have repeatedly chosen to give little support to them, and have preferred secular parties. The October 1993 elections proved this point again. Jamait-i-Islami, the largest and the most powerful religious group made an election alliance with a number of other like-minded groups and formed the Pakistan Islamic Front (PIF). PIF was acknowledged as a well-organized party and ran an efficient campaign, yet, it won only three out of the 103 seats it contested, in a total national assembly of 217 seats. Its leader, Qazi Husain Ahmed lost all three seats that he personally contested. The PIF parties had pushed for a hard line on Kashmir, opposed women entering politics, and pushed for the introduction of Islamic economic and judicial systems. The population chose to favor secular political parties in the freest elections held to date. The causes of PIF's defeat include:

a. disagreements and divisions among the Islamic parties;
b. a historic gap between the pronouncements and actions of the Pakistani religious leaders;
c. lack of faith in the abilities of the current party leaders;
d. the large influence of powerful local leaders (e.g., feudal lords);
e. the preoccupation of people with the local bread and butter issues; and/or
f. the desire to keep religion and politics separated.

Regardless of the causes, the voters avoided PIF candidates in spite of their emotional attachment to Islamic causes. Islam will always be important in Pakistan. However, the PIF's total election defeat is likely to reduce focus on Islamization in Pakistan, and likely to usher in economic and social reforms on secular lines.

200.   Sudan. Sudan is another example where an attempt to set up an Islamic government has angered the West. Around 1989, General Omar Hasan Bashir and other military officials seized power in a coup that gave control to an Islamic group in Sudan. The attempts to introduce strict Islamic law has alarmed many Western powers including the United States.

Widespread human rights violations including arbitrary detention, torture, executions without trial, and forced migration and starvation of thousands of citizens are alleged. The Iranian president's visit in 1991 has led to closer cooperation in economic and military matters. Observers fear that the two countries are supporting the overthrow of pro-West regimes in Egypt, Tunisia, and Algeria. Sudan's policy of allowing free entry to all Muslims has led to charges that it is a safe haven for terrorists and that it is training them. The arrest of some Sudanese citizens on charges of planning bombings in New York may lead to declaration of Sudan as a terrorist state.

In an interview with the *Washington Times*, Sudanese diplomat, Ali Alhag, accused some neighboring countries of using the issue of religious fundamentalism in Sudan to gain international attention:

In the past, when people wanted to get an audience from Congress and the White House, they spoke negatively about communism. But, now that communism is not there anymore, people tend to speak negatively about countries like Sudan and fundamentalism, and this gives them a visa or a passport to get people listening.[35]

201. Charges Against Fundamentalists in Egypt. News reports (*International Herald Tribune* dated February 4, 1994) indicate that among other things, the "fundamentalists" are seeking to:

a. denounce all foreign art and culture, particularly that from the West, including paintings showing nudity, plays, ballet, movie festivals, translation of Western literature;
b. denounce writings of secular writers of Egyptian origin;
c. deny high positions in government to atheists or people with secular views;
d. declare "secularists" as "apostates" who should be put to death;
e. avoid contact with Christians including shaking hands, or wishing them well on their religious holidays, or even walking on the same sidewalks with them;
f. introduce veil in villages for girls starting at age six; and
g. modify school books to emphasize Islam.

Clearly, Egypt is in the middle of a serious debate. People may be forced to take extreme positions in order to make their point. There is a need for clarifying just what the Islamic position is on issues like those mentioned above and to what extent diversity is to be tolerated within the Islamic position.

C. Reality Check

202. Implementation of the Ideal Model. The establishment of Muslim states along the lines of the ideal model in modern times has proven to be

---

[35] *The Washington Times*, Dec. 10, 1994, p. A9.

difficult. Muslims are in the middle of debating the form of Islamic government suited to current times. Some feel that a return to fundamentalism (i.e., both letter and spirit of the model set by the first Islamic government mentioned above) is essential. Others feel that the practice of Islam pursuant to the interpretation of progressive, liberal Muslim scholars is preferred. This group wishes to follow the spirit of the first Muslim government, while implementing details on the basis of the needs of current times.

203.   **Islamic Diversity**. Many Muslims believe that as long as one conforms to the teachings of the Qur'an, there is room for diversity in Islam. Muslims continue to search for a path which can be traveled together by Muslim scholars of different schools of thought. However, after several centuries, the controversy and even violence continues between dedicated Muslims, each claiming ownership of "the absolute truth." All are quick to declare the others "kuffaar" or non-believers. Non-Muslims have been exploiting the split from the start. As the words of the Sudanese official quoted above indicate, they are still doing so.

Islamic governments can have fundamental principles and still ensure diversity of views. Some argue that a government with such diversity cannot claim to be Qur'anically based. In modern times, at a minimum, an Islamic government should have:

a. a functioning constitution based on the Qur'an and *Sunnah*, which ensures that laws repugnant to the basic principles of Islam cannot be enforced;

b. leaders who display Islamic qualities in public and private life;

c. an election process free of undue influence by the military, powerful minorities, non-Muslims or foreign elements; and

d. systematic and periodic elections to permit the citizens to make choices on the basis of promise and practice.

Muslims live in all parts of the world. This chapter deals with the roles of (a) Muslims in Muslim majority countries, (b) American Muslims, (c) European Muslims, and (d) other Muslim minorities. The purpose here is to review the constraints and challenges facing them, and the required measures to increase their participation in the New World Order.

A. Role of Muslims in Muslim Majority Countries.

204.   Reform at Home. An overwhelming majority of Muslims live in Muslim majority countries which are generally located in Africa, Asia, and the Middle East. They live with their kin in familiar surroundings where to be a Muslim is normal and expected. Mosques, Islamic schools, Muslim teachers, Islamic literature, and brother and sister Muslims are everywhere in sight. Even many who do not practice Islam actively, wish that they did so. This is in complete contrast with life for Muslims living in non-Muslim countries, where effort must be made to create or find anything Islamic. In spite of anti-Muslim behavior by some Muslim leaders in Muslim countries, professing and practicing Islam is simple and officially endorsed.

Despite all the mosques and Islamic schools, life in most Muslim countries is not much different from life in non-Muslim countries in the same stage of development. There are good people and bad ones in all societies. Falsehood, arrogance, hypocrisy, deception, and tyranny are common characteristics of some peoples in all countries. There are numerous problems in all developing nations, as there are in modern states: a widespread system of bribery within the administration and even the judiciary; ethnic, linguistic and tribal disparity and injustice; violence used to achieve political objectives; power held by the unrepresentative few; prevalence of the usual crimes of theft, rape, kidnapping, and prostitution; and drugs. Obviously, many Muslims have not been touched by the spirit of Islam, but have been touched by modern society.

Allah makes the distinction between the conduct of believers and non-believers:

> . . .those who reject Allah follow falsehood. While those who believe follow the truth from their Lord. Thus does Allah set forth for men their lessons by similitudes *(Surah 47:3).*

One wonders if in practice, the majority of Muslims living in Muslim countries are any different from the "non-believers." Muslim commentators observe that some non-Muslims have adopted Islamic practices while many Muslims themselves have abandoned them. They lament that Islam appears to be confined to the mosques and does not reach the hearts of Muslims.

Good examples of Islamic behavior by top governments officials are rare but vitally necessary. Fair and just implementation of existing laws (or new ones, if needed) is also of great value. Government officials convicted of crimes deserve exemplary punishments. People must be convinced that the government exists to solve their problems and not just rule them. Islamic education at all levels is required.

205.   Invitation to Islam (*Da'wah*). Activities which aim at making the message of Allah known or better understood by others is called *da'wah*. All Muslims are encouraged to propagate Islam. It is generally agreed that the best way to propagate is to be a good role model yourself -- avoiding vice, embracing virtue, and demonstrating the goodness of Islam to Muslims and non-Muslims alike. Muslims are frequently reminded that by becoming good role models for their family, fellow countrymen, and non-Muslims, many of the problems facing the Muslim world can be reduced.

Muslims living in Muslim countries have the freedom and opportunity to engage in such *da'wah* work. Many Muslims formally invite other Muslims to make a deeper study of Islam and become better Muslims; they actively invite non-Muslims to embrace Islam, propagating in their own hometown, or traveling to other towns, or even other countries. Often *da'wah* workers are criticized for their display of long beards, flowing robes, recitation of Arabic verses, and ritualistic practices, while neglecting to emphasize the deeper spiritual significance of being a believer or just becoming a better human being.

206.   Influencing Government. As noted in the chapter, "Worries of Muslims," most Muslim governments have become eager to accept secular practices. Dedicated Muslims, generally, and Islamic political parties, particularly, actively seek to increase Islamic influence inside their own governments. The Islamic parties have generally claimed that they know Islam, and that they will bring more Islam to government if they are given the power. They often emphasize the need for regular prayers, separation of sexes, and stern punishment for those who do not follow the *shari'ah*. When it comes to the complex issues of government, and the immediate concern of people, however, they frequently manifest political naivety.

Many Muslims, especially Western educated women and men who make up a large portion of the governing class, are justifiably skeptical. They argue that Islamic parties need to address all key economic, political, spiritual, and military issues and spell out exactly how the life of common people will be improved under their government.

There is common acknowledgement by Muslim leaders, including kings and dictators, that, as a group, Muslims are not doing well in these times. They deplore their subservience to non-Muslims. Pakistan faces warning against nuclear development and threats of being labeled a "terrorist country"; Saudi Arabia is forced to rely on foreign intervention and then to make huge payments for the Gulf War and its aftermath; Libya is bombed and then forced to surrender citizens to foreign powers; Iraq faces bombs for every "wrong" move; and Iran has assets frozen. All hope to change their positions of relative servitude and impotence; all agree on the needs to protect their national interests and retain self-respect; and all admit that cooperation among Muslim governments will help them. Yet, all continue to disagree and fight among themselves.

Islam is recognized as the common rope available for all to grasp. The role of Muslims then becomes to remind officials and leaders of this reality, to translate Islamic beliefs and traditions into a language and a set of actions which can be understood and utilized by modern societies.

207. Unity of Muslims. Islam emphasizes duties toward God and duties toward mankind. The Qur'an declares that Allah does not change the condition of a people until they change what is in their hearts. Islamic movements are gaining grass-root support because Muslims are asserting their beliefs in a positive, emphatic manner.

Most Muslims appear willing to contribute as individuals to strengthening Islam. Many want "drastic surgery" and the immediate empowerment of Muslims around the world. They wish instant elimination of all oppressors and "enemies of God." Mature leaders have tempered this enthusiasm by reminding them of the need for hard work and sacrifice.

Muslims are becoming politically active, organizing, developing or joining Islamic groups. Many are dedicated and work hard to rise to policy-making levels hoping their vision can receive a fair hearing in their own sphere. They have worked to bring individuals and like-minded groups together to achieve common goals. At national levels, they have used their power for the welfare of Muslims at home.

Improving local government at home has led to the larger mission of developing the *Ummah* as a whole. Many favor relinquishing national interests for the benefit of the international *Ummah.* The concept of Muslim unity remains a dream to many, a myth to others. Until individual Muslim countries are willing to delegate their powers to a united "government," it will remain in the realm of the unreal.

B. Role of American Muslims.

208.   **Early Muslim Immigrants.** During the early 1900's, a number of Muslims migrated from the Eastern Mediterranean -- Syria, Lebanon, Iran, India, and Turkey. These newly arrived immigrants isolated themselves in clan-like settlements. A number of these Muslim immigrants settled along the eastern seaboard of the United States, and in the Midwest. Also, national and sub-national communities formed in Northern urban centers, particularly in Detroit. The first mosques, (or *masaajid),* and Islamic centers were built by Muslim migrants in the Midwest.[36]

Between 1900 and 1940, Muslim immigration increased considerably. Many came from Albania, the former Yugoslavia, the former Soviet dominated areas, and Poland. They settled in New York and New Jersey; many carved a place for themselves in the biscuit industry.

The farmlands of the Midwest and Far West attracted those who were of rural backgrounds from the Middle East. The Arabs and the Albanians preferred the Midwest while the pre-independence Indian Muslims from the Punjab area were inclined toward the California farmlands, where their knowledge of agricultural products such as rice and sugar cane became an asset. These Muslims responded to the food shortages in Punjab at the turn of the century by coming and settling on the west coast as farm workers. Willows, California was one of their early settlements. Some Pakistani and Indian Muslims also settled on the eastern seaboard.

Many of these early immigrants did not have much education or means of support back in their own countries and many of them believed that their arrival in the "New World" would open new avenues of economic opportunities. Because of their profound yearning to fulfill their "get-rich-quick" dreams, many of these immigrants became entrepreneurs. Their main areas of business settlements were the states of California, and Indiana. Most of them changed their names and stopped obeying the tenets of Islam.

---

[36] Adib Rashad, *Islam, Black Nationalism and Slavery: A Detailed History* (Beltsville: Writers' Inc., 1995), pp. 99-102.

This early period of Muslim migration was to a great extent psychologically devastating, primarily because these migrants found few ways of supporting their religious tradition. Some of them either lost or abandoned their Islamic cultural identity, and therefore became assimilated. Furthermore, the majority of Lebanese and Syrians already in the United States were Christians; therefore, new Muslim migrants had little or no option but to join their countrymen if they wanted the fellowship of persons speaking the same language and understanding the same culture.[37]

Immigrant Muslims, like immigrants in general, reacted to the social and political forces of their day. As more Muslims immigrated, especially around the 1920's, a more solid Muslim community developed. However, these Muslim migrants -- those who struggled to maintain their Islamic personality -- remained very clannish and isolationist. In addition, the extreme xenophobic behavior of Americans at that time undoubtedly contributed to the migrants closed society or isolationism. We should be reminded that the extremely racist Eugenics Movement was able to insure the passage in 1924 of the Johnson-Reed Act by the United States Congress. This law, for the most part, stopped immigration into the United States from Eastern European and Mediterranean countries.

Considering this factor, it is safe to say that perhaps the isolationism of early Muslims was justified. This isolationism and ethnocentrism inhibited them from reaching out (*da'wah*) to their non-Muslim neighbors -- particularly African-Americans. Islam did not become a provocative force in the Black community until it was subordinate to Black Nationalism in an altered form.

209. American Muslim Community. No one knows the exact number of Muslims in America. However, it is generally believed that there are between five and eight million Muslims in North America. Given the growth rate during the last two decades, Islam could easily become the second largest religion (after Christianity) by the end of the 1990's. The newspaper *USA Today* on January 28, 1994 reported that about 42 percent of American Muslims are native Blacks, 24 percent South Asians (immigrants or their descendants from Pakistan, India, Bangladesh, or Afghanistan), 12 percent Arabs, 6 percent Africans, and about 2 percent native Whites. About 90 percent are *Sunni* Muslims.

---

[37] Yvonne Yazbeck Haddad (Editor), *The Muslims of America* (New York: Oxford University Press, 1991), p. 22.

While all Muslims believe in the basic principles of Islam, they represent a diverse community which reflects varied cultural heritages, personal experiences, and national origins. They are spread all over the United States. California, New York, Illinois, and Washington, D.C. reportedly contain the largest concentrations.

210.   Adaption to the New Homeland. All Muslims living in Western countries face the some problems of cultural identity. Young Muslims, particularly women, face the most serious problem. There is a conflict between the values of decency, restraint, and morality established by Islam, and the license, promiscuity, and individuality accepted by Western culture. Temptations for healthy young Muslim men and women are many and not easy to resist. Many children are leading a double life -- one with their parents, at home or at Islamic functions, another at school and at secular social events. Children feel that they have to hide things from their Muslim parents.

Adaption to the new homeland and its culture in an honest, meaningful way, within limits, is often missing and is needed. Particular limits are put on young women by their parents, for protection of the women and peace of mind of the parents. This is particularly stifling for the girls. Constant supervision by parents causes frustration, friction with parents, and even serious rebellion in some cases. Muslim women in America criticize a double standard more so than the women in Muslim countries. In the West, they have encountered uninhibited women, both real and portrayed in the media, and have frequently been enticed into imitating them.

211.   Importance of American Muslims. Some have argued that American Muslims have an especially important role to play in helping unite the Muslim *Ummah*. The *Muslim World Monitor* of October 11, 1993 noted that America contains Muslims from every ethnic, cultural, and national group in the world. They represent a microcosm of the entire *Ummah*. Muslims in America have first-hand opportunities for interacting with Muslims from all parts of the world. They can come to understand issues, differences and controversies which originate overseas and are brought to America by immigrant Muslims. It is suggested that in America, these divisive issues can be solved in a more neutral and less rigid environment. Solutions implemented in America can then be used to resolve ethnic and ideological conflicts elsewhere.

This has not happened to a great extent. Both immigrant and native-born Muslims in America complain that the other has not paid attention to their respective situations. Indigenous Muslims in America resent the condescension shown by many foreign-born Muslims. They complain that immigrants have failed to preserve Islam in their own country and seek to bring their faulty practices to the new converts. To follow foreign Muslims is to follow "defeated, colonialized, westernized Muslims" who have came to North America, forsaking their Muslim homeland in search of material well-being. Some scholars add that the only role of a Muslim in a non-Muslim land is to propagate Islam; any other excuse is not accepted. Finally, indigenous Muslim criticize the immigrant Muslims for not being true to the egalitarian principles basic to Islam:

> **Early Muslim migrants made no attempts to introduce the downtrodden African-Americans to Islam. Despite the fact that some of them set up small businesses in the Black community, when it came to religious education or propagation, they completely ignored the African-American. Some of them openly violated the creeds of Islam by selling alcohol, pork, and lucky charms -- all in hopes of achieving the American dream of wealth. Therefore, it behooves those African-Americans who are still aspiring to culturally identify with the Arabs, Pakistanis, East Indians and other ethnic Muslims to historically examine why there was no effort on the part of these various ethnic Muslims to proselytize African-Americans. It was not until Noble Drew Ali, and especially Elijah Muhammad, started advancing their own Islamic movements that these various ethnic Muslims raised a loud voice about correct (Orthodox) Islam in the Black American community.**[38]

Immigrant Muslims find fault with indigenous American Muslim's disrespect for established traditions and practices. They complain that the leadership of American Muslims lacks basic Islamic education in important areas such as Qur'anic Arabic and *Fiqh* (jurisprudence). They give little respect to American *imams* who barely can read the Qur'an in Arabic but give long sermons on intricate doctrinal concepts. They criticize the influence Christianity has on their doctrines, and the disrespect they show to *Hadith,* (the Prophet's (PBUH) sayings). Some assert that what many

---

[38] Rashad, *Islam, Slavery and Black Nationalism*, pp. 101-103.

practice in America is not even Islam, criticizing leaders such as Louis Farrakhan for distorting orthodox teachings.

212.   Cooperation Among American Muslims. While there are examples of serious conflict among American Muslims, divisions among them are much fewer than those among Muslims as a whole. The typical immigrant is reasonably educated, and their children are generally free from the ethnic, linguistic, and national origin bias found in the native lands. Despite the tension between *Sunnis* and *Shi'ites*, native Muslims and immigrants, and Arabs and non-Arabs, relations are generally cordial and supportive.

Muslims of African origin and native-born African-Americans are the most detached group within the entire American Muslim community. Even though Islam is based on racial equality, there is still considerable color consciousness. American Muslims are struggling with this issue in attempts to remove barriers of all kinds among themselves, particularly on the basis of racial origin.

213.   Status. The immigrant American Muslims began to manifest publicly their commitment to Islam in the 1960's; they have been busy establishing mosques and schools for teaching Islam to the younger generation since then. They have worked hard and have made tremendous progress with hundreds of mosques, community centers, and weekend religious schools having been established. The number of mosques has reportedly grown, from about one hundred in 1960, to eleven hundred in 1993. More than 100 full time Islamic schools have been established.

Muslim scholars in the United States and England have produced much literature in the modern English language, specially for youth. It has been largely adapted to the needs of the current young generation in the United States. Other Muslim countries continue to use literature produced a long time ago. Muslims in all countries can benefit from the work done in the West.

The Iraqi invasion of Kuwait, civil war and starvation of Muslims in Somalia, and the bombing of the World Trade Center have all generated anti-Islam and anti-Muslim news coverage in the West. Subsequent arrests of other Muslims for allegedly plotting bombings of the United Nations and other structures have portrayed every Muslim in America as a potential terrorist and a threat to Western civilization.

Some Muslims in the United States feel humiliated and under threat. Others are not as discouraged. As a young American from California explained, kids get picked on at school for all kinds of reasons -- for being short, for having a funny accent, for having a strange name, and for having a different religion. It happens to everybody, not just Muslims. Even Prophet Muhammad had to put up with a lot of ridicule and abuse for 13 years in Mecca for introducing new ideas and a new religion. Like many religious minorities, American Muslims are holding their ground and explaining their religion and customs to others.

The current exposure in the press, though negative, may be a blessing in disguise. Many Americans are reading and hearing about Muslims for the first time. Previously-held fears, suspicions, and whispered notions are now openly discussed and often dispelled. Some Americans have begun to feel that the criticism of Islam has gone too far and are beginning to speak up for Muslims and their religion. Similarly, Muslims have become a more united and politically active group because of their common anger over the media's unfairness. For the first time, Muslims have begun to call talk show hosts and their congressmen. The American public has also become more curious, creating opportunities for *da'wah* work. Muslims are taking the time to explain Islam and its views to their neighbors and acquaintances.

Many Muslim organizations and scholars have become aware of the need to increase cooperation among Muslims. *Islamic Horizons* magazine devoted much of its Spring 1992 issue to this topic. The cover story emphasized that Muslims in the United States were held back by lack of cooperation particularly in areas of (a) Islamic outreach (*da'wah*), (b) coordinating media activities, (c) development of Islamic education, (d) establishing a political base, (e) economic development, (f) uniting the next generation, and (g) bringing Islamic centers and mosques together.

214. Development of Muslim Youth. Development of young Muslims is one of the highest priorities for all Muslims. It is particularly important in the United States. Muslims recognize the need to develop their youth in terms of understanding Islam, building skills in knowledge of the Qur'an, *Sunnah*, the Arabic language, and encouraging regular prayer and fasting. However, in dealing with young people, Muslims need to give equal importance to building their character and self-esteem, to having them become role models for Muslims and non-Muslims alike, practicing compassion and justice, and working for the advancement of the community as a whole.

215.   **Organizational Needs.** Based on interviews with community leaders and activists, Kamran Memon, former Chief Editor of *Islamic Horizons*, emphasized a number of required actions. He pointed out the need for:

a. encouraging the more than 80 percent inactive Muslims to attend the mosques;
b. expanded outreach program on college campuses;
c. joint use of media outlets to highlight critical issues, financing joint news bureaus in important cities, sharing advertising, establishing an Islamic TV channel;
d. responding to Muslim-bashing jointly with the help of Muslim scholars and inter-faith organizations;
e. use of Muslim leaders, scholars, and activists in different parts of the country as part of a Muslim speakers' bureau;
f. use of recently developed and tested curricula and textbooks for Islamic studies rather than reinventing the wheel in each Islamic school;
g. coordination of many existing political activists and donors in support of critical issues facing Muslims;
h. expansion and support of Muslim businesses;
i. keeping the youth focused on critical issues facing the community in order to minimize divisions; and
j. establishment of an effective national council similar to the one already begun in New York.

216.   **Image of Islam in America.** A nationwide public opinion poll conducted by the American Muslim Council in March 1993 indicated only 23 percent favorable rating for Islam, while 36 percent gave unfavorable rating, and 41 percent were unsure. For whatever reason, Islam and Muslims do not enjoy high popularity in America. American Muslims continue to face discrimination and exclusion. If Muslims wish to change the image of Islam, they have much work to do in educating Americans about Islam. The large number of people with no opinion indicated open-mindedness and was therefore encouraging.

C. Some Muslim Organizations in America

217.   **American Muslim Council (AMC).** AMC was formed in 1990 to serve the interests of American Muslims with the following mission:

a. identify and oppose discrimination against Muslims and other minorities;
b. organize conferences, seminars and training sessions;
c. organize American Muslims to become a political force in mainstream American life;
d. lobby Congress and the White House on issues of concern to American Muslims;
e. serve as a source of interagency and cross-cultural cooperation; and
f. build a network of Muslim organizations nationally.

AMC has a relatively small membership. It has a hard-working director who does his job with the help of a few dedicated part-time workers. Nevertheless, it has become for Muslims a visible and positive voice in Washington. In spite of its young age, AMC has proven to be an effective organization. Its management and staff have already been instrumental in the following areas:

a. Muslims were invited to open sessions of Congress with recitations from the Qur'an;
b. the first Muslim *imam* was recruited by the U.S. Army;
c. halal (Islamically pure) foods are available to many Muslims in the U.S. armed forces, and in U.S. jails;
d. American Muslims are getting invitations from the media to explain the Muslim points of view;
e. President Bush recorded an *'Eid* message for American Muslims;
f. the Religious Freedom Restoration Act was passed by Congress, and signed by President Clinton; and several Muslims were invited to the signing ceremony;
g. there is increased lobbying for Muslims causes within the government and the private sector; and
h. there is increased contact between American Muslims and visiting Muslim leaders from abroad.

243. Islamic Society of North America (ISNA). ISNA is a broad-based assembly of Muslims and Muslim organizations promulgating the message of Islam in North America. Its goals include: fostering unity among Muslims; establishing full-time Muslim schools; *da'wah* (propagation) activities and Muslim youth activities; and aiding Muslim causes around the world. It has full time staff of less than ten, and attempts to tackle a large and essential agenda with very limited resources.

244.   Islamic Circle of North America (ICNA). ICNA's declared mission is establishment of the Islamic system of life as spelled out in the Qur'an and the *Sunnah* of Prophet Muhammad (PBUH). ICNA is associated with Jamaat Islami in Pakistan. Its program includes:

a. *da'wah,* inviting mankind to submit to the Creator by using all possible means of communication;
b. motivating Muslims to perform their duty of being witnesses unto mankind by their words and deeds;
c. offering educational and training opportunities to increase Islamic knowledge, to enhance character, and to develop skills of all those who are associated with ICNA;
d. opposing immorality and oppression in all forms, supporting efforts for socio-economic justice and civil liberties in the society;
e. strengthening the bond of humanity by serving all those in need anywhere in the world, with special focus on neighborhoods across North America; and
f. cooperating with other organizations for implementation of ICNA program and unity in the *Ummah.*

ICNA is dedicated to the use of democratic, legal, and peaceful means according to Islamic principles.

245.   The Shi'ah Movement. The movement has many followers around the world, including the United States. In the 1960's, *Sunnis* and *Shi'ites* worked together to set up Islamic institutions in the United States. Following the Revolution in Iran, *Shi'ah* groups have become more independent, establishing their own mosques and centers in several large cities. Generally speaking, relations between *Sunnis* and *Shi'ites* in the United States are cordial despite dogmatic differences.

Shi'ites hold Malcolm X in great respect and have successfully introduced their school of Islam to the African-American community. Many militant African-American Muslims sympathized with the Iranian Revolution and supported it in the United States.

246.   The Nation of Islam. The movement organized by Elijah Muhammad during the 1930's was designed to elevated African-Americans. He taught the basic principles of Islam but added several concepts which nearly all orthodox Muslims find unacceptable, particularly the prophethood of Elijah Muhammad and the alleged divinity of the founder,

Fard Muhammad. The Nation of Islam, under Elijah Muhammad, developed notable figures including Malcolm X, boxing champion Muhammad Ali, and Louis Farrakhan. The advancement of Islam in America was aided by these figures, as well as by the social and economic accomplishments of the Nation.

Since Mr. Muhammad's death, Minister Farrakhan has reestablished many of the early programs of the Nation and revived its distinct doctrines. As a group, they continue to be enterprising people who believe in economic self-sufficiency. Like other Muslims, they preach abhorrence of alcoholic drink, unlawful drugs, fornication, homosexuality, etc. They blame the White race for slavery and for most of the suffering of Black Americans.

Minister Farrakhan has been the subject of considerable debate and controversy over harsh statements made by him and his followers regarding Jews. Some Muslims have made efforts to bring the Nation of Islam closer to traditional Islam while other have distanced themselves from it, asserting that his doctrines are incompatible with Islam. In any event, Minister Farrakhan's prominence has posed problems for some Muslims.

247.   Imam W. Deen Mohammed. The son of Elijah Muhammad, W. Deen Mohammed, was elected to lead the Nation of Islam upon his father's death in 1975. Imam Mohammed quickly moved to change the Nation's teachings to conform with traditional Islam. He dissolved most of his father's organizational structure and replaced it with a model more in keeping with Islam as practiced in the East. Unlike his father, he believes Prophet Muhammad (PBUH) to be the last prophet. He has affirmed traditional Islam completely and enjoys the support of most immigrant Muslims. He is the leading representative of the American Muslims of African descent.

Imam Mohammed has been active in interfaith dialogue with the Christian and Jewish religious communities. He has been successful in maintaining a stable African-American Muslim community and propagating traditional Islam among African-Americans. He is playing a prominent role in bringing all Muslims in the United States together.

Several Muslim organizations in the United States, including ICNA, ISNA and W. D. Mohammed's organization, have been planning to hold their conventions jointly. The effort for unity is continuing.

248.   Coordination of Muslim Organizations. In addition to the organizations mentioned above, there are many others working hard to serve their membership and the *Ummah* to the best of their ability. May Allah bless all those who are working for the welfare of His creation. There are some internal differences of opinion and even conflicts within the membership of some of them. Muslims will certainly benefit if the internal conflicts are resolved amicably, and the leadership of all the organizations cooperate with each other on key issues facing Muslims. Many of the organizations have membership in all parts of the United States. However, effective coordination could be improved; a well-organized and effective national council of all Muslim organizations would be useful and should be pursued.

249.   **Political Participation.** To date, Muslims in the West have been inactive in politics for various reasons. Some continue to debate if participation in politics is desirable or even allowed under Islam. However, most Muslims, particularly the younger generation, have accepted the importance of political participation and are becoming more active.

A number of Muslim newspapers, magazines and newsletters have been established, although with limited circulation, primarily directed to a Muslim audience. There was some effort at voter registration and political mobilization during the 1992 and 1994 general elections with no visible positive result.

No Muslim has been able to win any significant political office at the national or state level. Some Muslims have been elected to minor positions in large cities and to relatively important positions in small towns. Young Muslims, like most young Americans, have shown much interest in seeking future public office. Native-born African-American Muslims are growing in number and strength. Even though, they belong to a lower economic level, they are dedicated to Islam and know their way around the American political system. They are helping their communities in fighting drugs and crime. They have earned a reputation for being clean living people.

250.   **Relations with American Political Parties.** In spite of the growing numbers, and the political interest and awareness of American Muslims, they are shunned by both political parties. Both major candidates for president in the 1992 elections refused to have even a low level dialogue or any contact with Muslim voters in spite of several efforts by the Islamic Society of North America (ISNA) and the American Muslim Council (AMC). The 1994 Congressional, state, and local elections have helped in initiating some contact between a few mainstream candidates and some Muslims.

251. **The Bosnia Rally.** During May 1993, when the American media and prominent politicians, including the President, supported the Muslim cause in Bosnia, only one elected official out of several hundred participated in the Bosnia rally in Washington. While discussing the rally, the BBC correctly noted that Muslims can demonstrate in America but they are not the American public. *Islamic Horizons* magazine noted in its September 1993 issue that the rally helped to bring Muslims together under the same platform, however, it did not influence the U.S. government to support the Muslims in Bosnia. The organizers focused on bringing Muslims rather than all Americans together; it was a Muslim rather than an American rally. In the final analysis, American Muslims are not highly regarded by their countrymen or elected representatives. They could not achieve the desired action even when the media, many politicians, and a large part of the American public were supportive of the Muslim cause in Bosnia. It will be more difficult to garner support for more controversial issues.

252. **Muslims in Mainstream Politics.** America is a blend of nationalities, cultures, and religions. However, the American public is very nationalistic. To be proud of being an American comes first. While many immigrant Muslims have not forgotten their homelands and continue dreaming of going back, their American-born children value American citizenship above their roots. Many see complete participation in the American system as the only alternative and Islamically correct.

Immigrant Muslims often cite the experience of other minorities, particularly African-Americans. They note that as recently as the 1950's, segregation of Blacks from Whites was the law of the land in the United States. "Separate but equal" schools and public facilities were the norm, even though it was clear that inherently separate facilities could not be equal. After years of struggle and sacrifices during which they were harassed, abused, beaten, and killed in the process, Blacks and their supporters among Whites, succeeded in stopping legal segregation. Their homes and churches were burnt but they persevered until the courts and Congress brought some relief. The lives of Martin Luther King, Malcolm X, Thurgood Marshal, John Kennedy, and Robert Kennedy are noted for the lessons they contain for all minorities, including Muslims in America.

Muslim commentators point to Blacks today and their numerous accomplishments since the 1950's: the number of Black members in the U.S. Congress grew to 40 following the 1992 elections; they have a large power base; they can make the difference in critical debates and votes in the Congress. The President of the United States goes to their annual dinner, and pays attention to their serious concerns. President Clinton reports to them about the number of Black appointees in his administration, and promises to do more for Blacks in the future.

For many immigrant Muslims, therefore, Blacks are the example to follow for those who have no political representation in Congress. These Muslims see that many of the old opinions regarding Blacks have been erased and suggest that, with hard work and by lawful means, Muslims can achieve similar success. Similarly, they argue that American Catholics, Jews, Native Americans, and others have experienced discrimination and neglect at different stages. An effective anti-defamation league has proven to be beneficial for Jews. The National Association for the Advancement of Colored People (NAACP) has been useful for Blacks. Massive voter registration campaigns and participation in the electoral process have helped all. This has become the path advocated by many immigrant Muslims.

253.   Choice Between Republican and Democratic Parties. With some exceptions of leaders in both parties, on the whole, both parties (a) are strong supporters of Israel, (b) value Jewish money, votes, and media power, (c) wish to help fulfill biblical prophesies about a strong Israel, (d) have strong roots in Christianity and share a historic dislike for Islam, and (e) have little respect for Muslim leaders and citizens, either in the United States or abroad. Neither party wishes to help Islam. Support for Islamic causes (e.g., in Afghanistan and Somalia) to date has come for geopolitical and humanitarian reasons.

Republicans (a) are strong supporters of family values, (b) are against homosexuality and abortion, (c) have little representation of minorities, but are eager to have more, (d) have a soft corner for Cold War allies (e.g., Pakistan, Saudi Arabia), and (e) value business relations with Middle Eastern countries. They are in favor of bringing religion (i.e., largely Christianity) to schools. They support many Muslim dictators because of their solidarity with the United States.

Democrats (a) have the votes of most of the minority citizens and are, therefore, more tolerant of minorities, (b) are firm believers in separation of church and government, (c) support foreign aid for developing countries, and (d) are more flexible on immigration issues.

Each party has features which are of interest to Muslim citizens. Muslims wish to have political clout so that both parties would compete for the Muslim vote and Muslim support as they do for that of Jews.

Unfortunately, American Muslims have not mattered much to either party in elections because of lack of political activity -- no vote bank, no financial contribution. But, Muslims are gradually awakening; voter registration, formation of PAC's, and dialogue with candidates are increasing. Muslims have started to have contact with people in both parties.

At this point in time, Muslims feel free to work with any individual or party who will treat Muslims with respect, and support genuine Muslim interests. Over time, it shall be seen if one of the two parties emerges as the party of choice.

254. Political Agenda for American Muslims. There is a need for American Muslims to set an agenda for carrying out measures to improve the status of Islam and Muslims in America. Muslims need to work with the American public and political parties and decision-makers, including their elected representatives, on ways to establish a mutually beneficial relationship between the United States and Muslims -- those living in the United States, and the kith and kin spread all over the world. One could start by preparing a list of obvious Muslim interests, such as:

a. freedom to practice and develop Islam in the United States;
b. American support for current Muslim causes, including Palestine, Kashmir, and Bosnia, in terms of executive action, passing positive legislation and defeating laws having a negative impact;
c. protection for Muslim people and governments around the world;
d. support for development of Muslims around the world, in terms of maximizing beneficial relations between Muslim countries and the United States in economic, political, cultural, spiritual, and military fields;
e. elimination of frequently portrayed negative media images of Muslims, in general, and Arabs, in particular; and
f. encouragement for creating and maintaining a positive image of Islam and Muslims, as has been done with many other minorities, e.g., Blacks, Jews, Italians, Irish.

It would also be beneficial to define what actions Muslims themselves can take to improve their posture as a political group. These may include:

a. having regularly updated lists of reasonable and practical demands that Muslims can present to elected or appointed representatives;

    b. identifying American Muslim activists or specialists who are best able to handle this particular subject and entrust them with the particular assignment;

    c. encouraging development of specialist groups on subjects and in geographical areas where they are lacking; and ensuring provision of required financial, human, and other resources from the community to aid them;

    d. ensuring cooperation from all Muslim activists for the specialists in achieving the objective; and

    e. encouraging establishment of think tanks for thinking and planning ahead about forthcoming short, medium, and long-term issues.

Many Muslim national and ethnic groups are already working along these lines. Arabs, Pakistanis, Kashmiris, Palestinians, etc., have been at it for years. Muslims, as a group, are rather new at it. Nevertheless, various Muslim organizations, some of which are described above, are doing much and need Muslims' support. What Muslims need is a more systematic approach, more resources, and work on a much wider scale. The various Muslim groups, of course, need to support each other.

As shown by the results of the 1994 Congressional election, American voters are attracted by the right. School prayers, moral values, and the increased role of religion in the family and in society appear to be winning the support of voters. Even President Clinton is ready to help in finding ways to introduce prayer in public schools. The United States Constitution provides for separation of church and state. This was a natural reaction of the Founding Fathers, many of whom had fled oppression in Europe by the established state religion. However, Christian groups have argued that the amplification of the Constitution's doctrine of separation of church and state has resulted in placing religions and religious groups at a disadvantage in relation to secular organizations and programs.

American Jews are a strong force for maintaining that separation. This, too, is a natural response since they have a long history of oppression at the hand of religious governments. American Muslims need to study this issue carefully to understand the implications involved.

Most important, American Muslims need to (a) struggle against stereotyping and misinformation about themselves, (b) inform the American public about Islam and Muslims, (c) maintain their freedom to practice their religion, and (d) maintain freedom to continue dialogue with followers of other faiths.

254.   Financial Needs of American Muslims. The single most important constraint faced by American Muslims is money. In the 1960-1990 period, oil rich kingdoms provided a large part of the money for Islamic schools, mosques and books. However, following the Gulf War, many Muslims in the United States did not wish to be supported by or identified with those kingdoms. Similarly, the kingdoms and many of their rich citizens did not wish to support those who criticized them during the Gulf War. In addition, Saudi Arabia and other kingdoms expended large financial reserves in the war. As a result, money has become scarce for Islamic organizations. As a result, these organizations have become almost totally dependent on contributions of local Muslims.

Projects are many but the number of local donors and available funds are limited. ISNA, among others, is in debt and has had to lay off most of its staff members. Individual affluent Muslims such as doctors, engineers, businessmen, and other professionals are contributing. Many Muslims are participating in and benefitting from activities of Muslim organizations -- Sunday schools, Friday prayers, *'Eid* prayers, funerals, marriages, etc., yet, they fail to contribute even minimal membership dues.

D. Role and Concerns of European and Other Minority Muslims.

255.   European Muslim Population. About ten million Muslims live in the European Union.[39] The United Kingdom reportedly has about two million Muslim citizens who have primarily migrated from the subcontinent. France has about two millions who are primarily of North African Arab descent. Germany has about three million Turks alone, who have lived there for the last 30 or more years.

256.   The European Experience. Like Muslims in the United States, European Muslims started by establishing mosques and Islamic schools. Even though large numbers of Muslims of Turkish and Arab descent have become fully westernized, others continue to follow Islam. Muslims in the U.K. have established a Muslim parliament to provide a forum for discussion and expression of community views. The community is fairly active. Many conferences are held to discuss their common problems. The Conference on "Islam in a Changing Europe: Cultural identity, Citizenship, and Social Policy" held at the University of Bradford in September 1992, is an example.

---

[39] *The Economist*, August 6, 1994.

257.   **General Concerns.** The Muslims in Europe are alarmed by events on European soil in Bosnia. If native European Muslims cannot be protected by the rest of Europe, what is the future of other Muslims scattered all over Europe? They are also concerned about:

   a. demonization of Islam in the European press;
   b. decreasing physical security and harassment by right wing political parties and thugs;
   c. diminishing economic prospects for Muslim youths;
   d. increasing restrictions on further Muslim migration to Europe;
   e. maintaining identity as Muslims; and
   f. Muslim youth who go astray in non-Muslim societies.

European Muslims are far from being in agreement on how to face their current challenges in Europe. Nevertheless, the problems are recognized and the debate is underway.

258.   **The French Experience.** During the post World War II period, the French government invited workers from North African countries (Algeria, Morocco, Tunisia) to come and help in rebuilding the country. Manpower was needed to compensate for the French deaths during the war. Workers were eventually allowed to bring their families. Today, about half of the estimated four millions foreigners (about 7 percent of the population) are Arabs or Africans. Most are Muslims.

Islam is reportedly the second largest religion in France. Even though many second generation immigrants do not practice Islam, mosques and Arabic signs are common in many French cities. The right wing National Front and most French people do not like it. They talk about Islamic fundamentalists bent on de-stabilizing France and the West. The French authorities have arrested many Muslims for supporting Islamic parties in Algeria. France and the West prefer to see a secular government in Algeria and are prepared to take appropriate action.

Most immigrant Muslims live in separate ghettos. Unemployment in many areas is as high as 50 percent. Many have become engaged in drugs and prostitution as legal economic opportunities decline. Many young French Muslims fear that they have no future in France even though they were born there. However, they feel no ties to the countries of their parents. Banning of head scarfs (*hijab*) in classrooms, as order by the French National Minister of Education in 1994, is demoralizing to practicing Muslims and another example of their shrinking human rights.

Although some are becoming active in politics -- reportedly two of Marseille's 100-member city council are North African -- Muslims in France are economically and politically weak. They may need political support from their parent countries and the *Ummah* in order to ensure basic rights as citizens and immigrants in France.

259.   German Muslims. A large number of Turkish Muslims have lived in Germany since the end of World War II. They were welcomed by the government as cheap labor to carry out many manual jobs that Germans were unavailable or unwilling to do. Even though the Turks are White in skin, have lived in Germany for many years, and speak the local language fluently, they have not been well integrated into the society. They clearly live the lives of outsiders and second-class citizens.

Their lives have become harder since German reunification. The East Germans, experiencing high unemployment, blame foreigners, particularly the Turks. There have been several cases of violence against foreigners to force them to leave Germany.

There are Muslims in virtually every other European country, also. In fact, Bosnia and Albania have Muslim majorities. The Bosnia issue has been discussed elsewhere in the book.

260.   The Role. Like their American brethren, the European Muslims have to continue to: (a) emphasize religious and secular education of their children; (b) become politically active for the sake of protecting their interests and removing the biased image in the minds of their fellow citizens; (c) become socially active in their communities in service to the needy, regardless of race or color as taught by Islam; and (d) become economically strong for the sake of helping the weaker members of the community and gaining their rightful position in their society. Ultimately, the European Muslims have to please Allah and demonstrate the goodness of their faith to their fellow citizens.

260.   Other Muslim Minorities. There are Muslims minorities in almost every country of the world. The largest minorities, in the range of 100 million plus Muslims each, are in India and China. There are significant minorities in Latin American and Caribbean countries, and several countries of Africa (e.g., Eritrea, Ethiopia, Ivory Coast, Tanzania including Zanzibar, Malawi, and Togo). In Asia, the Philippines, Myanmar (Burma), Thailand, and Singapore have large Muslims populations.

Some issues facing Muslims in India have been addressed in another part of this book. The exact number of Muslims in China is not known. The *Encyclopedia Britannica* has estimated that about 10 percent of the population is Muslim. For example, Sinkiang, formerly known as Eastern Turkestan, is an autonomous Chinese republic in the west-northwest part of China where more than 80 percent of the population is reportedly Muslim. By all accounts China continues to be a communist country. It does not encourage any religion, including Islam. There are a token number of mosques in some parts, and a small number of Muslims is sent to perform Hajj (Pilgrimage to Mecca) every year. Nevertheless, the hardest part for Chinese Muslims is to maintain their religion in name and practice.

Muslims fear the loss of their religious and cultural identity in many other non-Muslim countries as well. For example, the struggle of Muslims in the Philippines is well documented. In Myanmar, they are regularly forced to leave their homes and migrate.

In Bulgaria, the government decided to change the Muslim names of the citizens to Bulgarian ones during the 1960's. No official communication, application, or letter is accepted under a Muslim name. There is a *Mufti* in Sofia, but he has no effective authority. Muslims are not permitted public celebration of religious holidays nor burial in Muslim cemeteries. Prayers are held in secret.[40]

Muslim governments around the world can work to help address the concerns of all Muslim minorities. The occasions of frequent meetings between the heads of Muslim governments and non-Muslim governments can be used to advocate the genuine concerns of Muslims. The Israelis and the Jewish-American community played very important roles in advocating the cause of Soviet Jews. Muslim governments and the *Ummah* can do the same to strengthen Muslims living in non-Muslim lands.

The primary role of these Muslims, as with all Muslims, is to work to please Allah by carrying out the established obligations of Islam. As the example of the newly independent Muslim countries in Central Asia indicates, Muslims in almost all non-Muslim countries require basic information about religion, the Qur'an, Hadith, and other related literature. They need well-trained scholars, imams, and funds to reestablish their places of worship and religious schools which have been closed for decades. All Muslims who can help must do so.

---

[40] *Journal of the Institute of Muslim Minority Affairs*, 5 (January 1984): 143.

> **Oh you who believe . . . hold fast all together, by the rope which Allah (stretches out for you) and be not divided among yourselves. . .** *(Surah 3:102-103).*

To establish one single Islamic state out of more than fifty individual Islamic governments is a very tall order. Many argue that the unity of Muslims of one government or even full cooperation among individual Muslim governments is an impossibility. There are substantive arguments for the position: (a) Muslims as a group do not really want it; (b) individual Muslim governments prefer partnership with the West to being part of a Muslim government union; (c) there are too many ideological differences between the various Islamic groups; and (d) there are no rulers who have the support of the majority of the Muslim leaders. This chapter explores these arguments and reviews different attempts at Muslim cooperation and solidarity in recent times.

261. Do Muslims Really Want Solidarity? Many educated Muslims believe that once they decide to cooperate sincerely, solutions will emerge for all outstanding political and military grievances against each other. Similarly, they are convinced that once Western leaders see durable Muslim unity, they will become more accommodating on many issues. Also, other non-Muslim nations, such as India and Burma, would be reluctant to take repressive action against Muslim populations in their countries. Such politically sophisticated Muslims are hopeful of union. Some denounce it. Many have questions, doubts, and even criticism.

Given the low rates of literacy in most Muslim countries, Muslims can be divided into educated and uneducated ones. The latter ones generally live from hand to mouth, have little idea of what is going on in the world, and have a strong faith in Allah, but few if any political preferences. They pray, persevere, and hope that tomorrow will be better for them than today.

The educated ones have been to schools, read some books, and done some travel. In spite of the many problems of the West, a majority of educated Muslims around the world want to have what the West has. They want for their children exactly what the West wants for their own: freedom to live their lives as they wish to; realization of their potential; and respect as citizens of this planet earth. They demonstrate their attachment to and admiration for the West by wanting to

    a. come to Western countries,
    b. reside there on a long-term basis,
    c. educate their children in schools and colleges there,
    d. train their children in Western organizations after their formal education,
    e. enjoy Western-type housing even in their own countries,
    f. import Western technology to ensure economic development of their respective countries along Western lines, and
    g. have freedom of speech, human rights, pollution control, economic growth, etc., as enjoyed by the Western people.

Islam, as practiced today, is still the main spiritual force, but not a complete way of life for most educated Muslims. They believe in Allah and his Prophet (PBUH), pray, perform Hajj, give in charity, provide Islamic education to their children, and hope to live and die as Muslims. They wish to maintain a spiritual relationship with Allah, but they do not look to Islam, as it is currently practiced, to solve their economic, political, technological, and other problems. Pending further research and clarification of Islamic thought, they are forced to seek secular solutions.

Many Western-educated Muslims are afraid of truly orthodox Muslims. They are afraid of rule by Iranian-style religious leaders who put considerable emphasis on religious procedures, and wish to run the society along the lines it was run fourteen hundred years ago. They would welcome the spirit of the traditional rule, but wish to adapt it to modern reality. Some feel that the initial success of the Muslim Brotherhood movement in Egypt can be attributed to its call for a modern Islam. Large numbers of educated Muslims, including a majority of educated Muslim women, belong to this group.

Some Islamic scholars tend to label this group as hypocrites, *munaafiq,* or even, disbelievers, *kuffar.* Most Muslims do not dismiss this group. Their concerns are frequently discussed, often leading to clarification of Islamic thought and practice in modern societies. It has made Islamic solidarity better understood and more acceptable.

Muslims who have lived in Western countries and have first-hand exposure to their culture have come to certain obvious conclusions:

    a. the West is ruled largely by White, Christian people;

b. Muslims have little if any role in decision-making outside their homes and place of work;

c. Muslim, as citizens of the West, are not likely to have prominent roles within their adopted countries for a very long time to come;

d. the future of Muslim children and future generations is uncertain in religious and even in economic terms; and

e. the West is insensitive to the needs of their relatives overseas in Muslim countries, while efforts are made to help White Christian people in other parts of the world.

Having achieved economic prosperity, the westernized Muslims begin to think of their heritage and the needs of their relatives and friends around the world. In short, many who live in Muslim countries hope to come to the West, while many already in the West have second thoughts. However, few who settle in the West ever return. As most people living in countries less developed than the West, Muslims are seeking a higher standard of living. Unlike many other groups, Muslims have an awareness of their spiritual commitment which makes it difficult to abandon their faith in exchange for material well-being.

262. Muslims Value Friendship with the West. Muslims in Pakistan, Saudi Arabia, Egypt, and sub-Sahara African countries have reasons for seeking the friendship of the West, and the United States in particular. The king and the royal family of Saudi Arabia are naturally interested in perpetuation of the monarchy. In addition, the Saudis are looking for modern technology for developing their energy sources, industry, agriculture, and infrastructure. They also wish to train their citizens, have access to markets for imports and exports, and maintain and, if possible, enhance their influence in the world or at least in Arab affairs. They recognize the threat of opponents within the country and abroad, including fellow Arabs, Iran and Western powers. They welcome foreign military and technological support, accepting the price that has to be paid in oil and international criticism.

Pakistan is looking for (a) alliances to counter India's sphere of influence, (b) political and military support, including arms for the liberation of Kashmir, (c) economic aid on a bilateral basis from individual Western countries and financial assistance from agencies such as the World Bank, IMF, and the Asian Development Bank, (d) private investment from Western countries, (e) markets for exports and sources of cheaper imports, and (f) transfer of science and technology.

Egypt is a poor country with a large population. Egyptian governments have spent much of the post World War II period in confrontation with Israel. They have fought at least three wars, with much sacrifice in lives and property, for the cause of Arabs, in general, and Palestinians, in particular. The current government is looking for (a) economic development and improved standard of living for its citizens, (b) peace within secure and protected borders, and (c) respect and influence within the community of nations. Good relations with the Western countries can meet their needs. Egypt receives more than $2.5 billion in aid annually from the United States.

Sub-Sahara Africa is facing declining standards of living. Most need substantial amounts of food to prevent widespread malnutrition. They look to the West to meet their economic requirements. Muslims in Sierra Leone, Chad, Mali, Somalia, Uganda, etc., are in the same position and are anxious to maintain good relations with the West.

In principle, most Muslim governments are eager to maintain good relations with the West for military, political, and economic reasons. During the Cold War period, it was possible to maintain these relations with the West while actively working for closer ties among Muslims. The West was thankful for any support against the communists. However, after the defeat of communism, politically active and militant Muslim leaders have come under criticism.

The West appears to view all Islamic movements with suspicion, particularly those advocating Islamic solidarity on military and political issues. Under the New World Order, one is either pro-West or an enemy. Accordingly, governments have the choice of being pro-Western, paying lip service to Muslim solidarity, or of being serious about promoting Muslim causes, and incurring the enmity of the West.

Can Muslim leaders maintain ties with the West and at the same time work for Muslim solidarity? Ironically, the answer lies with the West. As demonstrated in Saudi Arabia, Afghanistan and, to some extent, Pakistan, the attitude of the West toward Islam is determined by security and economic interests. There is only secondary consideration of ideological, moral, or human rights issues. This is true with regards to Islam and even socialism. Chinese policy reflects this.

Alternatively, can Muslim countries satisfy their developmental needs without the West? A Western mind can only think in terms of Western solutions. To the extent that Muslim leaders exhibit their Western education and training in asserting leadership, independence from the West is impossible. When the goals and objectives of a nation are based on

Western standards, there are no alternatives but those presented by Western ideals, technologies and paradigms.

263. Can Muslim Countries Satisfy Each Other's Needs? The needs currently met by the West include:

a. protection of existing regimes;
b. protection of territorial integrity;
c. provision of military hardware;
d. provision of assistance for economic development in terms of funding, technical assistance, and materials;
e. provision of the latest science and technology;
f. provision of access to centers of advanced learning for the next generation;
g. provision of safe heavens for money and banking; and
h. provision of places for rest and recreation.

Individually, it would be very difficult for any Muslim country to satisfy all the economic and military needs of all other Muslim countries. Collectively, Muslim countries are able to provide much of the required assistance. The more developed Muslim countries such as Turkey, Iran, Pakistan, Saudi Arabia, and Malaysia could meet many of the military, economic, and educational needs of poorer countries. Others, such as Egypt and Indonesia, could contribute to the manpower needs of richer but less populated countries like Saudi Arabia and Kuwait. Higher income countries like Saudi Arabia, Kuwait, and UAE could meet many of the economic needs of middle-income and low-income countries.

Would the stronger and richer Muslim countries be willing to help the weaker ones? Under current conditions, most observers theorize that they would not. However, the following points should be considered:

a. Rich Muslim countries are already providing significant amounts of the financial assistance going to poor Muslim nations.
b. Relatively stronger countries like Pakistan are already providing technical assistance to the weaker ones.
c. The cost of the Iran-Iraq War to both countries and the Gulf War to Iraq, Kuwait and Saudi Arabia was more than one hundred billion dollars. The cost was far more than any imaginable transfer of resources among Muslims under a Muslim union. Close

cooperation would minimize the need for similar expenditure on wars among Muslims in the future.

d. Economists have ascertained that when a relatively rich country such as Germany joins a relatively poor one such as Portugal, as they did in the European Union, both countries experience increased prosperity.

e. The U.S. government has argued that free trade with poorer Mexico under the North American Free Trade Area (NAFTA) will be economically beneficial to both countries.

264.   Unite and/or Be Closer to the West? Is it possible to be close to and friendly with the West while uniting into a single Muslim nation? Some Muslims say yes based on United States and Western support for regional cooperation and unity. In addition, while communism is not the threat it once was, there is considerable benefit in having Muslims as allies in the face of growing Russian nationalism and inflexible Chinese communism.

Others feel that the general rule does not apply to Muslims. There is a fear that if Muslims unite, all non-Muslims will unite in turn against them. Abdul Fatah Memon has asked in *Oil and the Faith*, "When and where have non-Muslims not aligned against Muslims?"[41] Unity among non-Muslims against Muslims is a frequent international event. Muslims must be able to convince the West that their unity is not a threat and that an Islamic union does not threaten their security or economic interests. Even better would be for Muslim to be able to convince the West that an international Islamic state would benefit them economically by providing huge new markets and adding to their security by improving stability throughout the world.

265.   Attempts at Muslim Solidarity to Date. Muslims have made several attempts at promoting solidarity among themselves since the breakup of the Ottoman Empire and the *Khilaafah* (Caliphate). King Husain of Hijaz tried to have himself declared as the *Khalifah* (Caliph) for all Muslims in 1924. King Abdul Aziz ibn Saud tried in 1926. Subsequently Kings Fuad and Faruq of Egypt tried. The Grand Mufti of Jerusalem, Amin Al-Husaini, tried during the 1940's. They failed to get sufficient support and eventually abandoned their claims. An Islamic Congress was

---

[41] Abdul Fatah Memon, *Oil and the Faith* (Karachi: Inter Services Press, Ltd. 1966), p. 138.

convened in Mecca in 1954 to explore the options. It failed to receive sustained support. In recent times, there have been more modest but significant attempts which are discussed below.

The Arab League, formed in 1945, includes practically all Arab countries. Even though it is not founded on their common religion of Islam, it has two major achievements to its credit: (a) the member countries accepted each others' borders which were generally drawn by colonial masters and were greatly disputed; and (b) it provided a mechanism for cooperation among the members. The League promotes cultural, economic, and political ties among its members. It seeks to mediate disputes among them and has been the coordinator of action against Israel. Even though, it has gone through an upheaval following the peace treaty between Egypt and Israel, it continues to promote solidarity among Arabs.

266.   Attempt at Merger of Muslim States. The breakup of the Ottoman Empire in the 1920's resulted in dissolution of the then-existing Muslim union. Since that time, there has been one noteworthy attempt at merger. Syria and Egypt decided to merge in 1958 under the United Arab Republic (UAR). Iraq considered joining it, too, but never did. Following a coup in Syria in 1961, the government decided to withdraw from the union. The United Arab Republic effectively dissolved in 1961. Subsequently, in 1971, Libya, Syria and Egypt negotiated formation of a federation. Frequent strains led to its virtual dissolution by 1974. The UAR was a result of Arab nationalism, rather than Muslim unity. Nevertheless, it involved Muslim countries and could be seen as a sign of emerging unity. Unfortunately, it did not last long.

The breakup of Pakistan into two nation states, Bangladesh, and Pakistan, in 1971, represented a movement in the opposite direction. A Muslim country failed to maintain its unity in the face of disputes among two parts of the country. Following a murderous civil war and military intervention by a non-Muslim regional power, the dissolution took place. The two new countries have significantly improved their relations since then. Nevertheless, no one is thinking of or interested in unifying.

267.   Economic Cooperation Organization. Ten non-Arab Muslim countries, namely Iran, Pakistan, Turkey, Azerbaijan, Kazakhstan, Kyrgyzstan, Turkmenistan, Tajikistan, Uzbekistan, and Afghanistan have formed a new organization for economic cooperation. It is too early to tell how effective it will be. The United States is eager to have relatively moderate Turkey take the lead in the newly independent former Soviet republics.

268.   Organization of the Islamic Conference. The OIC was established in 1971 with the following noble aims:

a. promote Islamic solidarity among the member states, consolidating cooperation among them in economical, cultural, social, scientific and other vital fields of activity;
b. carry out consultation among the member states in international organizations;
c. endeavor to eliminate racial segregation and discrimination in all forms;
d. eradicate colonialism;
e. take measures necessary to support international peace and security founded on justice;
f. coordinate efforts to safeguard the Holy Places;
g. support the struggle of the Palestinian people helping them to liberate their land and to regain their rights;
h. strengthen the struggle of all Muslim people with a view to safeguarding their dignity, independence, and national rights;
i. create a suitable atmosphere for the promotion of cooperation between member states and other countries.

The OIC currently has a membership of approximately 50 countries. To achieve its aims, a permanent secretariat has been established in Jeddah, Saudi Arabia with a permanent staff of over 100. A Conference of Muslim Kings and Heads of States and Governments is held every three years while the foreign ministers meet every year. The International Islamic Court of Justice is in the developmental stages. Special committees and subsidiary organs include: the Islamic International News Agency (IINA); the Islamic Development Bank; the Islamic Commission for International Crescent; the Islamic Educational, Scientific, and Cultural Organization; and the Islamic States Broadcasting Organization.

The formation and continued existence of OIC reflect the desire for unity on the part of all Muslim nation states and their leaders. OIC has been useful since it provides the mechanism for periodic meetings of all Muslim government leaders. Here they can discuss issues and problems of their Muslim populations. Even initial skeptics such as the secular governments in Turkey and Egypt have come to recognize its value.

There have been some practical achievements too. The Islamic Development Bank has provided funds to several needy countries. Islamic universities and cultural centers have been established for enhancing Islamic consciousness. OIC has advanced the causes of Muslim minorities in the Philippines, Eritrea and India. It has made efforts to resolve the issues of Palestine and Kashmir. As a result of OIC unity, there is a reasonably functional bloc of Muslim countries at the United Nations. However, the concept of secular nation states continues to have much stronger support among the members of OIC than that of one *Ummah*.

Wide differences about the nature, needs, and views of the members of OIC have prevented OIC from becoming truly effective. For example, rich oil producers have needs different from those of poor nations. Small kingdoms value their security above all else. *Shi'ah* Iran and westernized Turkey may be viewed suspiciously by orthodox, *Sunni* regimes. Some in Iraq and Syria view themselves as more secular than religious. There is no acknowledged leader of OIC, though Saudi Arabia, who pays most of the OIC bills, has day-to-day control. On the whole, OIC has not achieved most of what its founders had hoped for.

269.   Peacekeeping Force. In the Bosnia crisis, Muslims have regretted the absence of an OIC military peacekeeping force. Even though several Muslim countries were willing and able to help Bosnian Muslims against the Serbs, there were at least two obstacles. There was no mechanism for effective military coordination and the United Nations had been initially reluctant to accept forces from Muslim countries because they might have been biased in favor of Bosnian Muslims.

Presently, each Muslim country is responsible for its own defense. The OIC does not have any force to defend any Muslim country against external aggression, as in Bosnia or Afghanistan, nor to foster peace in conflicts between Muslims, as in the Iran-Iraq War, nor to support peace efforts during the fighting, as in Afghanistan and in Somalia.

Islam does not permit aggression but requires self-defense. Accordingly, Muslim forces should be defensive in nature. As the experience of multilateral forces such as NATO, the Warsaw Pact, and the United Nations indicate, forces are needed for peace-making and peace-keeping. An effective military organization among Muslims, with permanent forces or the ability to assemble them on short notice may be an acceptable concept to both OIC members and Western powers.

270.   **Proposed Draft Constitution.** Abdul Fatah Memon has proposed a draft constitution for "The Organization Of Muslim States" in his book in published in 1966. Some of the ideas were incorporated by OIC as discussed above. Additional suggestions are as follows:

  a. an economic council consisting of all member states to deal with economic issues, e.g., setting up a common market;
  b. a political council to deal with relevant issues;
  c. a defense council to help organize defense of all member countries including the supply and manufacture of arms;
  d. a religious council to interpret and apply Islam according to the needs of modern times, and to help propagate Islam;
  e. a Muslim world arbitration court to arbitrate disputes among Muslim states, and to help consolidate laws in member states on the basis of the Qur'an and *Sunnah*;
  f. a scientific council to promote scientific research and arrange distribution of resulting advancements among the member states;
  g. funding for the organization to be provided by all member states based on a certain percentage of national budgets;
  h. after a lapse of twenty years, language of the organization will be Arabic.[42]

271.   **Initial Phases.** Given their individual national interests (and those of individual rulers) it is unrealistic to expect that the existing Muslim national states will merge into one national entity any time soon. The best that the proponents of Muslim unity can expect is to gradually move in that direction. Consultations among Muslims on issues of mutual interests are already taking place in bilateral relations and in OIC. However, most of the collective decisions are *ad hoc*, in reaction to specific events and often non-binding. There is a need for strategic planning and formal commitment as was done in the treaties of Rome, Masterichs, etc., with the EU. A list of world trading block is found on page 138. It can be done in phases such as:

  a. further increasing the level and scope of cooperation among Muslim states on the basis of bilateral relations or preferably in the context of a strengthened OIC or another organization acceptable to Muslim governments;

---

[42] Abdul Fatah Memon, *Oil and the Faith,* pp. 139-141.

b. facilitating freer flow of trade, capital, and labor among them;
c. one or more agreements leading to linking currencies and the formation of a common market;
d. freer discussion of all spiritual, political, economic, and military problems facing Muslims. The current "exclusion of sensitive issues" may not be in the best interest of the *Ummah*.

272. **Intermediate Steps.** Formal steps leading to creation of a united Muslim state will have to wait a long time. Intermediate steps would require agreement on and introduction of:

a. a uniform currency;
b. common defense policy and arrangements;
c. common foreign policy; and
d. changes in existing constitutions.

273. **The Eventual Muslim Union.** The Muslim union that eventually develops can take any number of forms, including:

a. a separate "supplemental" government to whom existing national governments delegate certain functions while themselves retaining most other functions;
b. a confederation, with power decentralized, but individual national existence greatly diminished; or
c. a federation, with a strong central government.

All this would follow only if the parties involved are comfortable with the initial and intermediate steps. Citizens of all Muslim countries would have to be consulted each step of the way and there would be nations withdrawing and rejoining. Confidence-building measures including detailed explanations of proposed actions would be required. Interested parties, including non-Muslim citizens, officials of Muslim governments, and the West would require reassurance on numerous concerns.

Economic issues exist, such as the exchange value of each currency (several of which are non-convertible at the moment), rights over assets and liabilities of the existing treasuries (many of which are near bankruptcy), allocation of new jobs, the role of the private sector, etc. The recent German reunification is worth consideration in this area.

In addition, there will be constitutional issues including the role of Islamic law within the state (extent to which it will be implemented or enforced), whether to combine governmental and religious authority under one institution or person, and the introduction of checks and balances within the government.

Many Muslims see continual erosion of Muslim position, prestige, and power. They openly wonder if there is a bottom line to Muslim misery. Only Allah knows the answer. While we all are aware of Muslim decline, there have been some positive developments too. This brief chapter looks at both the positive and negative developments, and comes to a conditional conclusion.

A. Positive Developments For Muslims.

274. Past 50 Years. During the past 50 years, more than 40 Muslim countries have obtained independence in Asia, Africa, the Middle East, and the former Soviet Union. In spite of much publicized misery during the last ten years, approximately ten new Muslim flags are flying at the United Nations. This may be considered a political gain.

In spite of the death of many Muslims at the hands of brother Muslims and of non-Muslims, the total Muslim population continues to grow rapidly. This natural growth has been enhanced by a significant increase through conversion. A qualitative increase is also apparent, if the spiritual awareness (*taqwa*) of Muslims is an indication. Spiritually, Muslims are more aware of their religious heritage as evidenced by Islamic resurgence in all parts of the world. To some commentators, this rise in spiritual awareness among Muslims is the single most important development during the past 50 years.

Militarily, they have more troops and equipment than before. Successful struggles against the Soviet Union can serve to diminish the anguish caused by the Iran-Iraq and Gulf Wars. Some even argue that the Gulf War broke many barriers existing between the American military and Muslims. Certainly, the sharing of equipment and cooperation among the leadership could not have been expected a few years ago. Most observers, including Israeli leaders, would agree that Muslims, as a group, have superior military capabilities than they had 50 years ago.

While low levels of education, health facilities, food and shelter continue, Muslims have made progress in economic development. Some rich oil nations have jumped into the modern world with amazing speed, boasting of high technology, advanced infrastructures and high standards of living. Others have evolved, from ex-colonies dependent on their previous masters, into world traders competing as independent producers. From an economic point of view, Muslims as a group have made some progress in last fifty years.

275. Continuing Economic Existence. Pakistan can be used as an example of the recent political and economic progress made by Muslim nations. Yet, like most other developing countries, Pakistan has reportedly been bankrupt from the day of its independence. The economic situation is said to have gone from bad to worse. The nation's bankruptcy is publicized during the final days of every out-going government.

Yet every incoming government has been happy to take over. Members of each government have also found it possible to enrich themselves far more than the previous ones. Where does the money keep coming from? Borrowing -- both from local and foreign sources of money. International lending agencies and holders of local bonds are willing to provide more money after receiving assurances from the government. The government's ability to grant favors in the form of plots of land, industrial licenses, and cheap loans has also been a source of money for civilian and military rulers and politicians. Even the common people's lot improves through this mysterious form of economics.

B. Negative Developments

276. Decline of a Superpower. The breakup of the Soviet Union was caused, in part, by the victory of Muslim *mujahiddeen* in Afghanistan. Ideologically, Islam has always presented an alternative to communism which many who also opposed the West preferred. Even today, in the midst of secular decadence, some Westerners are discovering that Islam offers a perspective not found in most of their theological and metaphysical concepts.

Politically however, the presence of two competing world powers meant that one or the other was always looking for Muslim support. That competition has evaporated. Some feel that with the disappearance of communism, Muslims represent the main ideological threat, (even though a weak and distant one) to the newly established world order. The Gulf War was an example of the New World Order. In Bosnia, Serbs have openly and repeatedly declared that they are "cleansing" Muslims from Europe in the name of Christianity and so the whole Christian world ought to be grateful to them.

The mentality manifested in Bosnia augurs ill for Muslims, and other minorities, if it receives support elsewhere. Muslims can expect worse to come, even those living in Europe and in the United States. A greater threat may come from Russia whose history is replete with crimes against ethnic groups, who has been supporting the Serbs in Bosnia, was defeated by Afghanistan Muslims, and whose borders are threatened by several rebellions, some say inspired by Iran.

As discussed above, some Muslims suggest that the best course for Muslims living in the West is to become full participants in the democratic process of the adopted countries. They advocate building alliances with locally elected officials and seeking support from the legal system. They point to other minorities, such as Blacks in the United States and Jews everywhere, who have already taken the same route.

277. Going West. We have noted that, regardless of how badly the West may be treating them, millions of Muslims from all parts of the world are eager to come to the West. The poor and the rich, the weak and the strong, fully practicing Muslims and lukewarm ones, all are hoping to move to the West. Some want to improve their economic lot while other are escaping political or religious persecution. They feel that things are getting worse at home so they must do something for their own sake and for the sake of their children's future. They queue in front of embassies, bribe travel agents, or even reveal national secrets. It does not matter. Anything must be better than what they feel they have.

No one forces those already in the West to stay. Many Muslims go back to their country of origin for various reasons: they do not like the policies of the West; they do not want to expose their children to Western ways; they seek to have their daughters married to good Muslims back home; they prefer to live in greater comfort with their accumulated earnings from the West; etc. A number who return home find that the country they left is not the same -- it is Westernized. They encounter similar problems but also those of a less-developed country: drugs; poor medical facilities; corrupt government officials, politicians, and businessmen; weakened family network; etc. Many return after a time to restart their lives in the West and stay.

278. Muslim Suffering. Without fundamental change, current patterns of suffering are likely to continue: Muslims will continue to be ruled by leaders who owe allegiance to foreign powers rather than to their people; Muslim governments wishing to challenge the established world order will receive prompt punishment; and domestic Muslim movements will continue to be suppressed with as much force as necessary. Conflict among Muslim nations will be fueled by outsiders through pledge of support to each of the warring sides which will ensure continuance and possibly aggravation of the trouble. As in the case of the Iran-Iraq War, as one Western "statesman" put it, "The only bad thing about the war is that some day it will come to an end." In the case of the Gulf War, the West's worst fear was that Iraq would accept the United Nations resolutions before the start of the war and escape destruction.

Some Muslims feel that, as a group, they are not doing as well as other groups of people. Muslims are suffering in many parts of the world, and thanks to improved communications, the rest of the Muslims are becoming increasingly aware of it. What the media do not report and Muslims forget, however, are the achievements, the progress, and just the day-to-day accomplishments of Muslims. Whether it be the common man or political, military, or business leaders, Muslims' existence in this world cannot be analyzed solely in terms of material well-being and comforts, or a lack of suffering and pain.

> **Allah has promised, to those among you who believe and work righteous deeds, that He will, of a surety, grant them in the land, inheritance (of power), as He granted it to those before them; that He will establish in authority their religion-the one which He has chosen for them; and that He will change (their state), after the fear in which they (lived), to one of security and peace: "They will worship Me (alone) and not associate aught with me." If any do reject Faith after this, they are rebellious and wicked** (Surah 24:55).

Muslims are reminded that they must be sure they are seeking nothing more than the pleasure of God. He has mastery over all, and His help is forthcoming.

> **O ye who believe! Fear Allah, and let every soul look to what (provision) he has sent forth for the morrow. . .** *(Surah 59:18).*

> **. . .And those saved from the covetousness of their own souls -- they are the ones who achieve prosperity** *(Surah 59:9).*

279.　**The Future.** Only Allah knows the future. He is *Alim-ul-Ghaib*, i.e., the One who knows the unseen. No human can pretend to know the future. When the time for change comes, even the mighty fall very quickly. The defeats of powerful armies such as those of the Shah of Iran, Kuwait, Iraq, the Philippines (under Marcos), Pakistan (in East Pakistan), the Soviet Union (in Afghanistan) and the United States (in Vietnam) were difficult to predict. Nevertheless, one can try to anticipate future events based on the current status and past patterns of change. Planning and consideration of future consequences is encouraged in the Qur'an.

Both Western and Muslim governments have been developing future military, economic, and political scenarios to predict possible outcomes under various circumstances. All have been trying to maximize their chances of achieving the desirable objectives. The West is, of course, much more advanced. Allah is naturally free to introduce new variables and change the outcome completely. Allah however encourages Muslims to do whatever they can to try to improve their tomorrow in this world and the next.

> **. . .Verily never will Allah change the condition of a people until they change it themselves (with their own souls). . .** *(Surah 13:11).*

The purpose of this chapter is to (a) understand the changes already taking place in the world, (b) assess likely directions over the next ten to fifteen years if the trends continue, and (c) understand how changes may affect Muslims.

A. The Changing World and Implications.

The world has changed in many ways since World War II. Many authors have written on the subject. I have particularly benefitted from (a) Mahdi El-Mandjrah, a futurologist and a professor at Muhammad V University in Rabat, who presented a very useful paper in a symposium on "The Future of the Islamic World" in the summer 1993 issue of *The American Journal of Islamic Social Sciences*; and (b) Jessica Tuchman Mathews of World Resources Institute who made a presentation to a World Bank audience in 1992.

280.   **Spiritual Changes.** Muslims have little to boast about when they compare themselves to the West. Economically, politically, and militarily they are far weaker than the West. Muslims entering the international arena may note, nevertheless, that the Soviet Union lost the Cold War partly due to military or economic victories by the West and partly because Soviet leaders and the peoples of the republics lost their passion for communism. Gorbachev and Yeltsin were able to deliver their country to the West because they had lost faith in their ideology. Communism did not work.

The secular trend that heralded the communist adventure has crested and is rapidly waning. By contrast, these spiritual developments are noted:

a. Religion has lost much of its earlier influence on the life of prosperous, influential people in almost all parts of the world; but it continues to influence the ideals and mores of the middle and lower classes.
b. The relatively poorer people continue to practice their religions.
c. Conservative movements based on moral values are beginning to regain some power.
d. Both Christian and Muslim missionary movements are still active, and are gaining new converts particularly among the poor.
e. Partly due to dissatisfaction with their governments and societies, Muslims of all socio-economic classes are increasingly turning to their religion.

281.   **Future of Religion.** The post World War II period has seen a great rise of secularism in the West as well as in other countries. Pakistan and Israel obtained independence in the name of Islam and Judaism, respectively, but quickly decided to follow the secular model of government. India, containing a vast majority of Hindu population,

declared a secular constitution. The United States, Europe, Japan, the Soviet Union, Egypt, Syria, etc. all are secular. However, as people have recognized that growth of material goods and technology is (a) unevenly distributed and (b) not sufficient for human satisfaction in any case, interest in religions has increased considerably in the last twenty years.

The rise of "born again Christians" in the United States, growth of Hindu political parties in India, Zionism in Israel, and increased attendance in mosques everywhere, are manifestation of this increased interest. The Religious Revival has been visible in two different forms: people have chosen to (a) be more devout in their study and practice of their religion and (b) religion, coupled with violence, has been used to achieve political ends.

We can expect to see continued revival of all religions. This implies efforts to study, understand, and practice religion. In coming decades, it can take humanity in many possible directions, including:

a. rigidity of faith among followers of religion, leading to denunciation of other faiths, and eventually to conflicts;
b. disenchantment with religion once again, and reaffirmation of secularism;
c. understanding of common features of religions, including tolerance, leading to greater peace among followers of all religions; and
d. polarization of societies along religious versus secular lines, leading to increasingly disparate objectives and irreconcilable differences. This is already the case in many key issues including abortion, homosexuality, and prayer in schools; various religions and denominations are allied against secular approaches.

282. Changing Economic Relationships in the World. In recent years, many developing countries of the world have crossed the line of poverty. South Korea, Taiwan, Thailand, Singapore, and Malaysia have developed quite fast in East Asia. Indonesia, and China are catching up fast. In South America, Brazil, Mexico, Chile, and Argentina have come a long way. Life in these countries has improved significantly. They are playing increasingly important roles in international trade. The Western world is looking at them with greater respect. They expect closer relationships with the West in coming years. There are other trends too:

a. There are economic aspects of border erasing -- internationalization of markets, sources of supply, capital, and jobs.

b. International and global trends in the fields of economics, politics, environmental changes, etc., are immune to national boundaries and require international solutions.

c. About 40 percent of mankind depends on 214 river systems shared by at least two, and usually more, nations. Water shortage is one of the main causes of fear among nations of the Middle East and sub-Sahel Africa.

d. The current mal-distribution of world resources among developed and developing countries is likely to continue and become more acute. World stability is likely to be affected by the fact that 10 percent of the world population may consume 90 percent of the world's resources.

e. Massive numbers of economic refugees are expected to attempt to cross national borders. The United States and Europe are the preferred destinations for almost all, even though many end up settling at intermediate points.

283.   Freer Flow of Goods and Capital. Free trade is increasing; barriers are falling. Representatives of 117 nations have reached agreement on a new pact which is expected to make the trade freer in over 10,000 products. The details of the 550 page document are complex. The last round of negotiations was really between the United States and Europe. They thoroughly discussed each point of interest to them. Representatives of their agriculture, industry, and other sectors were fully involved and consulted. The rest of the countries reviewed and approved it. It is doubtful that they had sufficient expertise to understand the United States-Europe negotiations or enough clout to protect their vital interests.

Capital and financial markets are opening in many countries and are quickly being integrated into the existing ones. Capital is crossing borders in search of higher returns. New financial instruments are being introduced. Uniform rules of commerce are being adopted; economic trust and mutual understanding are growing among the developed countries and the fast developing ones. With rapid technological changes, all economies are likely to be affected. The innovative ones are reaping the most rewards. Being flexible and adaptable to change is the minimum requirement for staying in the race.

Slowly-developing and poorer countries on the other hand are generally outside the New World Order's economics. Aside from soft loans and frequent advice, they remain outside the mainstream. Most Muslim countries fall in that category.

284. **Economic Changes.** Since World War II, there have been numerous industrial and agricultural changes which have influenced labor conditions and standards. Among them are:

a. an acceleration of information, with the total amount in the world doubling every seven or eight years;
b. an increasing complexity of information and technology for defense, industry, and the home; developing countries including Muslims have been left far behind;
c. a move from a production-based society to an information-based society, with a declining value of traditional raw materials which Muslims have, and an increasing value of intellectual input and innovation;
d. a concentration of information and communications, with the developed countries controlling over 85 percent of all information related activities;
e. a significant increase in the number of people in the world and their rate of increase; the current world population of about 5.5 billion is projected to keep growing, with possible stabilization at twice or even three times the current level.
f. a fast growth rate and young age of the population of developing countries including Muslims; slow rate of growth and aging of the population of the developed countries (the West, including Japan);
g. a significant change in international economic aid; international aid agencies are receiving increasing guidance from their principal shareholders (i.e., the West), and are in turn passing it on to their clients in developing countries;
h. a failure of the public sector (i.e., governments) to find satisfactory solutions to economic problems;
i. an increasing emphasis on private sector participation in carrying out economic activities in developing countries;
j. a significant increase in the number of countries needing economic aid (due to the collapse of communism), with a minimal increase, if any, in the resources available for such aid; accordingly, those who are reluctant to implement "the guidance" can expect to receive less in the future; and
k. a reduction in aid from oil-rich Arab countries to needy Muslim countries due to the cost of the Gulf War, domestic reconstruction needs, and oil prices stabilizing at a relatively low level.

Most of the changes have adversely affected Muslims and will continue to do so. Muslims often complain of their relatively low, and in some cases declining, economic status, bemoaning the lack of material progress and prosperity. A large portion of the Muslim population living in rural areas continues to exist outside modern markets and survives at bare subsistence levels. They are less vulnerable to dramatic economic upheaval. With relatively little effort, the economic life of these Muslims can be improved significantly.

285.   Political Changes. There have been many political developments which have spectacularly changed the *status quo*, including:

  a. the Cold War has come and gone with the United States emerging as the only superpower;
  b. enemies during World War II (Germany, Japan, and Italy) have become tested friends of the United States for several decades;
  c. Cold War enemies of the West (Russia and more than twenty countries in Eastern Europe and Central Asia) have practically destroyed their economic and political systems and have reduced themselves to the status of developing countries, while their internal conflicts continue to grow;
  d. an erosion of the concepts of national governments in relatively developed parts of the world; governments in Europe and the Americas (North and South) are willing to delegate traditional power upwards to the United Nations and other regional unions of independent nations;
  e. information and telecommunication technologies (television, fax, and personal computers) have opened previously tightly shut national borders;
  f. special interest groups, including environmentalists, scientists, women, youth, urban interests, rural interests, and many others are successfully lobbying domestically and abroad;
  g. the human rights policies of governments are increasingly subject to the scrutiny of international forums and law;
  h. the number of independent countries has more than doubled; more than forty of these have Muslim majority populations;
  i. the supervision of elections by the United Nations in a number of countries has been accepted and even welcomed; and
  j. Muslim majority countries are gradually accepting the democratic process, but movement is at a snail's pace.

The pace of positive political change within Muslim countries may become accelerated. Under one scenario, the current leadership in Muslim countries may recognize the writing on the wall and introduce positive changes. Under another scenario, in spite of the Western support, the military government in Algeria may not last long. The Algerian people may succeed in bringing their Islamic party to power. If they succeed, and if they can make life better for their people, can similar changes in Tunisia, Morocco, Libya, and others be far behind? If the Muslim *Ummah* succeeds in transforming its current passive desire for political improvement into even a mildly active one, the results will become visible rather quickly.

286. Future of Russia. What happens in Russia is important to Muslims and non-Muslims. No one is prepared to make predictions. After auspicious changes, including relaxation of restrictions on religions, there is a reaction against the new leadership. As usual, it is easy to criticize from the outside and difficult to deliver. The Russian people are unhappy. Many warn of totalitarianism reappearing, 'especially if economic conditions deteriorate or protracted military action is required, in Chechnya or anywhere else.

Introduction of free-market economy and democracy have been less than successful to date. Some analysts feel that simultaneous introduction of the two was a mistake and that a country must achieve stability and a measure of prosperity before it can successfully practice democracy. The examples of China, South Korea, and Taiwan may be of benefit to Russia. Those Asian economic power houses are developing their economies under firm political control and stability. It is assumed that better education and full stomachs will lead to peaceful political participation and eventually to full democracy. Given Russia's earlier economic strength, the process need not have taken too long.

To Muslims, Russia may represent a continuing combative arena, on the heels of the Afghan War and the rebellion in several provinces. Currently, the Caucasus region is teeming with more ethnic conflicts than any other area of the former Soviet Union, all of which have repercussion for or involve Muslims. These include: Armenia; Chechnya; South Ossetia; Georgia; and Azerbaijan. By contrast, Russia also remains a competitive source of military weapons and equipment.

287. Future of the United Nations. The United Nations has always been as effective as its members, particularly those of the Security Council, allow it to be. With two superpowers who rarely agreed on any major action, the United Nations was reduced to a debating society. However, since disintegration of the Soviet Union, the United States has become, with some exceptions (e.g., on Bosnia), the undisputed leader of the Security Council and the United Nations.

As demonstrated in the Gulf War, restoration of President Aristide in Haiti, and troop movement on Kuwait's borders (in October 1994), it is much easier now for the United States to get action taken through the United Nations. Some would argue that the United Nations has already become an extension of U.S. foreign policy. If the United States really wants something done through the United Nations, it will be done. If the United States is undecided on a particular issue, European powers will play a larger role. The following are possible developments:

a. The United States is likely to seek and get major administrative changes which will result in a reduction of personnel at headquarters, and a reduced role for United Nations bureaucrats particularly from developing countries, including Muslims;

b. The United Nations Security Council led by the United States is likely to become aggressive about curbing nuclear proliferation among non-nuclear nations; this will result in continued or even increased pressure on Muslim countries with nuclear ambitions (e.g., Pakistan and Iran);

c. The United Nations peacekeeping missions in different troubled spots of the world which do not have strong support from the United States will be phased out; this may affect Bosnia, Kashmir, etc.;

d. Activities of the United Nations agencies dealing with development assistance are likely to be reduced, resulting in much less assistance to many Muslims in Africa and Asia.

All of the above factors are likely to have an impact on Muslim countries, too; in particular, reduced developmental assistance will have considerable impact. With the exception of the only remaining superpower, the United States, few leaders can afford to assert narrow nationalism. At a minimum, nations have to form blocks, formally or informally. Europeans have already formed their EU and have ambitious plans for expansion. Indonesia and Malaysia belong to ASEAN which is in the early stages of following the EU model. Arabs activate their Arab League when necessary, though sometimes it appears to provide little more than a meeting forum and opportunity for debate. In spite of belonging to OIC,

Muslim countries tend to rely on their bilateral relations with the United States for resolution of their problems. Africans have the Organization of African Unity (OAU) and are capable of providing a supporting block for Muslims within the United Nations. Latin American countries, with the United States included, have also recently entered into additional economic agreements among themselves.

The United Nations lacks economic foundations, and is historically wedded to Western traditions and jurisprudence. It is unlikely that it can shed the political baggage it carries without total restructuring. It offers only limited value to its members and is far outside the range of popular opinion, particularly in Muslim countries.

288. **Role of Think Tanks.** In the past, United States foreign policy was almost exclusively made by government functionaries. In recent times, think tanks (organized groups of scholars) in conjunction with the news media have become increasingly influential. These groups are established by powerful interest groups (conservatives, liberals, Christians, Jews, etc.) to propose and advocate policies of interest to them. They recruit former and aspiring government officials and distinguished intellectuals to analyze issues of concern to them and to develop policy options. Their expertise comes from having held government positions or studied and taught the subject at universities; from those perspectives, they advance the point of view of the sponsoring organization.

The media are always eager to report the policy options of these think tanks; they find them very useful. On specific issues, if there are conflicting views among the powerful (e.g., among the liberals and the conservatives), then there is keen debate. However, when it comes to the interests of Israel or action against Muslims, there is hardly anyone who is influential enough to present an opposing view. Such decisions are quickly and unanimously made and implemented. American and European Muslims need to understand the importance of think tanks and the media in making public policy and in playing power politics.

Muslims have also set up their own think tanks.[43] Almost every Muslim organization has thinkers who are continually writing and

---

[43] The Minaret of Freedom Institute in Bethesda, Maryland and the United Association for Studies and Research in Annandale, Virginia are two think tanks in the Washington D. C. area. The International Institute of Islamic Thought (IIIT), in Herndon, Virginia, is active in the Islamization of knowledge.

publishing. In fact, there has been an explosion of writings in the English language by Muslim scholars on Islamic subjects. However, the overwhelming majority of the presentations and writings tend to be historic in nature, analyzing events of the last several centuries. Everyone is looking for historic precedents to justify whatever is being said or suggested. While Muslims need to be sure that their actions are consistent with the Qur'an and *Sunnah*, Muslim thinkers need to be forward-looking, bringing the *Ummah* to the twentieth century and getting them ready for the fast-approaching twenty-first century.

Some Muslims feel that it may be a disservice to keep the Muslims entangled in old issues, since at least partially, it results in leaving them unprepared for dealing with the present and future. Of course, the press and the media of the West have almost completely ignored the work of contemporary Islamic thinkers. Muslims should not be discouraged. They should continue to do high quality work and make it available to governments and to the media. The *Ummah* ought to encourage such work through financial contribution and participation.

289. A View of American Muslims. A conference on "Islam and the West" organized by the American Muslim Council in Washington in October 1993 made useful suggestions on soul searching, image building, and policy making. It was pointed out that Muslims should:

a. recognize that while most media are biased against Muslims, some of their reporting about lack of human rights (unfair treatment of women, unfair distribution of wealth, lack of democracy, treatment of religious minorities, lack of ability to hold objective, open debates, emotionalism, etc.) is true;

b. realize that the West, its media, and the United States are not monolithic, and all of them do not have closed minds in relation to Muslims;

c. search to find members of the media who understand Muslims' concerns and work with them toward expanding the group through setting good examples, and disseminating positive information to them, including Muslims' contributions to knowledge and to the evolution of civilization;

d. emphasize the values which are shared by Muslim and Western societies including the common moral codes of Judaism, Christianity, and Islam;

e. work with religious groups in the West to combat "secular fundamentalism" which disregards the value systems of all religions;

f. keep pointing out to the media that the terrorist activities of a few who happen to be Muslims are not "Islamic terrorist activities";

g. point out that acts of poor governance in individual Muslim countries are not examples of normal Islamic behavior, and that Muslims aim to improve governance based on Islamic teachings;

h. indicate that representative government is not alien to Islam, but a desired objective;

i. point out that, under Islam, each human being has rights as well as duties toward others.

Many advocate that Muslims should convince Western governments, including the United States (through their representatives, media, think tanks, etc.), that the West should:

a. be sensitive to the opinion of the Muslim masses;

b. not intervene on behalf of the elite, who are unpopular with a majority of their own Muslim citizens;

c. understand and support the intense desire for freedom and self-assertion current among Muslims;

d. allow Muslims to make their own mistakes rather than intervene at every excuse;

e. realize that in view of its power, the West has nothing to fear from Muslims; therefore, it should extend a hand of cooperation; and

f. not single out Islamic governments for economic sanctions and military interventions.

291. Military Changes. Muslims know that advanced military technology continues to wield tremendous power. Israel is the obvious example. However, China also presents a lesson. Though known to have nuclear weapons, the large number of relatively trained and hard working people under Chinese control is also impressive to the West. It is important to note the following changes:

a. Russia and the East Europeans have dismantled their own collective security arrangement (the Warsaw Pact), and are now eager to join NATO;

    b. the West, led by the United States, has already gained absolute military superiority, and is getting stronger by the hour partly due to additional research and development in military fields;

    c. international aid agencies are critically examining the level of military expenditure in determining the level of economic aid for needy countries. This will make it difficult for the economically needy countries (e.g., Iran, Syria, Sudan, Pakistan) to become too strong in military terms. China may prove to be an exception; and

    d. trade in military hardware can be monitored easily; the West can detect and prevent adverse transactions and shifts in the military balance relatively easily.

As discussed elsewhere in the book, if Muslims can assume a defensive posture, resolve disputes amicably, critically review and streamline military expenditures, focus on technology and manpower development, introduce universal military training, and, above all, pool their resources, or at least effectively coordinate their actions with each other, they have little to fear.

292.   **Causes of Future Wars.** For centuries, wars were mainly among kings for reasons of religion or territory. This was followed by wars between nation-states primarily for economic and imperialistic reasons. This continued into the twentieth century, with ideology being added to the mix, including fascism, communism, and capitalism. In most wars, a just cause and an underlying idealism prevailed, giving leaders ammunition with which to inspire the people.

In light of the increase in religious fervor mentioned above, it is interesting to note the results of a recent poll conducted by *US News & World Report*. It found that 59 percent of Americans believe the world will come to an end; a third of them think so within a few years or decades; and 44 percent believe it will end with a Battle of Armageddon as described in the Bible. Muslims are also convinced about the nearness of the end. The famous Muslim, Ibn Kathir, recorded the Prophet's (PBUH) description of the "signs of the Day of Judgment." Muslim activists have argued that most of these signs have been fulfilled by Western society. Both Christian and Islamic eschatology foresee a final war between good and evil in which the promised Redeemer defeats Satan.

Some political scientists believe that future wars will be fought among civilizations. Western powers hope that Western civilization will be one united group. Muslim civilization is viewed as one possible opponent.

Third-world nations, including the peoples of China, Latin America, and Africa are other possible opponents. A North-South polarity has also been mentioned.

U.S. government spokespersons have repeatedly rejected the thesis of future wars among civilizations. The U.S. feels that if there is any "ism" they wish to confront, it will be extremism. They are happy to work with any government and people who are for (a) stopping oppression of people, (b) broadening political participation, and (c) resolving local, regional, or international conflicts.

The United States enjoys good relations with many Muslim governments and people and, of course, went to war in support of Saudi Arabia. The U.S. continues to provide assistance to many Muslim countries in building their societies and economies. It has participated in several efforts in resolving conflicts involving Muslims, including the Arab-Israeli conflict which has led to a large foreign aid package commitment for each party.

The U.S. government has never denied its global interests. If its direct interests are in conflict with those of anyone else, the U.S. government obviously assigns first priority to protecting them. The U.S. denies having any policy designed to repress Muslims or to keep them from uniting.

Muslims living in OIC countries can expect to be targeted only if they are perceived to be a threat. Muslims of Iran, Iraq, Libya, Algeria, and Palestine have already faced wars or boycott. Sudan and, occasionally, Pakistan appear to be on a collision course, again. Even Indonesia is coming under increased scrutiny despite being a "good Muslim country" from the West's point of view. It has emphasized economic development, treated non-Muslim minorities well, and kept religion out of politics. Yet, it is being asked to settle with Portugal in East Timur through self-determination. Also, it has been asked to reduce expenditures on technology.

The only Muslims safe from possible friction may be those who agree with the West on almost every point, e.g., Egypt, Saudi Arabia, and other economic allies and/or militarily dependent kingdoms. Muslim leaders who focus on developmental issues, such as Malaysia, or those who have little strategic or economic significance can also expect to be left alone, at least for some time.

Regardless of circumstances and causes, any future conflict between the West and Muslims will result in great hardship and suffering. In any struggle, the combatants need to conscientiously examine the issues to be certain that fighting is justified; all means of resolving differences must be exhausted before fighting can even be considered. Under current circumstances, it is most unlikely that Muslims and Christians would conclude that widespread fighting between them was justified for any reason.

293.   Future of the Conquered Lands. During the colonial period, conquered lands were deemed property of the conquerors and held indefinitely. In the post-World War II era, taking permanent possession of conquered lands is generally not practiced in the West. Under the New World Order, a main factor discouraging return to earlier practices is fear of getting involved in unstable areas, resulting in financial burdens and possible loss of life. This theory may not apply to sparsely populated deserts or offshore waters containing huge oil and other natural resources. Next time around, the conquerors may not vacate parts of Iraq or Kuwait as quickly as they did the last time. Muslims should not count on continued application of the old rules of the game. It really depends on the desire of the conqueror.

294.   Impact on Muslims Living in the West. If there is conflict between Muslims and non-Muslims, Muslims living in non-Muslim countries are likely to experience adverse consequences too. Muslims need to be politically strong in their countries in order to avoid suffering. If they are unable to defend their interests through political and peaceful means, they can expect adverse actions at the hands of non-Muslims. Attacks on mosques and homes, discrimination at jobs, harassment by local police, problems in schools, and even ethnic cleansing have already taken place in different countries at different times. These may happen more frequently in more places. To defend themselves, an increasing number of Muslims are stressing the need for voting power and for exhausting the protections provided under the local legal system. Some refuse to turn to non-Muslim institutions for relief.

B. The Middle East.

295.   PLO-Israeli Accord. The accord between the Palestine Liberation Organization (PLO) and the government of Israel, and subsequent overwhelming support from President Clinton led to the historic meeting at the White House in September 1993. It has raised much hope. All analysts, including Henry Kissinger and strong supporters such as President Mubarak, have predicted a long and painful process of implementation.

Most of the key issues have not been resolved, including the return of Palestinian refugees, the rights of Israeli settlers in the Occupied Territories, the status of Jerusalem, sharing of scarce water supplies, and the fixing of national boundaries. The PLO may be monetarily exhausted because of financial aid being cut off by rich Arab countries, while Israel may be emotionally exhausted from the years of the *Intifadah*. However, both sides appear to be willing to deal with each other and the leaders involved received the Nobel Peace Award. The atmosphere for peace and cooperation has never been better.

Palestinians have already received some land and financial assistance to develop it. If the peace process is not derailed by the two parties themselves or the agreement's many opponents among Arabs and Israelis, Palestinians may eventually get more. In spite of open support from several Muslim governments and people, many remain skeptical and even opposed. Syria, Libya, Iran, Hamas and several factions of the PLO itself remain unhappy. On the Israeli side, almost all Jewish settlers, many orthodox religious parties, and the Likud (the Conservative Party) remain strongly opposed. Some on each side are actively working for the "death of the accord."

296.   Jordan-Israel Accord. The next major event in the Middle East took place in July 1994 with "The Washington Declaration" by King Husain and Prime Minister Yitzhak Rabin. It was followed by the signing of a treaty at the Jordan-Israel border, with President Clinton in attendance, in October 1994. Both sides have agreed to end the state of war between the two countries. Some feel that the agreement simply formalizes what has been a reality for many years. Nevertheless, the declaration moves the peace process forward.

297.   Full Peace in the Middle East? The PLO-Israeli accord has led to a flurry of "peace process" activity all over the Middle East. With the exception of Iraq and Libya, Israel has made diplomatic contacts with all the other Arab countries. Almost all Arabs have accepted Israel as a permanent part of the Middle East. The Gulf Cooperation Council (comprising Saudi Arabia, Kuwait, Oman, Qatar, Bahrain, and the UAE) has already ended most aspects of the economic boycott against Israel. Syria and Lebanon are in the process of negotiating a comprehensive peace with Israel. It is widely felt that stable peace is not possible without Syrian participation. Even though there have been acts of violence, many of the

Israeli citizens who were skeptical of the peace accord with the PLO are
slowly changing their minds, too.

Most Jews in the United States are supportive of the peace process.
Obviously, they are much more comfortable with King Husain than with
Arafat.

298.   Possible Impact of Genuine Peace in Palestine. A recent report,
"Securing Peace in the Middle East: Project on Economic Transition,"
prepared by a group of 34 Israeli, Jordanian, Palestinian, and American
economists (from Harvard and MIT) has outlined a scenario under which
the presently occupied West Bank and Gaza Strip can be turned into centers
of shopping, industry, and tourism. Two of the authors, Leonard Hausman
of Harvard, and Lester Thurow of MIT, reported in the *Washington Post*
of August 1, 1993 that a few essential steps will be required:

  a. Reforming the existing administrative system in the area through
     replacement of Israeli administrators with the Arabs, and orderly
     transfer of power;
  b. Providing credit through creation of new banks and expanding the
     existing ones;
  c. Providing jobs to the Palestinian labor force through creation of
     new positions and reserving about 100,000 jobs for them in Israel
     (as done until recently imposed restrictions);
  d. Establishing a free trade zone in the area for goods, services, and
     capital;
  e. Seeking foreign aid for infrastructure projects, including water
     supply and transportation;
  f. Creating an integrated economy of the West bank and Gaza.

It is felt that the changes will not be easy, but given the cooperation
among enemies of previous wars in Europe and Asia, anything is possible
after peace is achieved. High quality labor from Palestine, Israeli
technology, and outside capital can make it possible.

299.   Joint Ventures Among Muslims and Israelis. There have been
rumors of secret contacts, economic dealings, and political plots between
some Arabs and Israelis for a long time. The *Asian Wall Street Journal*
reported such contacts through well-known Saudi arms dealer and financier
Adnan Khashoggi on February 8, 1994. It was reported that Khashoggi has

been making contacts with Israelis as far back as 1967 with the knowledge of many leaders of Muslim governments.

His main partner Yaacov Nimrodi is a well-known Israeli spymaster and fellow arms merchant. Nimrodi reportedly lived in Iran for fourteen years as Israel's secret military attache. He "built the Shah's intelligence agency while earning huge commissions on some $250 million a year in arms sales to Iran." Reportedly, he is currently working with Israeli businessmen to prepare proposals for investment in Gaza. Regardless of the opinions of Muslims on Khashoggi's dealings in the past, many more examples of such cooperation among Muslims and Israelis can be expected in the future.

300.   Development of Gaza and Occupied Territories. The task is going to be a long and hard one. The interim Palestinian government is already faced with many aspects of development and related issues. It is hoped that the PLO will be able to solve these and other issues as they arise. No doubt, they will continue to receive some technical and financial assistance. However, the main burden is on the Palestinians' shoulders.

Political opponents of both the PLO and the ruling labor government in Israel have not accepted the treaty quietly. Many efforts at sabotage have been made and many more can be expected. There will be many emotional scenes and loss of life. May Allah bless the genuine peacemakers.

301.   Settlers in the Occupied Territories. One of the most difficult issues may prove to be the Jewish settlers in the Occupied Territories. The PLO has reportedly indicated that the settlers were welcome to stay, under the protection of the new Palestinian government. The settlers and the government of Israel find that impossible, and are demanding Israeli military protection. The issue has proved volatile, as has the issue of building additional Israeli settlements.

The arrangement made with Jewish settlers in Sinai at the time of the Egypt-Israel Camp David Accord may serve as a model. The settlers were simply compensated for their assets and moved to Israel. Nevertheless, it was an ugly scene. They bulldozed the settlements before leaving. Further more, who will come up with the huge compensation? The United States is not likely to contribute as much as they did in Sinai. Oil rich Arabs have been drained by the Gulf War and its aftermath; they do not have money available even if they wanted to pay.

The West Bank and Gaza issues may prove to be even much more difficult. Many Jews feel that they have a biblical right to the land, and may refuse to move at any cost. Even if they agree to move, the initial estimates indicate that it could cost up to ten billion dollars. No one in the area has that kind of spare change. The United States, Europe, and others may be faced with contributing large amounts.

C. Rapprochement with Other Muslims.

302.   **Impact on Muslims Elsewhere.** One side effect of the "peace in the Middle East" is already visible in the United States. For example, even though the jury selection was underway, hourly news broadcasts and daily newspaper reports about the New York World Trade Center bombing trials and associated commentary on alleged Muslim terrorists became much less frequent. Similarly, the tempers are cooler in the case of Shaykh Abdul Rahman's trial. It appears that the United States media have decided to play down the war of words against Muslims. After all, the Palestine issue has been at the core of the conflict between Muslims and Jews.

Meanwhile, the Pakistan media have reported that the United States is taking an evenhanded position *vis-a-vis* India's nuclear program. The Indian foreign minister has also suggested possible secret talks with Pakistan (PLO-Israel style) to resolve the Kashmir problem. The religious-nationalist Hindu party, BJP, has of course condemned the idea. Rapprochement between Muslims and non-Muslims (Jews, Christians, and Hindus) has taken a turn for the better. If the peace process continues, Muslims may no longer be targeted.

> **[Allah is the] Originator of the heavens and the earth: When He decreeth a matter, He saith to it "Be," and it is** *(Surah 2:117)*.

303.   **Muslim Unity Plus Improved Relations with the West.** The two conditions can result in a truly New World Order. It will mean non-interference from the West and full cooperation among Muslims. It will introduce the Islamic atmosphere that Muslims have been dreaming about. It would have positive implications for all aspects of life. In such a case, Muslims can expect:

   a. to enjoy the many benefits of the unity -- many issues which divide Muslims will be either solved or will be handled in a peaceful atmosphere;

b. international peace for Muslims -- no threats from fellow Muslims and much fewer threats from non-Muslims;
c. peaceful political and economic transitions of domestic governments as desired by the people without outside manipulation or interference;
d. domestic governments devoted to the welfare of people rather than the welfare of the regimes;
e. focus on economic development;
f. emphasis on productive armed forces which will participate in nation building, and truly defensive capability;
g. freedom of religious practice for followers of all Islamic sects, as well as followers of other religions;
h. emphasis on reform in economic, political, and military fields with the pace of change dependent on internal rather than external factors.

Among Muslim countries, the Middle Eastern ones may benefit the most if genuine peace is achieved there. Those in sub-Sahara Africa and South Asia are likely to remain poor for a long time. Basic human needs are largely unmet there. Macro-economic reforms would need to go with institutional, legal, and financial sector reforms. Competition and investment, mostly domestic, will be needed. The public sector must provide a regulatory framework, invest in infrastructure and human resource development, and establish welfare programs for citizens unable to care for themselves.

South Asian Muslims in Pakistan, India, Bangladesh, and Sri Lanka are suffering largely because of regional issues, many of which are traced historically to Britain. The West is currently avoiding involvement in issues dealing with Kashmir, mosques in India, the Farakha Barrage affecting Bangladesh, the expulsion of Muslims from Myanmar, and the civil war in Sri Lanka. It is up to the countries themselves to solve the problems. Religious hate and intolerance are on the increase in each of those countries.

In the event that Muslims remain disunited but improve relations with the West, there will be less provocation and attacks from abroad. Muslim countries will be treated like other developing countries. It will be up to them to develop and solve their own problems.

The Ultimate Future. While planning for the future in this world, Muslims remain aware of the ultimate future -- the Day of Judgment when the righteous shall be rewarded.

The Hour will certainly come: there is not doubt: yet, most men believe not *(Surah 40:59).*

305.   **European Renaissance.** Renaissance means rebirth or revival. In European history, it refers to the period, beginning in the fourteenth century and lasting approximately three hundred years, which saw great increase in study, learning, experimentation and intellectual growth. It focused on the study of Greece, Roman and Islamic civilization. Scientists and scholars sought solutions for everyday problems surrounding them. They achieved excellence in literature, the arts and sciences. Francesco Petrarch (1304-74), an Italian, started the humanism movement devoted to problems of humanity. Sir Thomas More (1478-1535), an Englishman, wrote *Utopia* portraying an ideal society where injustice, war, and ignorance did not exist. Montaigne (1533-92), a Frenchman, wrote *Essays* describing ethical principles by which humans should live. Shakespeare (1564-1616), an Englishman, wrote plays and poems dealing with problems of individuals and the society.

The period produced great artists -- painters, sculptors, architects, and composers of music. People were encouraged to study science, broaden their horizons, and find scientific laws which governed God's universe. Copernicus (1473-1543), a polish astronomer, concluded that the sun is the center of the solar system, and that the earth is merely one of the several planets rotating about it. Galileo (1564-1642) perfected a telescope for observing the heavens. William Harvey (1578-1657) discovered that blood circulates through the body. Sir Isaac Newton (1642-1723) discovered the law of gravitation explaining the attraction of physical bodies to each other. The period included the development of printing, navigation and the discovery of the Western hemisphere, including what is now the United States, the development of cities, and increased food production. The Reformation and reduction in power of the Catholic Church were also taking place during the period.

The European Renaissance was the forerunner of modernization leading to the rise of Western civilization as we know it. After the fall of earlier Greek and Roman cultures, it extended civilization into Europe, which had always been considered barbaric and uncivilized. Many scholars believe that intemperance of governments, dissatisfaction with the Church, and threat of a rival religion, Islam, led to the Renaissance in Europe.

306. Need for an Islamic Renaissance. Since the decline of Islamic civilization, Muslims have longed for a similar revival. As with Europeans in the fourteenth century, Muslims appear disillusioned by their corrupt and inefficient governments, dissatisfied with the performance of their religious leaders, and humiliated by the supremacy and arrogance of the West. Muslims, of course, believe that all the required knowledge is already available to them in the Qur'an. There is little concern about the fact that they do not understand much of it yet -- particularly from a scientific and technological point of view. Research, coming largely from Western countries, has begun to explore concepts mentioned in the Qur'an. Their practical application for the welfare of mankind is still being studied.

Some feel that, following a number of shocks, an Islamic renaissance is already under way. James P. Piscatori mentions several reasons for Islamic revival in his book, *Islam in a World of Nation-States*, including:

a. the defeat of Egypt, Syria, and Jordan in the 1967 War with Israel provided spiritual, political, economic and military shocks, not only to Arabs but all Muslims who lost the holy city of Jerusalem;
b. the process of development has provided speedy means of communications and easy means of dissemination of domestic and international information;
c. modernization has strained the social and cultural fabric of Muslim societies, thereby encouraging people to turn to traditional symbols and rites; and
d. conditions of political development (which have been less than fully democratic) have heightened the importance of Islam as a political ideology, and encouraged the rulers to invoke the name of religion to justify their continuance in power.[44]

The causes are complex but the manifestations of Islamic revival are obvious. They can be seen in Islam's spectacular rate of growth and conversion, both in the West and the East, the Iranian Revolution, the number of Muslims annually performing *Hajj* (the pilgrimage to Mecca), the results of political elections in Algeria and Turkey, and in the number of Muslims assembling for Friday prayers. Other manifestations include:

---

[44] James P. Piscatori, *Islam in a World of Nation-States* (Cambridge: Press Syndicate of the University of Cambridge, 1986) pp. 26-32.

a. the success of Muslim fighters against Soviet and Afghan communists in the Afghanistan War;
b. the relative success of stone-throwing Palestinians against Israel;
c. visible interest, interference and control of the Western powers in many Muslim countries; and
d. widespread *da'wah* and easier availability of Islamic literature and other media in many languages.

As described elsewhere in this book, during the last fifty years, more than forty Muslim nations have obtained freedom from colonial masters. In spite of their current low literacy rates, Muslims have paid much attention to education, scientific knowledge and its application of new knowledge, and nation-building. Religious education at home, school, and university is finding favor with Muslim youth.

Muslims are much more open-minded today than ever before. They travel abroad, enjoy intimate contact with technologically-advanced nations, and boast the finances to restructure their societies. Some would cautiously argue that the changes accomplished in the ruling family of Saudi Arabia are as great as those accomplished by the Italian Medicis in the Middle Ages.

The role of Islam in modern politics is undergoing changes. Bernard Lewis has noted in his book *Islam and the West*:

Islam is a powerful but still an undirected force in politics. As a possible factor in international politics, the present prognosis is not favorable. There have been many attempts at pan-Islamic policy, none of which has made much progress. One reason for their lack of success is that those who have made the attempt have been so unconvincing. This still leaves the possibility of a more convincing leadership, and there is ample evidence in virtually all the Muslim countries of the deep yearning for such a leadership and a readiness to respond to it. The lack of an educated modern leadership has so far restricted the scope of Islam and inhibited religious movements from being serious contenders for power.[45]

Many are impatient and believe that to accelerate revival, it is necessary to blossom and participate fully in the new world. For Europe, the

---

[45] Lewis, *Islam and the West,* p. 154.

Renaissance was spread over a 300-year period and has, in a way, extended to current times. With modern means of communications and easier access to information, a Muslim renaissance need not take a long time.

> . . .Verily never will Allah change the condition of a people
> until they change it themselves (with their own souls). . .
> *(Surah 13:11).*

A. Strategic Planning.

307. Visions for Muslim Nations. The vision of many is that Muslim nations be at peace with each other and with the West, particularly the United States. The hope is that Muslims can develop and participate as equals under the New World Order. In summary, Muslims, as a group, hope to be able to:

a. meet their own basic needs of adequate food, shelter, education, and health care;

b. have stable and representative governments which cooperate closely with each other;

c. tolerate and, whenever possible, peacefully resolve differences in religious interpretations among each other;

d. be strong enough to defend their own borders, and render help to other Muslims in defense of their vital interests; and

e. develop enough, in the long run, to be at the cutting edge of technology, and assume a leadership role, alongside others, for the betterment of humanity at large.

308. Vision for Muslim People. Muslims expect to be thriving, contented, and successful people who are:

a. working hard in a non-antagonistic way to improve themselves (individually and collectively), and the rest of humanity;

b. controlling their own destiny, free of coercion, bullying, or domination at home or from abroad;

c. resolving internal and external conflicts in peaceful and harmonious ways;

d. free from compulsion in choice of religion or manner of practice;

e. free from discrimination and exclusion from every quarter; and

f. at the top of their professions of choice and looked up to by all concerned.

Muslims living in the West hope to share power with other religious groups. This would help Muslims emerge as a self-sufficient, peaceful, and strong people in the world. It would gain them self-respect, and the respect of others. They will be treated as equal partners, and full participants under the New World Order.

309.   Options and Strategies. History indicates that success in any endeavor has many ingredients. Divine decree has always been first on the list. However, as the above *Surah* indicates, "the inner self" has always played a critical part. Many factors are important, among them, clear vision, judicious strategy, hard work, focused purpose, exhaustion of legal remedies, justified mission, perseverance, desire to succeed, etc. All the factors were illustrated during the life of Prophet Muhammad (PBUH) in his struggle to establish Islam. The earlier achievements of Muslims in spiritual, scientific, military, and economic fields contained all these ingredients.

Other have followed his example, proving the same points in their endeavors. The success of modern Western civilization contains them also. Individual Muslims who are succeeding in their respective pursuits today seem to follow the same recipe. If the Muslim *Ummah* is seeking success, they should follow the same path. Within the *Ummah*, the Qur'an shows the way, however, leadership in day-to-day matters has been lacking. Not all Muslims need to have all these qualities, but the leaders at all levels must, though all individuals in the *Ummah* are called to play, sincerely, their respective roles.

Muslim leaders have options which vary in the manner in which their religion is asserted, including:

a. continue the present policy of individually dealing with the current powers of the world;
b. achieve some form of unity and deal as a group;
c. insist on the superiority of their religion, refusing to acknowledge the validity of non-Muslims until they accept Islam; and/or
d. believe in their faith, but accept the principle of non-compulsion in religion and dealing with others on the basis of equality and coexistence.

The overwhelming majority of Muslims aspire for maximum unity. Most Muslims believe in the superiority of Islam over other religions since the Divine message conveyed in the "religions of the book" has been perfected through the Qur'an. A large majority, particularly those living in the West, accept coexistence with other religious groups and reject any form of compulsion in religious matter. A significant number are vehemently opposed to compromising their religion in exchange for secular modernity and technology, but are eager to improve their societies.

310. **Coexistence.** Most Muslims advocate coexistence with the West. They advise leaders to cooperate in areas of mutual benefit and to avoid conflict to the extent possible. However, acceptance of coexistence by Muslims may not be sufficient anymore. Sometimes the West seems to be determined to restrict Islam to private spiritual practice as generally done in the case of Christianity and among many ethnic Muslims in Eastern Europe. They do not accept Islam as a complete way of life. They wish to detach the political and military side of Islam from the religion, and either ignore it or render it ineffective. This arrangement appears to be perfectly acceptable to many secular leaders of Muslim countries.

From a theological point of view, the separation of religion and state is not a viable alternative for practicing Muslims in any Muslim society. In addition, it does not remove the political and military issues facing Muslims in many parts of the world. The Palestine issue could not be solved under the leadership of secular leaders such as Gamal Abdul Nasser of Egypt, Hafiz al-Assad of Syria, or King Husain of Jordan. Yasser Arafat of the PLO has made a start, but needs the full support of religious groups to succeed. The religious reality of Israel took precedence even though it remains a secular state. It is religion that defines Israel and it is religion that defined Pakistan, Bangladesh, and other Muslim countries.

Similarly, the Kashmir issue was not solved under secular Ayub Khan, Zulfiqar Ali or Benazir Bhutto because largely Hindu India will not allow it. On one hand, the West does not wish to see Islam outside the mosque; on the other hand, it has not shown interest in helping the secular leaders solve national or international issues of vital interest to them. Meaningful coexistence then becomes very difficult.

311. **Fear of War.** Weapons of war can kill and maim a very large numbers of individuals, destroy years of economic development and disrupt community and domestic institutions for generations. The United States, the U.K., Germany, Israel, Vietnam, Iraq, Iran, Egypt, Syria, Pakistan, and

Bangladesh have all lost large number of people in wars. They continue to survive as nations, to a great extent because they fought wars. War is a reality of human existence, but war must be only a last resort; and even after hostilities begin, peace must remain present in the vision of the leaders.

Most Muslim leaders have maintained a balanced posture in international politics; few have provided excuses for opponents to initiate aggression. When they have presented a united and determined front capable of inflicting damage to aggressors, they have deterred war. However, most aggression against Muslims has been by Muslims, perhaps instigated by the West, yet conducted by Muslim leaders.

A war waged merely on the ground of religious intolerance, by definition, is an unjust war. No combatant can long persevere in such a struggle. The danger to Muslims is not of a direct attack on their religion. Their enemies are not going to march against Islamic holy cites, provoking a holy war. Those who seek to repress Islam are sufficiently clever to make their attacks subtle, indirect, and almost undetectable. In the long run, it is not war that Muslims need fear, but the continuing dilution of their spiritual affirmations.

Muslims wish to implement Islam as established by the Prophet (PBUH), emphasizing duties to Allah as well as to mankind. They seek to become better human beings than others around them, and to transform their societies. Those with vested interests in the *status quo* resist such change; they include narrow-minded religious leaders and their illiterate followers, rulers who get and keep power through manipulating and controlling them, and Western conglomerates and governments who control the rulers. They are more or less content with the present. Voters in Algeria, Iran, Sudan, and elsewhere in Muslim countries are looking for implementation of the ideal model of Islamic government through democratic and peaceful means.

312. **National and International Sacrifice.** To achieve the desired objectives, Muslims agree that they have to work hard at reform. Many non-Muslims oppose Muslim unity and progress for a variety of reasons, including historic mistrust, fear, jealousy, and potential competition. Economic and political pressures are likely to be exerted to dissuade Muslims. The international boycott, exclusion, and surveillance currently faced by Iraq, Iran and Libya may be a preview of the future. Muslims can expect developmental assistance coming from the West to be critically reviewed and curtailed. Pressure may eventually be reduced when

opponents are convinced of peaceful and constructive reform and no longer see Muslims as a threat to their security.

313. **Work at the Individual Level.** Muslims who wish to strengthen Islam have to make their contribution in a number of ways according to their abilities. Some essential steps are:

a. be a part of the Islamic renaissance in your own country by becoming a better Muslim. Strengthen your practice of Islam in whatever way you deem necessary. Recognize your duties toward God and your duties toward mankind;

b. join an Islamic group of your choice in your hometown and country, working hard to please your Creator through active involvement in matters of this world;

c. work hard to bring your own group and like-minded groups to power through democratic elective process in your own country;

d. once in power at your national level, use it for the welfare of the *Ummah* at home and abroad;

e. be prepared to delegate all national power or a part thereof to the *Ummah* at the international level; and

f. be prepared to sacrifice for the development of Muslims and their effective participation in the New World Order. The sacrifice can be in terms of time, money, relationships, or more.

At all times, work toward consolidating strengths, reducing weaknesses, and establishing solidarity.

B. Military and Technological Planning.

314. **Solving Military Issues.** Muslims' main conflict with the powerful Jewish community is over the Palestine issue. In order to maintain control over Palestine, Israel and its defenders in the United States and elsewhere appear determined to weaken all Arabs and their supporters. Iraq, Iran, Sudan, Libya, Pakistan and other Muslim countries thus become victimized, too. If this problem can be peacefully resolved, the Palestinian people who have suffered for the last fifty years can begin to live a normal life. It is hoped that this will also encourage the Jewish community to put less emphasis on opposing Muslim interests everywhere in the world.

Kashmir is another issue requiring urgent solution. Past wars by Pakistan have failed to solve it. Diplomacy and United Nations resolutions have failed. Enormous sacrifices by Kashmiris themselves over the last several years have not yielded any better results. Reportedly on the advice of its Israeli supporters, India has initiated a more vicious policy of collective punishment, which is likely to result in much more death and destruction for Kashmiris. Pakistan has fought three wars with India, largely over Kashmir. However, India's nuclear technology threatens Pakistan; another war with India may cost much more than Pakistan is willing to pay. Some see a glimmer of hope in the United States's desire to maintain peace in the subcontinent and control nuclear weapons. Most Muslims welcome the U.S. initiative.

315.   **Attempt to Reach Military Balance.** Some Muslims dream of military balance *vis-a-vis* non-Muslims. However, that appears impossible in the foreseeable future. Muslims are not even able to achieve military balance against immediate adversaries. Arabs have been left behind in relation to Israel. Pakistan is substantially behind India. However, if Muslims had unity, a Muslim-Israeli or Muslim-India balance would be possible.

Now that the Cold War is over, most Muslim countries cannot expect to get military assistance on a grant basis. In addition, lacking foreign exchange, they cannot expect to buy advanced equipment. Relying on their own research and development may prove beneficial in the long run, particularly to the extent Muslims seek to improve their defensive capability. Allah said:

> **Oh Prophet! Rouse the believers to the fight. If there are twenty amongst you, patient and persevering, they will vanquish two hundred: if a hundred, they will vanquish a thousand of the unbelievers: for these are a people without understanding** *(Surah 8:65)*.

This of course assumes a degree of spiritual commitment and advancement which may not be present in most Muslims of today.

316.   **Technology and Manpower Development.** The technology gap and accompanying manpower advances are the most important causes for the domination of Muslims by others. Muslims owe a good part of their historic successes to superior technology. Muslims fell behind in technology after they became a conquered people. The superior technology

of the West kept them within the colonies until economic and political factors arising out of World War II led to their freedom.

Muslims have acquired much technology and developed much manpower since World War II. However, there has been a sizable leap in the knowledge of the West since then. While they have learned to manufacture basic consumer goods and small conventional weapons, others have mastered technology relating to nuclear weapons, missiles, space, oceans, biological and chemical warfare, computers, etc. The more progressive leaders have accorded high priority to technology and related manpower development in national budgets.

317. **Military Expenditure.** Muslim leaders seek sufficient military power to deter aggression. No one attacks others if they fear retaliation and significant damage. Some deterrence is being maintained and it represents a significant part of the budgets of several Muslim governments. However, these expenditures have become too large to be sustained by the economies of most Muslim countries. These expenditures should be carefully reviewed and revised. Simply spending money for the purchase of advanced equipment which quickly becomes obsolete is not the answer. Military strength has to be self-sustaining and permanent.

318. **Universal Military Training.** The introduction of universal military training and service is an option to be considered by several Muslim countries. It increases the pool of available personnel with a minimum degree of military training at relatively small cost. Such training also provides physical fitness for youths. This is valuable in light of the currently poor fitness of youth in Pakistan, Bangladesh, and many African countries. Other benefits include increased discipline and training to previously unemployed people in marketable vocational skills such as those available in telecommunications, construction, and logistical support activities (automobile driving, cooking, tailoring, accounting, etc.). Finally, universal military service promotes national integration by having people from all parts of the country work together; Muslim countries with domestic ethnic diversity would find this of considerable benefit. It has been avoided in some cases because governments do not trust the people and fear that widespread military training may lead to their own overthrow. The Ummah cannot afford such shortsightedness.

319. **Population Issues.** Natural reduction in high population growth rates through educational programs and improved economic status and

health care for women is justified and is already on the agenda of most Muslim nations. On the other hand, social and economic safety nets for most Muslims around the world are provided by the extended family and by adult male offsprings. Wars in Muslim countries also continue to cost many lives. The strong economic arguments in favor of population control are well known, nevertheless, most Muslims believe that Allah has promised sustenance for all creatures. The Qur'an is frequently quoted to point this out:

> **Kill not your children for fear of want: We shall provide sustenance for them as well as for you. Verily killing of them is a great sin** *(Surah 17:31).*

In particular, Muslims argue that there is little justification to deliberately curtail the size of affluent families who can afford to provide adequate education and sustenance for their children. These families need not place a heavy emphasis on birth control. Many assert that, after they have grown older and their children have moved on in pursuit of their own careers, they wish they had other children.

320.   Firm Unified Stand. If all Muslims, particularly the member governments of OIC, take a firm stand on a vital issue and convince the West that they are ready for any sacrifice, the West will think twice. The West is not ready to have 50-plus enemy nations who will be willing to sacrifice for their cause. Al-Aqsa mosque in Jerusalem may be safe so far because Israel and the West sense that any damage to it will unite all Muslims. The moment Israel and the West sense a division of opinion about it, the mosque is sure to be attacked by some "fanatic." The West has not sensed similar unity in respect of Bosnia, Kashmir, Palestine, etc.

There is a convergence of views with the West in a number of areas as mentioned in this book. The Islamic economic system is also similar to that of the West in many ways. However, Islam insists on a moral filter for all actions. The combination will be a powerful one. Focusing on areas of agreement can provide a useful start.

321.   Ways to Participate in the New World Order. Muslims have to avoid self-imposed isolation. Prophet Muhammad (PBUH) was willing and able to deal with people of all faiths and ideologies. While he continued to invite people to Islam, he remained a part of the society in Mecca and Madinah. The desire of some Muslims to isolate themselves from non-

Muslims appears to be contrary to the Prophet's practice. Muslim participation at all levels -- family, neighborhood, town/village, provincial, national, and international levels -- is beneficial from a social and economic perspective, as it offers an opportunity to demonstrate the ideals of Islam to others. Instead of brooding in isolation, Islam encourages active participation in supporting good and opposing evil.

322.   **Strategy and Action Plan.** A model strategy is rather simple and would consist of several steps for Muslim governments and people:

a. emphasize long-term of interest of local citizen and work diligently to resolve domestic issues;
b. start with implementation of activities for which Muslims have convergence of views with the West;
c. solve outstanding military issues among Muslims and with non-Muslims as soon as possible;
d. accept genuine coexistence with followers of other religions and world powers;
e. consolidate strengths, and reduce weaknesses on all fronts as discussed above;
f. increase cooperation and solidarity with fellow Muslims;
g. enhance defensive capabilities through expenditure for technology, manpower development, and universal military training; and
h. continue study of the many unresolved spiritual, military, economic, and political issues as recommended in this book.

323.   **The Islamic Agenda**. Muslims have a great message in the Qur'an and *Sunnah,* or traditions, of Prophet Muhammad (PBUH). There are many common factors which unite Muslims. Muslims have a large population in the world; diversity of geography, race and culture; large land; huge financial resources; sizeable industrial base; large well-trained manpower; experience in media; a system for good governance; strong community feelings; and belief that they are one nation. Muslims have all the ingredients to be a powerful force for good.

324.   **Difficulties**. However, the brotherhood has many weaknesses and the leadership can be better. Most elements of the Muslims' agenda are clear. Yet, experience indicates that the responsiveness of the *Ummah* to the needs of Muslims is negligible. Muslim leaders and many of their people are moving from bad to worse, frequently following the bad habits of Westerners, while neglecting their good ones, and developing their own forms of corruption. Muslims wish they could stop infighting and move forward, but this has not been possible. Why is the Islamic agenda so difficult to implement? There may be many reasons:

a. Although some required actions are obvious to everyone including government leaders, a comprehensive agreed-upon agenda is not available.
b. The agenda must deal with a malaise which is several centuries old and has inflicted about a billion people around the world. The cure is likely to be complex, time consuming, and expensive to many, in more than one way. Even though everyone talks of the changes, neither the *Ummah* nor the individual leaders have shown the required perseverance and patience to follow up on the agenda.
c. There are always alarming issues and emergencies that require immediate attention, leaving little time for focusing on long-standing concerns.
d. There is fear of external forces which are unlikely to look at the revival of Islam kindly, and are likely to sabotage Muslim efforts through the many channels accessible to them.

Ironically, the fear of Islam in the minds of Muslim leaders may be the most serious problem. Many Muslim government leaders are reluctant to accept a definition of Islamic behavior which does not coincide with their own. They refuse to shoulder the rigors of Islam in a personal or collective sense. Confrontations with the established religious leaders are common but feared.

Religious leaders themselves are not blameless. Apparently, there are irreconcilable differences between them; often these are clouded by personal interests they seek to protect. Some fear confronting government leaders. Others have something in their personal life inconsistent with the high standards set by Islam.

Major changes cannot be made quickly. Yet, priorities need to be set. Plans for a year, for five years, and for 20 years are necessary for any kind of development. The question asked is who will make the plans and who will implement them. Religious, political, and military leaders have to be persuaded to do something. Once a level of support is reached domestically, in at least some of the Muslim countries, an influential forum such as OIC has to be used for discussion and eventual consensus.

325.   **Conclusions and Recommendations**. The long list of obvious conclusions and recommendations has been separated according to the four subjects -- spiritual, military, economic, and political. It can also be divided into several subgroups:

a. **conclusions (C)** which do not contain action;
b. relatively non-controversial recommendations primarily referring to economic and political development in individual countries. These can be put into practice within a reasonably **short term (ST)** by individual Muslims or governments, with applause from everyone;
c. actions relating to religious interpretations and adaptations which would require **studies (S)** by mutually acceptable competent authorities; and
d. recommendations needing open and sincere cooperation among Muslims, primarily in political and military fields. These actions would require political and even physical courage on the part of the Muslim leaders, and may be the hardest to carry out. These are **long-term (LT)** wishes.

Many of the conclusions and recommendations presented in this book are general, rather than precise. However, if the priorities are accepted, detailed and exact steps can be worked out. There is no shortage of expertise on spiritual, economic, political, or military matters. The required expertise can be obtained within the *Ummah* to work out the details.

A. Spiritual Issues.

1.　　Muslims must study, understand, and follow (a) teachings of the Qur'an, which is the basic source of knowledge, and (b) the authentic practice of the Prophet (PBUH). They should stop being observers and become active. **(C)(ST)**

2.　　Muslims must pay special attention to the younger generation's moral education in order to produce citizens of superior character, values, and competence. They must be prepared to make all necessary sacrifice for the next generation of Muslims. **(ST)**

3.　　There is a need for a systematic interpretation of Islamic precepts in light of twentieth and the twenty-first century conditions. It must be carried out. It will require a large effort and will involve much thought, research, discussion, and consensus. However, it will remove confusion and help regain lost assurance and self-confidence of many Muslims. **(S)**

4.　　As permitted by Islam, there is a continual need for study, debate, and eventual consensus on many subjects/issues among Muslims. A working mechanism must be established for reaching such a consensus. The value of the on-going work must be recognized and thinkers must be brought together. **(LT)**

5.　　There is an urgent need to deal with the Arabic language issue to ensure wider understanding of the Qur'an. As a result of *ijma* and *ijtihad*, Muslims may consider several options including compulsory study of Arabic in all Muslim countries, and greater use of their local languages in religious matters. *Ijma* and *ijtihad* must be open to all practicing Muslims and not be restricted only to those who have command of the Arabic language. **(LT)**

6.   Establish effective Islamic councils in each town, province, and country leading to an effective World Islamic Council. Delegate sufficient authority to the councils to prevent conflicts and clarify disputed interpretations of Islamic teachings. **(S)(ST)**

7.   Upgrade training and enhance the education of religious leaders at all levels, particularly at the level of village and neighborhood mosques. **(ST)**

8.   While a vast majority of Muslims follow the Islamic teachings and avoid drinking alcohol, other substances, which have similar or even worse effects, are gaining popularity in Muslim countries. These substances require a large amount of money, and destroy the health of users. Countless families have been destroyed in Pakistan, Afghanistan, and Somalia because of their use. Corrective action and regulation by the religious and government authorities are required. **(ST)**

9.   Many Muslim women believe that numerous social, cultural, political, and economic rights given to them by Islam are being denied to them. There is an urgent need for definitive interpretation of the Islamic position on issues relating to the role of women. The genuine rights must be restored. **(ST)**

10.   Islam must come outside the mosques and enter the hearts of Muslims. Grievances of all oppressed groups must be addressed. **(S)**

11.   Muslims should support (by financing and participating in) research and peaceful discussion on all controversial issues. Existing think tanks must be supported, and new ones must be established as needed. **(LT)**

12.   Traditionalists and modern Muslims look at each other with suspicion and some contempt for neglecting either the duties to Allah or to mankind. Each group feels a sense of superiority over the other. There is a need for an open dialogue and practice of at least the minimum non-controversial rules of Islam. **(ST)**

13.   There is an urgent need for each Muslim to look inside him/herself in order to ensure that he/she is on the right path. The answer is generally hard to follow but always clear. **(LT)**

14.   Muslim governments should treat religion as a personal matter, even if their ministries of religious affairs and private organizations are active in supporting Islamic education, construction of mosques, performance of *Hajj*, payment of *zakat*, fasting, offering of prayers, and missionary activities based on freedom of choice. **(ST)**

15.   Muslim governments must eliminate corrupt practices which have caused so much harm to them, including bribery, food and drug adulteration, thievery, and use of drugs. **(ST)**

16.   Muslims must avoid misinterpreting Islam as something more difficult than it is. This would refute the Islamic assertion of being the most natural religion. There is need for some research to determine "pleasures" allowed by Islam. **(S)**

17.   There is a need for review of Muslim marriage arrangements, making them natural and based on true consent of the bride and the groom, as intended and practiced earlier. **(S)**

18.   Muslim dress is not synonymous with Arab or Pakistani dress, however there are some prescribed rules. If necessary, Muslims should seek legal recourse to safeguard their right to wear prescribed clothing in the Western countries without fear. **(ST)**

19.   In the 1990's, when the West prides itself on being fair, the Western media are being very unfair to Muslims and Islam. Muslims need to work on improving their image. A test case in a court of law for slander ought to be considered. **(ST)**

20.   Muslim scholars in the United States and Europe have produced much religious literature specially for youth in modern English language. They deserve recognition and encouragement. Muslims in all countries can benefit from it. **(ST)**

21.   Muslims are divided on the basis of race, ethnic origin, language, economic status, sects, etc. They need to remove barriers of all kinds among themselves and work closely with each other. **(S)(LT)**

22.   Good examples from top government officials help set the pattern for the rest of the society. Fair and just implementation of existing laws (or

new ones, if needed) will help, too. Government officials convicted of crimes deserve exemplary punishments. People must be convinced that the government is there to help in solving their problems and not just rule them. **(ST)**

23.   *Da'wah* at a massive scale is required to call people to Islam, both those from non-Islamic traditions and those who are Muslim in name only. **(ST)**

24.   If Muslims can become good role models for their family members, fellow countrymen, and non-Muslims, many of the problems facing the entire world will be solved. Unfortunately, the present *da'wah* activities in Muslim countries and abroad overemphasize "Muslim appearance," recitation of verses (which few understand), and rituals. Little is visible in terms of becoming a better human being. Rituals are stressed over God-consciousness and duties to mankind. The first test of successful *da'wah* must be improved human behavior particularly among Muslim themselves. **(ST)**

25.   If Muslim countries decided to work together, they will experience an amazing spiritual uplift. Many of the spiritual issues identified above will disappear. The current divisions and the ease with which many can purchase and manipulate Muslims will be reduced. In such an atmosphere of spiritual renaissance, individual Muslims can deal with the issues of the partial practice of Islam, need for self-reform; and the allurement of the Western way of life. **(C)**

B. Military Issues.

26.   During 1992, the total size of all Muslim armed forces amounted to about 4,493,000 persons, of which armies had 3,739,000, navies had 232,000, and air forces 521,700. By all measures, Muslims have a very large total armed force. In numbers, they can match any other power on earth. Several armed forces of Muslim countries are relatively modern. As a group, Muslims have a right to feel self-confident. **(C)**

27.   Since the attacks on Iran and Kuwait by Iraq, and on Libya and Iraq by the United States, the morale of individual Muslim countries has been lower. Other Muslim countries did not come to their defense. Accordingly, almost all feel isolated and vulnerable. With a degree of

cooperation from each other, they can feel safer and reasonably more secure. (C)

28.   Military success requires: (a) a just and moral cause; (b) wisdom, bravery, and sincerity of the leadership; (c) proper timing in terms of suitability of the political conditions and physical circumstances; (d) adequate size, organization, and discipline of the troops; and (e) superior equipment. Muslims should not think of initiating a conflict unless all peaceful means have been exhausted, there is an undisputed interest to be served and the welfare of people is assured. (C)

29.   Muslims should settle internal and international disputes peacefully, leading to reduced expenditure on the military; (ST)

30.   There is an urgent need to evaluate the cost and contribution of the military in Muslim countries. Ways must be found to make it cost effective. (ST)

31.   In order to control military budgets, many experts have suggested (a) substantial reduction in permanent standing armies, (b) universal military training for all citizens with increasing reliance on national draft or conscription, (c) development of their armament industry, and (d) extreme selectivity in acquiring advanced but expensive conventional equipment from abroad. Muslim countries ought to consider their options carefully. (LT)

32.   Spending money for the purchase of some advanced equipment which would be obsolete shortly after the time it arrives, is not the answer. Military strength has to be self-sustaining and permanent. (C)

33.   Universal military training and service has been avoided mainly because governments do not trust their own citizens. It should be considered by all Muslim countries. Its relatively small cost will be offset by its many benefits. (ST)

34.   Muslims need to recognize the current superiority of non-Muslims in (a) military power, (b) economic power, (c) science and technology, (d) homogeneity of values, objectives, and strategies, and (e) a well-defined mechanism for cooperation among each other. Muslims need to work hard on all fronts in order to fill the gap and to earn respect and equality. (C)

35.   Muslims appear to be permanently relegated to the position of military weakness in terms of advanced technology. Muslims can find defense in the unity of spiritual affirmations, large numbers, universal military training, collective strengths, and willingness to sacrifice for their own defense. (C)

36.   There is an urgent need to assure and demonstrate to the West that Muslims wish to peacefully coexist, and progress without hurting anyone; and that its fear of Muslims is not justified. (ST)

37.   There is an urgent need to undertake steps to increase professionalism of the military in Muslim countries. (ST)

38.   Islam does not permit aggression but requires self-defense and resistance against oppression. Accordingly, Muslim forces should be defensive in nature. (ST)

39.   Military forces are needed for peacemaking and peacekeeping among Muslims. An effective military peacekeeping organization among Muslims is urgently needed. Peacekeeping forces would need to be paid for by all OIC members on the basis of a mutually agreed transparent formula. Troops should be preferably selected among volunteers. Every peacekeeping operation should have the full support and backing of OIC. Once dispatched, the peacekeepers should be able to stay as long as required to ensure peace and establish credibility for future operations. Experiences of other multilateral forces, such as NATO, Warsaw Pact, and United Nations forces should be carefully studied. (LT)

40.   The suffering of Muslims is unacceptable in any part of the world -- Palestine, Bosnia, Kashmir, Somalia, or Chechnya. All Muslims must use their influence to persuade the West and other non-Muslim powers to bring about peaceful resolutions. If all else fails, Muslims have to be prepared to make whatever sacrifices are necessary. Muslims must learn from the example set by Jews in defense of their own people. (LT)

41.   Achievement of military balance with non-Muslims is impossible in the foreseeable future. Even an Arab-Israeli or Pakistan-India balance appears to be out of reach. However, a Muslim-Israeli or Muslim-India or Muslim-Serbia balance is not impossible. (C)

42.   Given the current disunity among Muslims, those who confront the world powers can expect trouble in the form of personal and national threats, economic blackmail, attacks from third parties, sabotage of different kinds, and eventually direct attack. **(C)**

C. Economic Issues.

43.   Neglecting basic economic needs of Muslims in the respective countries while talking of a Muslim *Ummah* unifying 50 countries is not going to work. Some effective mechanisms have to be found for accelerated national economic growth, balanced regional development and strengthening safety nets within individual countries. **(C)**

44.   Finding productive employment is the number one priority for most Muslims. All Muslim governments need to accord high priority to reduction of unemployment at home. The main answer lies in economic growth. As a group, Muslims should plan and implement a well-coordinated international action program. **(ST)**

45.   Bribery is an unnecessary economic burden on people. Muslim governments must make the practice uneconomic for those who practice it. Successful efforts of world leaders, Muslims and non-Muslims, ought to be widely replicated. **(ST)**

46.   If Muslims are united, their large population, natural resources, land, and other strengths, coupled with responsible leadership, will discourage others from taking unreasonable positions against them. **(C)**

47.   Muslims need to demonstrate that the concept of "one Islamic nation" is attractive for the rich as well as the poor Muslim nations. The Divine command can be reinforced by the practical benefits of cooperation, as demonstrated by EU, ASEAN, and others. **(S)**

48.   Abuse of guest workers in Muslim countries must stop. It may be noted that: (a) if the concept of one Islamic nation is ever implemented, there will be considerable movement of labor; (b) without respect for contractual rights, the rest of the world will not seriously respect Muslims in commercial matters; and (c) Muslims cannot insist upon other nations (e.g., Germany *vis-a-sis* Turks) respecting their guest workers, if Muslim Arabs cannot treat their own Muslim guest workers well. **(ST)**

49.   Dependence on foreign aid from non-Muslims must be reduced. Lessons in self-reliance may be partly learned from the experiences of (a) China from the 1940's through the 1970's, (b) Iraq since the end of the Gulf War, and (c) Iran since the Revolution. Initially, it will mean hardship and the lowering of already low living standards. However, eventually Muslims will emerge stronger, and will be able to deal with the rest of the world on equal terms. **(LT)**

50.   Muslims should study taxation options, including *zakat,* and improved arrangements for collection. Improved taxation systems, and efficient collection could greatly reduce fiscal deficits and the need for foreign aid from non-Muslims. **(S)**

51.   In order to ensure sufficient resource mobilization, Muslims need to develop an alternative to interest payments in return for the use of the capital of those who are unable to take risk or do not wish to share in profit and loss. **(S)**

52.   Muslims can expect to fall further behind in scientific research and advanced technology unless there is (a) major improvement in their education policy, (b) increased expenditures on education, and/or (c) improvement in relations with the West. **(ST)**

53.   Muslim governments and private organizations need to spend large shares of their resources on development of science and technology. A science-friendly atmosphere needs to be created. Muslim students need to learn applied science and technology on a massive scale and conduct research of all kinds. Some well-justified, planned, and executed expenditures on advanced technology projects need to continue in spite of competing demands. **(ST)**

54.   Muslims as a group should examine the issues relating to scarcity of water affecting many Muslim countries, and take appropriate action for sustained long-term improvement. **(S)**

55.   In view of Islamic teachings, economic safety nets provided by extended Muslim families, and the large number of Muslim deaths in recent conflicts, government officials should carefully consider their population growth policies. Individuals with the economic means to provide

adequate education and upbringing for their children should not overly emphasize birth control. **(ST)**

56.   Muslim governments should improve the economic well-being of their people through higher priority for and increased public and private expenditure on education, food, and shelter. **(ST)**

57.   Muslims should devote national and collective resources for reduction of poverty, elimination of illiteracy, raising education and health standards, improving environmental conditions, and developing infrastructure. Large number of Muslims living below the poverty line in Africa and South Asia deserve special help. **(ST)**

58.   There is merit in increased decentralization, in terms of the division of powers among central, provincial, and local governments; it should be considered by all Muslim government officials and leaders. **(ST)**

59.   Much of what needs to be done in economic, political, military, and spiritual terms is non-controversial among Muslims and supported by the non-Muslim world. It will strengthen Muslims and can at least raise standards and the quality of life. Malaysia is a good example to consider. **(C)**

60.   Unless a drastic positive change occurs in strategy and pattern of development, the gap between per capita incomes of Muslim countries and the Western countries will widen. All major factors affecting economic development (e.g., revenue mobilization, expenditures, borrowing, human resource development, defense, etc.) have to be reviewed and redirected. Muslims should agree on targets they wish to achieve in the next five, ten, twenty, and fifty years and act accordingly. **(ST)**

D. Political Issues.

61.   Establish a commission to study current and old constitutions of Muslim states in various parts of the world and propose a practical model constitution based on the teachings of the Qur'an for consideration of each Muslim government. **(S)(LT)**

62.   Muslims need to create active and effective associations for advancement of Muslim people everywhere, with the objectives of discussing, finding, and implementing improvements. **(ST)**

63.   Muslim governments should respect the human rights of their citizens in general, and women in particular; elected representatives, religious organizations, and people in general should come to the support of victims. **(ST)**

64.   Muslims need to create anti-defamation leagues in non-Muslim countries to defend themselves and explain their viewpoints to non-Muslims, particularly in the West. **(ST)**

65.   Muslims cannot afford to ignore the media. They must seek out journalists and other media personalities and try to convince them about the validity of the Muslim point of view. **(ST)**

66.   Muslims need a better coordination of media policy and the creation of international mass media. To have their message reach all concerned, Muslims need communication vehicles similar to the New York Times and Washington Post in newspapers; BBC in radio; and CNN in television. **(ST)**

67.   Muslims have a long way to go in terms of extending media coverage (particularly TV) to less developed areas of their countries; they need to strengthen the role of media in instructional, educational, and national/international fields. **(LT)**

68.   Muslims need to consider implications of new broadcasting technology in terms of receiving these signals and using the opportunities to transmit their own news, views, and culture. **(LT)**

69.   Muslims need to study and possibly reconsider their position on controversial political issues of today. Political relationships with non-Muslim powers must be based on overall interests of the Ummah. **(S)**

70.   Muslims need to promise to each other that they will: (a) accept all Muslims as part of one brotherhood; (b) renounce internal conflict on the basis of ethnic, linguistic, and racial grounds; (c) not go to war with any other Muslim country; (d) spend resources on getting to know each

other through tourism, cultural exchanges, learning languages, inter-marriages, etc.; and (e) spend resources on strengthening their judiciary, and international conflict-resolution among Muslims through establishment of a permanent organization (Muslim international court) for resolution of issues, and abide by its decisions. **(ST)**

71.   The education and development of common Muslim people will encourage all Muslim rulers to improve their behavior toward their people. **(C)**

72.   Muslim objectives should be to demonstrate the excellence of Islam, to invite others to Islam and to peaceful coexistence. To assert domination over others in the world is unwarranted under Islam. Peaceful intentions must be demonstrated through action. **(ST)**

73.   For peaceful coexistence, Muslims have to assure the West that they do not intend to deny to the world economic resources within the borders of Muslim countries (particularly including oil and gas). **(ST)**

74.   With the Soviets defeated, the West has lost interest in Afghanistan. Now, the West is afraid of Muslim unity and the possibility of a fundamentalist government in Afghanistan. As in the Iran-Iraq war, they have no interest in stopping bloodshed among Muslims. The Afghanistan civil war may be an example of how difficult it is to promote unity among Muslims, how individual Muslims may act in promoting their own narrow self-interest, and how Muslim differences can be exploited by outsiders. **(C)** Muslims as a group must do more to bring peace and unity in an Islamic Afghanistan. **(ST)**

75.   Kashmiris deserve an explicit opportunity to decide whether they wish to remain with India, join Pakistan, or become independent. **(C)** Muslims must work together to ensure self-determination in Kashmir. Pakistan and the people of Kashmir should encourage the U.S. initiative for comprehensive peace in the subcontinent. **(ST)**

76.   There is a need to remove overt and covert legal and regulatory discrimination against women. Political leadership, Islamic scholars, and the media can play a vital role. Increasing opportunities for women will be essential to improving economic performance, promoting equity, and improving relations with the West. **(ST)**

77.   Muslim governments should realize that individually they mean little to the West and the rest of the world. They can be manipulated easily. Like Western Europe under the EU, Muslim governments will mean much more if they are united in an effective working block. (C)

78.   The concept of Muslims relying on each other appears to be too far-fetched to be taken seriously by even Muslim leaders themselves. However, the teachings of Islam, self-respect, geographic proximity, and common interests require it. It must be developed. Some confidence-building measures have to be taken. (S)

79.   Muslim governments must demonstrate their respect for the human rights of their own people, before demanding others to do the same. (ST)

80.   National legal systems, and other conflict-resolution mechanisms must be used to stop intra-Muslim violence in Muslim countries. (ST)

81.   Freedom of the press needs to be guaranteed; legal recourse must also be afforded to those who are unjustifiably defamed, slandered or injured, individually or collectively, by the media. (ST)

82.   Muslim governments should review and modify the laws relating to blanket amnesty provided to officials. Amnesty should be minimized to enhance the honest and efficient operation of governments. (ST)

83.   Islam supports the stability provided by the righteous ruler, but encourages disobedience to, and even rebellion against, the corrupt one. Muslims must learn to exercise rights granted to them through national constitutions and Islam. (C)(ST)

84.   The Western people are beginning to take note of the excessive power of money and media in their own elections for public office. They are increasingly reluctant to give political power to people with accumulated wealth, or to be manipulated by the media. Similar recognition and reluctance should be encouraged in Muslim countries in order to move them to truly representative governments. (C)

85.   Citizens want elected officials to be sensitive to the problems faced by the common people. The voters want officials to be accessible to them and to help them improve the quality of their lives. (ST)

86.   Islam does not have a doctrinal system for succession or removing leaders from office. Since the four Rightly-Guided Successors to the Prophet served for life, a model for periodic change in a peaceful manner has not be agreed upon. Later successors practiced family rule with heirs coming to power on the death of the rulers. A mechanism of succession is stipulated in the constitution of most countries, but is often sabotaged. Muslims need to adjust to the orderly transition of governments. (S)(ST)

87.   If about fifty Muslim countries join in a just cause supported by their more than one billion citizens, they can generate a positive force which would be hard to defeat. (C)

88.   There is a need for OIC, Muslim governments, and think tanks to design a strategy which will maximize the benefits of Muslim positions, and minimize the costs. (C)

89.   Muslims need better leadership. Muslims need leaders who recognize the strengths and weaknesses of the *Ummah*, who can question the status quo, and who believe in a better future for all Muslims. (C)

90.   With patience and effort, it is possible to increase cooperation among the followers of Islam and other religions. Muslims and non-Muslims need to respect each other's vital interests. The weaker one is, the more respect one has to give. (C)

91.   Arabs are not only divided, but, according to the Western press, they privately urge Western powers to punish their Arab enemies excessively. They need to search their souls about their long-term objectives, make special efforts to improve inter-Arab relations, and put their houses in order. (ST)

92.   Muslim governments should do all in their power to ensure protection of non-Muslims in their territories. (ST)

93.   There is an urgent need to convince the West and its media to differentiate between criminal actions of individuals and the teachings of Islam. (ST)

94.   Many Muslims have noted exemplary behavior by many Westerners and recognized good Islamic qualities in them. Some even

attribute the success of the West to the fact that they are following the teachings of Islam more closely than Muslims. (C)

95.   The affirmations which are non-threatening to the world powers also happen to be fundamental to Islamic behavior and can lead to improvement in the life of common Muslims. Muslims should start with carrying out these activities. (ST)

96.   Based on experiences in Saudi Arabia, Jordan, Pakistan, and Bangladesh, it is wrong to label all Islamic governments as (a) incompatible with modern politics and government and (b) hostile to the West. (C)

97.   Muslims should work with non-Muslims and try to form as many alliances as possible even if these relate to single issues. Internationalists, minorities, and peace groups everywhere can be allies. (ST)

98.   All Muslims should encourage a peace settlement in the Middle East. It may bring an end to the long misery of Palestinians, Syrians, Jordanians, Lebanese, and Israelis. It may also reduce Israeli and Western pressure on the rest of the Muslims.(ST)

99.   Muslims should launch a public relations campaign to educate people in Western countries about their common heritage and beliefs. There is much that unites Jews, Christians, and Muslims. (ST)

100.   There is a need to research, understand, emphasize, and build on the common heritage with Hindus in the subcontinent. The welfare of over one billion people of India, Pakistan, and Bangladesh depends on it. (ST)

101.   Muslims have a good basis for coexistence with Buddhists as well as with the followers of other great religions. Efforts must be made to improve relations. (ST)

102.   Muslims should work with minority groups everywhere to protect mutual rights. Blacks, Jews, American Indians, and Spanish Americans have all struggled side by side in the United States and helped each other's cause in the past. Muslims have to work with and help others, too, if they wish to receive their help in the future. (ST)

103.   Muslims should take advantage of any consensus among Muslims, even with non-representative governments, and move forward with implementation of useful ideas. (ST)

104.   The influence of American Muslims in U.S. politics can be an effective vehicle in tomorrow's world. Many American Muslims, particularly the younger generation, have recognized the importance of political participation in their homeland and are becoming more active. They face much prejudice and opposition. All Muslims should help and encourage young American Muslims in politics. (ST)

105.   Adaption to a new homeland and its culture in an honest, meaningful way, within acceptable limits, is often rejected by immigrant Muslims. To adapt to new environments is not un-Islamic, so long as Islamic affirmations are not compromised. (C)

106.   American and European Muslims must follow the law of the land concerning separation of religion and government. Political participation must be on the basis of public service. However, Islam must remain the dominant factor in the individual's life. (ST)

107.   Any Muslim seeking political office in a non-Muslim country will find it difficult to win the support of a majority of voters unless the electorate consists of a majority of Muslims or other like-minded people. Among Muslims, secular ones have a better chance of success. Righteous, practicing Muslim candidates will have to wait until prejudice against Islam is substantially removed in the West. Some may question whether such a secular person is a true Muslim, however, Muslim voters should support anyone who is sympathetic to their causes. (C)

108.   American and European Muslims need to understand the importance of think tanks and of the media in public policy-making and power politics. They need to set up and finance their own think tanks and empower them to assert and defend Muslim interests. (ST)

109.   It is clear that American and European Muslims are not held in high esteem by their countrymen or elected representatives. They have to do more to raise their standing in the community. (ST)

110.   Muslims in non-Muslim majority countries must strengthen themselves in spiritual, economic, and political terms. They have to convince their fellow citizens that their religion is worthwhile and deserves respect like Christianity, Hinduism, Buddhism, and Judaism. (LT)

111.   Massive voter registration campaigns and participation in the electoral process has helped all minorities in America. Modest but wide-based political contributions have helped many political candidates. Muslims have to learn from others, and open their pocket books to political parties and candidates of their choice. Participation in the political process is a right of each citizen and a duty of each American Muslim. (C)

112.   Without generous contributions to Islamic organizations from all those who can afford, Muslims cannot reach their full religious or political potential. All Muslims must pay their share in contributions. Even small individual contributions can add up to a lot. (ST)

113.   Muslims in France, China, Germany, India, and other non-Muslim majority countries are economically and politically weak. They are likely to need some political support from Muslim governments to ensure their basic rights as citizens and immigrants. (C) The occasions of frequent meetings between heads of Muslim and non-Muslim governments must be used to advocate the genuine concerns of Muslims. Israel and the Jewish-American community played very important roles in advocating the cause of Soviet Jews. Muslim governments and the *Ummah* must do the same to support Muslims living in non-Muslim lands. (ST)

114.   Under the present world order: (a) Muslims will continue to be ruled by leaders who owe allegiance to foreign powers rather than to their people; (b) Muslim governments wishing to challenge the established world order will receive prompt punishment; (c) domestic Muslim movements posing a serious challenge to the *status quo* will continue to be suppressed with as much force as necessary; and (d) conflict among Muslim nations will be fueled by outsiders, by all possible means including pledge of support. All of the above will continue until common Muslims everywhere are willing to work for the protection of their interests. (C)

115.   Some feel that after the defeat of communism, Muslims are the main threat, though a weak and distant one, to the established world order. In order to protect their interests, Muslims living in the West should (a)

become full participants in the democratic process of their adopted countries, (b) build alliances with locally elected officials, (c) work with those who believe in coexistence, and (d) seek support from the legal system. (ST)

116.   The OIC has been very useful. It provides the mechanism for periodic meetings for leaders of all Muslim governments. The Islamic Development Bank has provided much needed funds. However, wide differences among the members of OIC about the Bank's nature, needs and views have prevented it from becoming truly effective. (C) Ways must be found to make OIC more effective. (ST)

117.   Many factors are important for success, including: clear vision; well-planned strategy; hard work; single mindedness of purpose; belief in the justification of the mission; persistence in the face of set backs; desire to succeed; and use of all available legal tools. Muslim leadership needs to possess all these qualities. The rest of the *Ummah* need to play their part too. The total collective effort will determine success. (C)

118.   Muslims appear to be too preoccupied with their day-to-day economic survival. They should learn to participate at all levels, family, neighborhood, town/village, provincial, national, and international levels. Instead of brooding in isolation, there should be active participation in supporting good and opposing evil under the New World Order. (ST)

119.   Leaders of all Muslim countries are seeking a better life and way. They all can be persuaded to work for Muslim solidarity if their basic concerns are met. (S)

120.   There is no compulsion in Islam, therefore, the long-term solution lies in coexistence. However, given its massive power, the West does not appear to be seriously interested. The West prefers to maintain its upper hand partly through continued division among Muslims. However, if Muslims become united, the situation would change. If the other side foresees united and determined Muslims, the potential damage, the futility of war, and, in this case, the injustice of war, they will also seek coexistence with honor. (LT)

121.   It is unrealistic to expect that the existing Muslim national states will merge into one national entity any time soon. The best that the

proponents of Muslim unity can expect is to gradually move in that direction. There are many intermediate steps for increasing cooperation; the EU model is worth considering. Formal steps leading to uniform currency, common defense, and foreign policy may follow. A merger resulting in a confederation or a federation may happen much later if the parties involved are comfortable with the ideas. **(ST)**

122.   Muslims can expect to be left alone if they avoid actual or perceived threat to the powers of the day. They can expect to fare well, and even receive help under the New World Order if they focus on priorities on which there is convergence of views between Muslims and the West. **(ST)**

E. Overall.

123.   The vision of Muslims is to develop, and participate as equals under the New World Order. Development is equally urgent on economic, political, spiritual, and military fronts. Objectives in each of those areas have been discussed above. In summary, Muslims as a group should be able to (a) meet their own basic needs of adequate food, shelter, education, and health care, (b) have stable and representative governments which cooperate closely with each other, (c) tolerate and, if possible, peacefully resolve differences in religious interpretations among each other, and (d) become strong enough to defend their own borders, and render help to other Muslims in defense of their vital interests. The above should help Muslims to emerge as a self-sufficient, peaceful, and strong group of people in the world. It would earn them self-respect, and the respect of others. They will be treated as equal partners, and full participants under the New World Order. **(LT)**

124.   The strategy would consist of several steps for Muslims: (a) emphasize the long-term of interest of local citizen and work diligently to resolve domestic issues; (b) acceptance of genuine coexistence with followers of other religions and world powers; (c) implementation of activities for which there is convergence of views with the West; (d) consolidation of strengths and reduction of weaknesses as discussed above; (e) increased cooperation and solidarity; (f) resolution of outstanding military issues as soon as possible; and (g) enhance defensive capabilities through expenditure for technology, manpower development, and universal military training. *Insha'Allah* Muslims will make progress. **(LT)**

125.   Muslims ought to consider the world military power structure very carefully. They should avoid military conflict with any nation, particularly one with nuclear weapons. They should strengthen themselves through increased unity and by other means. They should be cautious of emotional and irrational leaders among themselves, and commit themselves to peace. This will lead to the best possible outcome under the New World Order. (ST)

126.   When Muslims start implementation of their program for self-reform and self-help, they can expect all economic, political, and military aid from the West to be critically reviewed and curtailed. However, the pressure will hopefully reduce when others (a) are convinced of Muslims' peaceful and constructive reform and (b) see Muslims as a force for good, inevitably to be respected. (LT)

127.   This book has barely scratched the surface toward integrated development of Muslims. Many Muslims are thinking about and working for the same goal. May the God of the universe show the right path to all Muslims and help in making this a better world. Amin!

O Allah! Forgive my sins, ignorance and extravagance in my affairs, and what Thou knowest best about it from me. O Allah! Forgive my earnestness and frivolity, my mistakes and intentions and everything of what is with me. O Allah! Forgive me of sins I sent in advance and I will send in future, and what I kept secret and what I disclosed, and what Thou knowest about it better than myself. Thou art the First, and Thou art the Last, and Thou art powerful over all things.

1. Action program to consolidate Muslim strengths and reduce weaknesses in spiritual, economic, political and military fields.

2. Proposed constitution of Islamic governments which can be practiced in current times.

3. Principles of conflict resolution in the Qur'an.

4. Role of *ijma* and *ijtihad* in Islam in resolving outstanding controversial issues.

5. Ways to demonstrate that concept of "one Muslim nation" is attractive for the rich as well as the poor Muslim nations.

6. Optimum steps for achieving Muslim solidarity.

7. Ways to establish Muslim religious leadership (e.g., court) which would be capable of preventing religious conflicts, and clarify disputed interpretations of the teachings.

8. The concept of Muslims relying on each other.

9. Definitive interpretation of Islamic position on issues relating to women based on the Qur'an and *Hadith*.

10. Improved arrangements for collection of *zakat;* it could greatly reduce the need for foreign aid from non-Muslims.

11. An alternative to interest payments in return for the use of capital of those who do not wish to share in profit and loss.

12. Some research to determine "pleasures" allowed by Islam.

13. Review of Muslim marriage arrangements, to make marriage natural as intended and practiced earlier.

14. The issues relating to scarcity of water, and the appropriate action for sustained long-term improvement.

15. Research, understand, emphasize, and build on the common heritage with followers of other religions.

16. A systematic evaluation of Islamic propositions in the context of conditions of the twentieth and the twenty-first centuries. It will require a large effort, and will involve much thought and research. However, it will help regain lost self-confidence of many Muslims and deserves the undertaking.

17. The feasibility of enhanced cooperation among and possible union of Muslim countries, including comparison of their relative strengths and weaknesses, intermediate steps, confidence-building measures, and a time-table.

Holy Qur'an. Translated by Abdullah Yusuf Ali. Brentwood, Maryland: Amana Corp., 1989.

al Ahsan, Abdullah. *OIC: The Organization of Islamic Conference (An Introduction to an Islamic Political Institution)*. Herndon: IIIT, 1988.

Asad, Muhammad. *Islam at the Crossroads*. Islamabad: Da'wah Academy, 1990.

Chapra, M. Umar. *Islam and the Economic Challenge*. Herndon: The Islamic Foundation, The International Institute of Islamic Thought, 1992.

Enayat, Hamid. *Modern Islamic Political Thought*. Austin: University of Texas Press, 1982.

Haddad, Yvonne Y., ed. *The Muslims of America*. New York: Oxford University Press, 1991,

Fromkin, David. *A Peace to End All Peace*. Henry Holt and Company, 1989.

Gordon, Irving L. *Reviewing World History*. Amsco School Publications, 1964.

Huntington, Samuel P. "The Clash of Civilizations?" in *Foreign Affairs*, Summer 1993.

ibn Kathir. *The Signs Before the Day of Judgment*. London: Dar Al Taqwa Ltd., 1991.

Khan, Mohammad Asghar. *Islam, Politics and the State: The Pakistan Experience*. London: Zed Books Ltd., 1985.

Lewis, Bernard. *The Political Language of Islam*. Chicago: The University of Chicago Press, 1988.

Lewis, Bernard. *Islam and the West*. Oxford: Oxford University Press, 1993.

McNeill, William H. (ed.) and Waldman, M. Robinson (ed.). *The Islamic World.* Chicago: University of Chicago Press, 1973.

Memon, Abdul Fatah. *Oil and the Faith.* Karachi: Inter Services Press, Ltd., 1967.

Memon, Abdul Fatah. *Invitation to a New Society.* Karachi: Inter Services Press, Ltd., 1968.

Mohammed, Imam W. Deen. *Al-Islam Unity & Leadership.* Chicago: The Sense Maker, 1991.

Nielsen, Niels C. Jr. *et al. Religions of the World.* New York: St. Martins's Press, 1988.

Piscatori, James P. *Islam in a World of Nation-States.* Cambridge: Press Syndicate of the University of Cambridge, 1986.

Rashad, Adib. *Islam, Black Nationalism and Slavery: A Detailed History.* Beltsville: Writers' Inc., 1995.

Siddique, Kaukab. *The Struggle of Muslim Women.* Kingsville, Maryland: American Society for Education & Religion, 1986.

Stoessinger, John G. *Why Nations Go to War.* New York: St. Martin's Press, 1982.

The Message Magazine, ed. *Commandments by God in the Qur'an.* New York: The Message Publications, 1991.

The World Bank. *The Europa World Year Book.* 1992 and 1993.

The World Bank. *World Development Report.* 1993 and 1994.

Thompson, Ahmad. *Dajjal: The King Who Has No Clothes.* London: TaHa Publishers, Ltd., 1986.

Toer, Pramoedya Ananta. *This Earth of Mankind.* New York: Avon Books, 1975.

Vatikiotis, P. J. *Islam and the State.* Beckenham, Kent: Croom Helm Ltd., 1987.

ABOUT THE AUTHOR

Ali Nawaz Memon was born in the city Shikarpur, the province of Sind, Pakistan, on September 28, 1941. He received his early education in Shikarpur, Larkana, and Karachi, Pakistan; he obtained a BS degree in Electrical Engineering from the University of Illinois in 1964 and an MBA (Honors) in International Finance from the University of Oregon in 1967. Mr. Memon has been an international civil servant for more than 27 years and has traveled, lived, and worked in the United States as well as in many parts of Europe, Africa, Asia, and the Middle East. He has been uniquely fortunate to have interaction with and exposure to the views of peoples from the West and from Muslim countries.